THE HISTORY OF MR WELLS

MICHAEL FOOT

THE HISTORY OF MR WELLS

COUNTERPOINT

WASHINGTON, D. C.

Library of Congress Cataloging-in-Publication Data
Foot, Michael, 1913–
H. G.: the history of Mr. Wells / Michael Foot.
1. Wells, H. G. (Herbert George), 1866–1946—Biography.
2. Novelists, English—20th century—Biography.
3. Journalists—Great Britain—Biography. I Title.
PR5776.F66   1995
823'.912—dc20   95–34151
ISBN 1–887178–04–X (alk. paper)

FIRST PRINTING
Printed in the United States of America
on acid-free paper that meets the
American National Standards Institute
Z39–48 Standard.

℞ A CORNELIA AND MICHAEL BESSIE BOOK

COUNTERPOINT
P.O. Box 65793
Washington, D.C. 20035–5793

Distributed by Publishers Group West

CONTENTS

ACKNOWLEDGEMENTS

The author and publishers gratefully acknowledge permission to reprint the following material:

Extracts from the writings of H. G. Wells, reprinted by kind permission of A. P. Watt Ltd on behalf of The Literary Executors of the Estate of H. G. Wells; extracts from *The Diary of Beatrice Webb Volume 2 (1892–1905)* edited by Norman and Jeanne Mackenzie, reprinted by kind permission of the publishers, Virago Press; extracts from *The Young Rebecca* edited by Jane Marcus, reprinted by kind permission of the Peters, Fraser & Dunlop Group Ltd; extracts from *James Joyce* by Richard Ellmann are reproduced by kind permission of Oxford University Press Inc.

Picture acknowledgements: Tania Alexander 66; Ashmolean Museum, Oxford 50; British Library Newspaper Library 28, 54, 58; Local Studies, Bromley Libraries/Godfrey New Photographic 4, 6, 7, 37, 46, 63, 75; Camera Press 76; Division of Rare and Manuscript Collections, Carl A Kroch Library, Cornell University, Ithaca, New York 30; Hulton Deutsch Collection 10, 25, 43, 45, 65, 69, 74, 78; Illustrated London News Picture Library 47; David Low, Evening Standard/Solo Syndication, Centre for the study of Cartoons and Caricatures, University of Kent, Canterbury 61; The Mansell Collection 15, 62; A C Michael/Pall Mall Magazine 27; National Portrait Gallery 17, 32, 33, 38, 41, 48, 49, 52, 53, 55, 56, 77; National Trust Photographic Library 2; North West Film Archive at the

Manchester Metropolitan University 71; Novosti Photo Library 67; Popperfoto 26, 64; Punch Picture Library 32; The Royal Photographic Society Picture Library 16; Sheffield City Archives/Carpenter Collection 42; Solo Syndication 79; University of Illinois Library at Urbana – Champaign 1, 5, 8, 11, 13, 19, 20, 21, 23, 35, 39.

The cartoon on page 28 is © Estate of H. M. Bateman.

The following Beerbohm caricatures are reproduced by permission of Mrs Eva Reichmann: 24, 44, 49, 50, 53, 58.

The Literary Executors of the Estate of H. G. Wells have given permission for the reproduction of the following picshuas and photographs: 1, 3, 5, 8, 9, 11, 12, 13, 14, 18, 19, 20, 21, 22, 23, 29, 35, 37, 39, 40, 51, 57, 60.

Thanks also to the following individuals and organizations for their assistance: Mick Scott and staff, Local Studies, Bromley Library; Chris Rolfe, HG Wells Collection, University of North London; National Portrait Gallery Archive.

The publishers have made every effort to contact the owners of illustrations reproduced here. If in any case they have been unsuccessful they invite the copyright holder to contact them direct.

Inscription

I owe a particular debt to Una Cooze. She has added to her secretarial duties a herculean mastery of modern technology. Without her this book would have been an impossibility. Sheila Noble, for years the presiding grammatical genius at *Tribune*, came to our rescue at the last moment: any remaining solecisms are mine, and not hers. Jill Craigie's role is, I trust, properly recognized in the Preface. Sorrel nags of the true Swiftian breed may be able to recognize themselves. And, finally, the nearer I have come to the completion of this task, the more I have appreciated how much I owe to the Labour Party members, first in the Devonport constituency of my home town, Plymouth, and then in the constituency of Ebbw Vale, later named Blaenau Gwent, who taught me what democratic Socialism was about, and who would themselves so often acknowledge their debt to H. G. Wells.

Without Sally Gaminara of Doubleday and Transworld, the whole project would never have started and would have foundered on a series of occasions. Authors sometimes offer formal and polite thanks to their editors. Something much more than that is required in this case.

All critical misjudgements, touches of hyperbole, occasional lapses from taste or accuracy in these pages must be laid at the door of V. S. Pritchett, who kindly encouraged me to proceed with this book on 10 July 1992 at a meeting at his house, witnessed by Lady Pritchett. Despite this moment of aberration, he remains for us all not only the greatest of short story writers, but also the most perceptive and generous of all modern critics.

Preface I

I had a unique and, I trust, instructive glimpse into the world of H. G. Wells and Rebecca West. Apart even from such a love affair, which can add piquancy to any public debate, the whole argument between them – or perhaps, to put the point more accurately, the whole action between them – strikes me as one of the great ones of the century, at least for those of us who call ourselves Socialists. That was the name which each did adopt or adapt; but the curious link between them, Lord Beaverbrook, could not make any such boast, and yet his evidence as an expert witness is not to be dismissed.

It was under his roof that I first met the hero of my youth, H. G. Wells, and his last love, Moura Budberg, who, for me, became something of a heroine, too. It was under that same roof, some fifteen years before, quite unsuspected by the world at large, that Rebecca West had been wooed by Max Beaverbrook. I introduced my wife, Jill, to Max; and she in turn introduced me to Rebecca. It was a fair exchange by any reckoning. Indeed, Jill was responsible for persuading Rebecca to republish some of her earliest writings, which led to the reassessment of Rebecca's contribution to our twentieth-century politics. If it had not been for Jill's incitement, the pieces which appear in *The Young Rebecca* would never have been reproduced in their present form. And those pieces are, apart from their other shining merits, the best examples of feminist writing in the language. But the connection between those pieces and today could never have been foreseen; it was known to none of the survivors but Rebecca herself. And then, when all of them, Max and Rebecca and Moura and HG were safely dead, with the publication of a posthumous novel by Rebecca the last piece of the jigsaw became available.

It is worth standing back to see the whole picture. Two such political minds as HG's and Rebecca's have seldom been matched, and both in their differing styles felt they were living through – indeed, were helping to unleash – an era of unprecedented emancipation for mankind and womankind. That was what their Socialism was, and that is what all Socialism should be. Has the dream faded for ever, and how was it that in their hands it shone so brightly, and can still shine? So this is a book about Socialism, but personalities will be constantly allowed to intrude. I recall that when I told my old Liberal father that I intended to join the Labour Party he referred me to a passage in H. G. Wells's *Tono-Bungay* where one enquirer after truth says to another:

'We ought to join on to other Socialists. They've got something.'
'Let's go and look at some first.'

Always there have been two Labour Parties: one problem has always been how to keep them together. My favourite has always been the one which Wells inspired or, at least, since the whole affair had started earlier, which so lovingly folded him to their bosom. As good as any place to start disentangling the libertarian from the bureaucratic strand in British Socialism is the controversy which Wells had with Sidney and Beatrice Webb in the first decade of the century. Yet to concentrate on this dispute would be to set much too narrow confines to the whole debate.

The Socialism of the 1890s and the early 1900s appealed to a whole variety of tastes and traditions: the sheer richness of it should make us pause in wonder. So much came as a direct English legacy, and yet it was truly and properly woven into an international fabric. No other political creed of the age could claim such richness or command such widespread intellectual contributions: scientists who saw their Socialism as the essential fulfilment of the Darwinian discoveries; artists or the prophets of the world of art, like William Morris, who believed that no civilized society could be imagined without the artist's gift; men and women of passion and compassion who could not sit quiet amid the human misery they saw all around them; bureaucratic centralizers who believed, with an equal ardour, that only the power of the state could alleviate such chronic ills; students of Karl Marx who thought they could foretell (and help to shape) the revolution which would bring these prizes within the grasp of those who suffered such hardships and insult; men and women (Rebecca was one of these) who argued that they could use their new-found strength in the trade unions, a revival of the old guilds, to win immediate gains; men and women of every brand and breed who inherited a peculiar English tradition of dissent, the sons and daughters of the Chartists, the Radicals, the Levellers who would always watch with a healthy scepticism any established authority. All these helped to make the Labour movement of Edwardian times or, to speak more exactly, the Labour Party, founded at the Farringdon Hall in 1900.

But what order of priority should prevail amid such commendable rivalries? H. G. Wells and Rebecca West might often find themselves on the same side against the same opponents. But not always. What would happen when the irresistible feminist force met the immovable Wellsian object? The question, in the physical world, might be one of comparative simplicity. How would it be resolved when Rebecca, even in her early twenties, showed herself a furious, highly effective opponent in an age of great controversialists? G. K. Chesterton was terrified; a host of others skedaddled in the face of her invectives; Bernard Shaw paid respectful homage; H. G. Wells became her lover. However, that was not his first resort. A good moment, first of all, to make an estimate of what H. G. Wells meant for British Socialism and for Socialism in the world at large was in that pre-1914 world, before the Great War, before the flood, before Rebecca.

One other association with HG I hope I can claim without any charge of inaccuracy or pretension: a common or nearly lifelong interest in Jonathan Swift. HG read *Gulliver's Travels* in an unexpurgated edition when he was 10 years old or thereabouts: he constantly returned to that same source of inspiration and would always acknowledge the debt. Swift was one of the writers who helped to give him his interest in satire; and, re-reading most of his writings in recent years, I have been more and more reminded, with HG himself doing the direct reminding, how much he honoured Swift, how much he took Swift as a model in his mockery of the human condition, which was brought to its highest pitch in *Gulliver's Travels*. 'A perpetual assault on human self-satisfaction' – that was one essential task which HG said he learned from his master.

It might also be deduced that Swift, the prince of journalists, influenced the HG who became as dedicated to his journalism as he was to his fiction; or perhaps we may say, more appositely, that it was Swift who taught him not to draw any sharp distinction between the two. The Swift of the *Drapier's Letters* or the *Conduct of the Allies* introduced into the trade of journalism a combined force and simplicity which had rarely been attempted before or since. The style formed part of the Swiftian creed that politics was suited to many heads (male and female, by the way), and that the participants, especially if they happened to be poor people maltreated by rich conquerors, had a right to be able to understand what the argument was about. HG never quite won such a single, spectacular victory as did the Drapier. But he set himself the same task of being understood by every reader. If the theme was too abstruse or elaborate for this purpose, so much the worse for the theme. We may note here also that HG the allegorist, or HG the journalist, was an avid reader and imitator of Swift's *Journal to Stella*. He appreciated the baby language and thus instructed all his own Stellas and Vanessas, who would readily concur: 'A bad scrawl is so snug.' All the close members of the HG family and almost all his lovers (all the real ones) were to be treated to that particular intimacy. And, if anyone questions the claim about the early acquaintance of the young Wells with the old Swift, I may refer them, here and now, to a casual reference in a hitherto unnoted essay published before the real HG had ever been heard of, in which he heaps scorn on 'a gallinaceous Swift.'* It was the more remarkable that the young HG should have folded Swift to his bosom when we recall that the Jonathan Swift of that age was still protrayed as the madman or the monster, the perverted, treacherous lover, or the whole conglomeration of vices, which Dr Johnson had delineated a century before. Those indelible traits were drawn even more darkly by the Macaulays and the Thackerays and a host of lesser hands. No orthodox political writer, if the word can be used in that sense, had said a good word for him. His only real defenders were men on the extreme Left in England, Hazlitt, Leigh Hunt, Byron, Charles James Fox – and their rush to his defence could be added to the indictment – or by Irishmen of his own breed whose taste could not be recommended. In the London of the 1860s and 1870s, Swift was still not accepted as a respected figure in our literary history. The wicked streaks in his nature still clouded his fame as a writer. Thomas Carlyle mentioned the matter to Moncure Conway when they passed the place in Chelsea where Swift used to live: 'a man grossly maligned in his own time and never properly reclaimed from the libellers.'

However, the boy HG formed his own conclusions on these mighty matters, and thereafter nothing could ever shift him. He

---

* *Select Conversations with an Uncle (Now Extinct)*, ed. David C. Smith and Patrick Parrinder (1992), p. 59.

confessed there were a few writers who could make him laugh out loud, and Swift was the first among them, even before he could introduce him to his other worlds as well. Indeed, Jonathan Swift was something else in addition to all these characteristics which made him such a noteworthy commentator on his own age and such a good model for practising satirists or practising journalists. He was an unmistakable specimen of one of the rarest breed of rare birds. He was a comic genius, like Rabelais or Cervantes or Byron or Charles Dickens or Benjamin Disraeli or Oscar Wilde or Charlie Chaplin or Groucho Marx. This was never the single quality of any of these on his list – except possibly Rabelais or Groucho – but it was the rare gift which gave them the final distinction. I believe H. G. Wells belonged to this company, too.

Preface II

Note on Debts and Larcenies, Petty and Otherwise

When I went with my brother, John, to Paris to celebrate my twenty-first birthday in July 1934, we took with us a copy of *Tono-Bungay*. We both derived so much enjoyment from it that we had to ration our reading, limiting ourselves to some thirty pages at a time. All the other delights of Paris, from the Louvre to Montmartre, from the Panthéon to the rue Pigalle, had to wait.

Thereafter, for a few decades, other interests intervened, but I never quite gave up the idea of both reading and writing properly about the author. However, I had one grave deficiency for the task: my scientific knowledge was not quite so extensive as that taught to HG's father or, say, Brynhild, among his latter-day heroines; and this scandalous ignorance, I fear, has not been repaired, as every reader may quickly recognize. The scandal remains a scandal, especially after all the Wellsian invocations which must be noted in any decent book about him for a revolution in our country's educational system as one of the first essentials for national recovery.

To turn to a happier note, it has been thrilling to see how H. G. Wells's reputation has been protected by a range of writers in different fields, and especially by those who formed and sustained the H. G. Wells Society. Several of these – John Hammond, Patrick Parrinder, Sylvia Hardy and Michael Draper – have themselves written critical or biographical books of first importance, and I hope my debt to them and to others is properly recognized in the extensive footnotes.

Another recent invaluable product of the H. G. Wells Society was a volume entitled *H. G. Wells under Revision. Proceedings of the H. G. Wells Symposium, London, July 1986.* Edited by Patrick Parrinder and Christopher Rolfe, and published in 1987, it contains so many riches supplied by Wellsians, old and new, that it is invidious to mention any particular ones. Even so, the risk must be taken. Patrick Parrinder and John Hammond offered the evidence from their own special knowledge how the great Wellsian revival was proceeding. Brian W. Aldiss set the tone with a chapter on Leopard Ladies and linked gardens, and a few days later Robert Crossley threw open unexpected floodgates which should help to sweep aside for ever some of the worst anti-Wellsian prejudices.

He has been the subject of seven excellent biographies, and the various authors – Geoffrey West (1930), Vincent Brome (1951), Lovat Dickson (1969), Norman and Jeanne MacKenzie (1973), John Batchelor (1983), Anthony West (1983), David C. Smith (1986) – have each made notable additions to our knowledge. Strong traces of all of them are present in these pages. And, especially in the light of my own deficiency noted above, I must recommend Patrick Parrinder's writings on Wells's science fiction and Roslynn Haynes's *H. G. Wells, Discoverer of the Future* (1980). H. G. Wells's own writings provide the main part of my story. I read and reread the two volumes of his *Experiment in Autobiography* and, most important of all for my purpose, *H. G. Wells in Love*, published in 1984. And I have dealt – adequately, I hope – with the critical attacks made upon him, either in the text or in the footnotes. The most serious of these in recent times is the essay included in John Carey's *The Intellectuals and the Masses* (1992). He seeks to drive a wedge between the two popular writers, H. G. Wells and Arnold Bennett. Which of the two would be the more amazed at this discovery it may be difficult to determine. However, John Carey's general case is a serious one. The same cannot be said of another volume recently appearing which accused H. G. Wells of being a misogynist. One excuse for my book is the notable company of women of varying professions, tastes and accomplishments – indeed, the whole feminist galaxy, in the best sense of both words – who will be summoned to the witness-box to repudiate the charge.

Apart from the books about Wells himself, I must express my debt to some others covering the whole period or considerable sections of it: Michael Holroyd's biography of Bernard Shaw in all its six-volume glory; Norman and Jeanne MacKenzie's edition of Beatrice Webb's diaries; and the Dan H. Lawrence Bernard Shaw diaries.

A word about epigraphs at the head of chapters. David C. Smith selected for his biography passages which displayed his and my hero's eloquence. To offer the best examples, space was needed, and he has surely indicated what a special feature of HG's writings this could be. My own selection is designed to illustrate his humour, and how it could often be expressed in single shafts directed against himself. Indeed, one of these, plus my memory of Moura Budberg's accent, has prompted my choice of a title for the whole book. He wrote in his *Brynhild* (1937): 'But Wells at the best was a discursive, intractable writer with no real sense of dignity. A man is not called "H.G." by all his friends for nothing.'

Hampstead,
May 1995

MICHAEL FOOT

ONE

Adam and Eve

I was at war with the world and by no means sure
I could win.

The Book of Catherine Wells, p. 8

He was born in Kent, where Socialism was also born, and he was always happy to celebrate the association. He believed that men and women could learn from a true knowledge of their history lessons nobler and more efficacious than anything prescribed in the rudimentary exercises of religion and other myths. He became the boldest prophet of the century; not one who would ever claim infallibility or anything to be distantly related to that term but still one who never abandoned his youthful Socialist aspiration of what the human mind might achieve.

The date was 21 September 1866, and the place was 47 (now renumbered 172) High Street, Bromley. His father, Joseph Wells, and his mother, Sarah, had been married in 1853 and they had four children. An elder sister, Fanny, had died at the age of 9 two years before HG (Bertie was his name in the family) was born. Almost from his mother's womb, Bertie had a fight on: he seemed to be a weakling, and for several years the fear

1

persisted that he might suffer the fate of Fanny. His father kept the little hardware shop in Bromley which he christened Atlas House, was a gardener of some ingenuity, but was most distinguished as a professional cricketer of real ability. Wells recorded that 'his was a mind of inappeasible freshness, in the strangest contrast to my mother's'.

Almost everything he wrote about his parents – and he constantly returned to the theme – was deeply moving. He realized that his father was an imperfect partner for his mother and had often contributed directly by his thoughtlessness or folly to the failures of the home. He saw that his father had neither imagination nor sympathy for the woman's side of life. 'Later on', he acknowledged, 'I was to betray a similar deficiency.'* He had been brought up in a home where the women did all the work without apparent complaint. But this did not qualify HG's admiration for his father; and, when he died, he could hardly control his grief:

A rush from my memory of many clumsy kindlinesses, a realisation of the loss of his companionship came to me. I recalled the happiness of many of my Sunday tramps by his side in springtime, on golden summer evenings, in winter when the forest had picked out every twig in the downland hedgerows. I thought of his endless edifying discourses about flowers and rabbits and hillsides and distant stars. And he was gone. I should never hear his voice again. I should never see again his dear old eyes magnified to an immense wonder through his spectacles. I should never have a chance of telling him how I cared for him. And I had never told him I cared for him. Indeed I had never realised I cared for him until now. He was lying stiff and still and submissive in that coffin, a rejected man. Life had treated him badly. He had never had a dog's chance. My mind leapt forward beyond my years and I understood what a tissue of petty humiliations and disappointments and degradations his life had been. I saw then as clearly as I see now the immense pity of such a life. Sorrow possessed me. I wept as I

* *Experiment in Autobiography* (1934), vol. 1, p. 60.

stumbled along after him. I had great difficulty in preventing myself from weeping aloud. *

But his sympathy for his mother and the women of that age and what they endured was no less real.

Bearing a child was not the jolly wholesome process we know today;† in that diseased society it was an illness, it counted as an illness, for nearly every woman. Which the man her husband resented – grossly. Five or six children in five or six years and a pretty girl was a cross, worried wreck of a woman, bereft of any shred of spirit or beauty. My poor scolding, worried mother was not fifty when she died. And one saw one's exquisite infants grow up into ill-dressed, under-nourished, ill-educated children. Think of the agony of shamed love that lay beneath my poor mother's slaps and scoldings! The world has forgotten now the hate and bitterness of disappointed parentage.

And his memories of that mother could move him too.

But she was indeed just the creature and victim of that disordered age which had turned her natural tenacity to a blind intolerance and wasted her moral passion upon ugly and barren ends. If Fanny and Ernest and I had shown any stoutness against the disadvantages of our start in life, if we had won for ourselves any knowledge or respect, we inherited that much steadfastness from her; such honesty as we had was hers. If her moral harshness had over-shadowed and embittered our adolescence, her passionate mothering had sheltered our childhood. Our father would have loved us, wondered at us and left us about. But early in her life, that fear, that terror-stricken hatred of sex that overshadowed the Christian centuries, that frantic resort to the suppressions, subjugations and disciplines of a stereotyped marriage in its harshest form, a marriage as easy to step into and as hard to leave as a steel trap with

* *Autobiography. The Dream* p. 104.
† When did HG imagine the process ever became so jolly? So Jill enquired when she read this sentence.

its teeth hidden by the most elaborate secrecies and misrepresentations, had set its pitiless grip upon my mother's imagination, and
blackened all the happier impulses in life for her. She was ready, if
necessary, to pass all her children through the fires of that Moloch,
if by so doing their souls might be saved. She did it the more bitterly
because she was doing it against the deeper undeveloped things in
her own nature.

The schools he was sent to were, first of all, a dame school at 8
Smith Street, Bromley, and later an establishment called
Morley's Commercial for Young Gentlemen where he remained
until the age of 13. Then, in 1880, when his Bromley home
came near to complete financial collapse, his mother took a post
as housekeeper at Up Park, a magnificent old country house near
Petersfield, a post which she held until the early 1890s. Amid
these shifts and disturbances, HG had two lucky breaks which
started to lift the pressure and tedium of his upbringing. He had
been born into a home of genteel poverty and he learned to hate
everything about it except his loving parents. But, when he was
7 years old, still in Bromley, he broke his leg or his hip and was
confined for months to his bed. His father brought him books,
stacks of them: bound copies of *Punch* and other magazines,
Wood's *Natural History*, geographical works. Then he turned to
books about war, Wellington's war and Columbus's adventures,
and the American Civil War. And then, even more extraordinary, 'the march of tall and lovely feminine figures,
Britannia, Erin, Columbria, La France, bare armed, bare
necked, showing beautiful bare bosoms, revealing shining
thighs, wearing garments that were a revelation to an age of
flounces and crinolines. My first consciousness of women, my
first stirrings of desire were roused, by these heroic divinities.'
His kinship with his adoring and adorable father was soldered
by the treatment each gave the other as the situation demanded.
Bertie's accident at school was a serious one; his fractured hip
bone had to be set and re-broken and reset again. And this was
the moment to which HG would trace his intellectual awakening. But, a few months later, his father slipped and fell while

pruning the grapevine in his back garden one Sunday morning –
a judgement upon him, it was agreed in the town, for not being
at church. He could never play cricket again, and the family
income was severely cut. The pressure was on to see whether
Bertie could start making his contribution, along with his two
brothers, to the common store. That must mean his apprenticeship in a draper's shop. But, before and after that disaster,
nothing could check the miscellaneous tuition he received from
his untutored father. Either at the Literary Institute in the
Bromley Town Hall or at home he was introduced or made his
own introduction to Washington Irving and David Hume,
Humboldt's *Cosmology*, Grote's *History of Greece*, Scott's poetry,
a little Shakespeare, lots of Dickens; and the pictures of Wood's
Natural History gave him 'an inkling of evolution and a
nightmare terror of gorillas'.

It was indeed an extraordinary assortment, especially since
HG never ceased to rail against the denial of any decent
education to his father, and indeed his mother, too, both
'intelligent, book-reading persons' to whom the great Darwinian
discoveries of the previous twenty or thirty years had never been
imparted. 'To this day', he wrote later, 'I will confess I dislike
this restriction and distortion of knowledge, as I dislike nothing
else on earth. In the modern world, it is, I hold, second only to
murder to starve and cripple the mind of a child.'[*] The crippling
of his own mother and father was something he never forgot.
'My mind was born anew,' he wrote, a Thomas Paineite
reflection, prompted by another bout of illness; and, profiting
still further from that 7-year-old introduction to the art of
reading, he found his way to the library of Up Park which had
been partly furnished through the Enlightenment tastes of its
owner, Sir Harry Fetherstonhaugh, who happened to be an
eighteenth-century-style freethinker. Among the volumes
which he found on those shelves was Thomas Paine's *Rights of
Man* and Plato's *Republic*. Of course, he could not swallow the
whole feast at once. But he himself offered a most persuasive

[*] *The Fate of Homo Sapiens* (1939), p. 9.

report of the scene years later in *Tono-Bungay*. He approached the matter delicately but decisively; he told how he made himself into one of the great readers of the century:

Sitting under a dormer window on a shelf above great stores of tea and spices, I became familiar with much of Hogarth in a big portfolio, with Raphael – there was a great book of engravings from the stanzas of Raphael in the Vatican – and with most of the capitals of Europe as they had looked about 1780, by means of several big iron-moulded books of views. There was also a broad eighteenth-century atlas with huge wandering maps that instructed me mightily. It had splendid adornments about each map title; Holland showed a fisherman and his boat; Russia a Cossack; Japan, remarkable people attired in pagodas. I say it deliberately, 'pagodas'. There were Terrae Incognitae in every continent then, Poland, Sarmatia, lands since lost; and many a voyage I made with a blunted pin about that large incorrect and dignified world. The books in that little old closet had been banished, I suppose, from the saloon during the Victorian revival of good taste and emasculated orthodoxy, but my mother had no suspicion of their character. So I read and understood the good sound rhetoric of Tom Paine's *Rights of Man* and his *Common Sense*, excellent books, once praised by bishops and since sedulously lied about. Gulliver was there unexpurgated, strong meat for a boy perhaps, but not too strong I hold – I have never regretted that I escaped niceness in these affairs. The satire of Traldragdubh made my blood boil as it was meant to do, but I hated Swift for the Houyhnhnms and never quite liked a horse afterwards. Then I remembered also a translation of Voltaire's *Candide*, and *Rasselas*; and, vast book though it was, I really believe I read, in a muzzy sort of way of course, from end to end, and even with some reference now and then to the Atlas, Gibbon in twelve volumes. These readings whetted my taste for more, and surreptitiously I raided the bookcases in the big saloon. I got through quite a number of books before my sacrilegious temerity was discovered by Ann, the old head-housemaid. I remember that among others I tried a translation of Plato's *Republic* then, and found extraordinarily little interest in it. I was much too young for that; but

'Vathek'. 'Vathek' was glorious stuff. That kicking affair! When everybody had to kick! The thought of 'Vathek' always brings back with it my boyish memory of the big saloon at Bladesover.*

Of these first mentors, it was Jonathan Swift who left the most indelible impression, and it is interesting to note how discriminating was his first reading about the Houyhnhnms: some modern Swiftian scholars have reached the conclusion that Swift intended us to question their perfectibility. But the whole galaxy together rivets attention. Swift, Hogarth, Voltaire, Gibbon – of course, the 17-year-old or 18-year-old adolescent could not be expected to absorb more than a smattering of these masters, but nor should anyone doubt the capacity of this reader to read. He folded to his heart most closely the iconoclasts of the Enlightenment, and one early service they performed for him was to scatter those fantasies of military adventure first acquired only a few years before in the sickroom at Atlas House in Bromley.

And how much HG owed – how much a new race of Socialist readers came to owe – to his training in that Up Park university of all the horrors, dreams, disproportions between giants and dwarfs, with human cruelty and human pride unmasked by the final Swiftian indictment. How could any other item weigh in those scales which, whatever their scandalous nature, seemed often to carry his beloved father's blessing? Even more surely it was through the eyes of his father, the expert gardener, that he was introduced to another lifelong interest: 'There was a slope of bluebells in the broken sunlight under the newly green beeches in the west wood that is now precious sapphire in my memory; it was the first time I knowingly met beauty.'†

Then he turned his mind – or, rather, had it persistently turned for him – to examine the world of the spirit. His dear mother forced him, and his dear father would not object. 'I was indeed a prodigy of Early Impiety,' he wrote in his auto-

---

* *Tono-Bungay* (1909), pp. 20–1.
† *Tono-Bungay*, p. 20.

biography, but it was not in any sense an exhibitionist display. He could recall those events with some vividness until his dying day. These words are quoted from one of the last articles which HG wrote, and which appeared in *Tribune* on 28 January 1944. The vividness with which he could still recall, seventy years later, the injury inflicted upon his young mind seems to add to the story.

My conflict with the Religious Complex began very early in life, but the internal struggle left its scars and twinges for many years. I was told there was a 'God Almighty' of intricate but essential unity, a Person, who knew everything, past, present and future; who had made everything just as he liked and who was, in fact, the absolute monarch of being. But also I perceived that life was full of painful events and frightful possibilities. Why had he made it like that? Quicker-witted people could just jump that question, leaving it unanswered, but I could not. My fear and distress were very great. I dared not ask anyone I knew about this overwhelming sadist! Whom we praised and pretended to adore! My mother took me to Bromley Church on Sunday mornings and to Shortlands Children's Service in the afternoon, where a great parson, named, very appropriately, Woolley, baa'd at us about how God loved us. He asked us easy questions of a conventional type, which I steadily refused to answer in spite of my mother's urgency. She did so want me to be a credit to her.

She had been disappointed in my being born a boy instead of a girl, because before I was born, she had lost an elder sister of mine, also precocious, whose essentially feminine mentality had proved less resistant than mine. She dilated upon the wonderful and exemplary sayings, and doings of this lost sister, 'Possy', comparing them humiliatingly with my own excess of original sin. It failed to produce the ready response she hoped for, poor dear! I understand her now but in those days I did not understand, and so I had no pity. Let every parent and teacher keep in mind that excellent proverb 'Comparisons are odious,' particularly to the young. It was certainly true, I brooded, that this God Almighty did not love any of us, but although I felt a very natural desire to escape that hell of his, I

8

found it absolutely impossible to be abject and love him. I prayed for faith. How many poor little souls have tried the self-abuse of such prayers! I might easily have gone into some crazy religious mania. One finds every type of that stress among mystical confessions. But I escaped – through a dream.

I was a precocious reader by seven, and in an old number of *Chambers' Journal* I read an account of a poor creature being broken on the wheel. I went to bed and had a frightful nightmare in which my mind took a rational leap. I jumped all the intermediaries in the business. I dreamt it was God Almighty himself who was breaking that man on the wheel. Because that followed logically upon its happening at all. The Almighty was responsible for the whole world; the evil in it, therefore, just as much as the good. That dream was a perfect resolution of my distresses. I knew He, that awful He, was impossible. I was left to struggle with a vast number of minor philosophical issues, but I believed in God Almighty no more.

What has not been exactly determined, either in his own autobiographical writings or anywhere else, is when he was introduced to two other writers who helped to shape his mind. One was Laurence Sterne whose *Tristram Shandy* became the discursive model for so many of his own novels, and the other was his Kentish kinsman John Ball. In the latter case, the strong presumption must be that the introduction was made by William Morris, whose poem *The Dream of John Ball* was published in 1867 and quickly became a favourite with Socialist readers. HG himself was never so devoted a disciple of Morris as many others of that generation. But John Ball, almost the only Catholic priest ever to receive Wells's unqualified approval, had the essence of the matter in him.

When Adam delved and Eve span/Who was then the gentleman? All the real work was done by Adam and Eve; and the gentleman, if he existed at all, was a parasite. And when HG first heard the couplet, which he would perpetually quote, it is hard to believe that he did not see Adam as his wayward, unlucky, but still inspirational garden-addicted father and Eve as his broken, shamefully overworked mother. It was the injustice done to them which made him a Socialist.

TWO

The Wheels of Love

There's nothing in life like loving someone,
Harry. People don't talk to you about it and lots
of people don't know what they are missing. It's
all the difference between being nothing or
something. It's all the difference between being
dead or alive.

Fanny to Harry, The Dream, p. 228

If the teenage HG had not been extremely lucky on a series of occasions, he would have been broken, as his father and mother were broken. Owing to their bad luck or bad management, they were not able to make a success of the shop in Bromley. His mother decided that the best solution for all their domestic trials was as soon as practicable to get her children out of schools and into actual work as drapers' assistants or some other form of apprenticeship. The arrangement worked with his two elder brothers, Frank and Fred, and she eagerly pressed Bertie in the same direction. She did it out of love, and could never understand how each such exertion on her part ended in resentment and calamity. He spent nearly four interminable years, with only occasional breaks for Christmas or illness at Up Park, obeying his mother's instruction, hating every aspect of his servitude, pleading with his father to help his release but finding that his ineffectualness added to the burden. He might be able to escape on holidays into other worlds, but this made his senseless imprisonment all the more unendurable.

Thanks to his special relationship with his family, he did not blame them. His resentment turned on 'the social and religious organizations responsible for me that had allowed me to be thrust into the hopeless drudgery of a shop, ignorant, mis-informed, undernourished and physically underdeveloped, without warning and guidance, at the age of thirteen'. His superiors of every kind 'took my inferiority as part of the accepted order. They first trod on me . . . I *hated* them as only the young can hate, and it gave me the energy to struggle, and I set about struggling, for knowledge.'* At last he did turn a dream into action on one day which became famous later – in August 1883 – when he walked seventeen miles from the hated Southsea Emporium to Up Park to tell his mother that he could tolerate the sentence no longer. 'I felt then', he said, 'most desperately wicked, and now I know that it was nearly the best thing I ever did.'

Thereafter, he won the chance to continue the process of his self-education. He did it first teaching at Midhurst Grammar School, a place which naturally won an enduring reward in his affections, for it was there that he read on a form the offer of free studentships at the Normal School of Science, South Kensington, carrying with them a maintenance grant of a guinea a week and second-class railway fare to the capital:

> I read the blue form with incredulity, filled it up secretly and with trepidation, and presently found myself accepted as a 'teacher in training' for a year in the biological course under Professor Huxley, the great Professor Huxley, whose name was in the newspapers, who was known all over the world! I had come to Midhurst a happy but desperate fugitive from servitude; I left it in glory. I spent my summer vacation partly at Up Park with my mother and partly with my father at Bromley, and I was hardly the same human being as the desperate, footsore, youngster who had

* *The Fate of Homo Sapiens*, p. 9.

tramped from Portsmouth to Up Park, breathing threats of suicide. My mother did not like to cast a shadow on my happiness, but yet she could not conceal from me that she had heard that this Professor Huxley was a notoriously irreligious man. But when I explained that he was Dean of the Normal School, her fears abated, for she had no idea that there could be such a thing as a lay Dean. Later on my mother thought and learnt more about the Dean. I have described the quaint simple faith in Providence, Our Father and Our Saviour, by which to the best of her ability she guided her life and the lives of her family. I have guessed at a failure of belief in her after the trials of Atlas House and the loss of her 'poor Possy'. Whatever reality her religion had had for her ebbed away after that. She wept with dismay when I came blustering from Southsea to say I would not be confirmed, but I think it was social rather than religious dismay. I said I was an 'Atheist', a frightful word for her to hear, as bad as swearing. 'My dear!' she cried. 'Don't say such a *dreadful* thing!' And then, good little Protestant that she was, she found consolation. 'Better than being caught by those Old Priests,' she said, 'anyhow.'

Thus Midhurst was the place where he could celebrate a new liberation even more than those associated with the upper rooms at Bromley or Up Park. Once again, books came to his rescue. Somehow at Midhurst he read more attentively than before Plato's *Republic*:

Plato was like the hand of a strong brother taking hold of me and raising me up, to lead me out of a prison of social acceptance and submission. I do not know why Christianity and the old social order permitted the name of Plato to carry in intellectual prestige to my mind far above that of Saint Paul or Moses. Why has there been no distraction? I suppose because the Faithful have never yet been able to escape from a certain lurking self-criticism, and because in every age there have been minds more responsive to the transparent honesty and greatness of Plato and Aristotle than to the tangled dogmatism of the Fathers. But here was a man wearing the likeness of an Olympian God, to whom every scholarly mind and every clerical back bowed down in real or imposed respect, who had written things of revolutionary destructiveness beyond my darkest mutterings. Hitherto there had always been something insurgent, inferior, doubtful and furtive in my objections to the religious, moral and social systems to which my life had, it seemed, to be adapted. All my thoughts leapt up now in open affirmation to the novel ideas he opened out to me.

Chief of these was the conception of a society in which economic individualism was overruled entirely in the common interest. This was my first encounter with the Communist idea. I had accepted property as in the very nature of things, just as my mother had accepted the Monarchy and the Church. I had been so occupied with my mental rebellion against the ideas of God and the King, that hitherto I had not resented the way in which the Owner barred my way here, forbad me to use this or enjoy that. Now with Plato's picture of an entirely different social administration before me, to make a comparison possible, I could ask 'By *what right* – is this for you and not for me?' Why are things monopolised? Why was everything appropriated and every advantage secured against me before I came into the world?

Had Plato ever had such a reader, we may pause to ask. If so, why had the challenge to the established system and, in particular, to the system of property-owning taken so long in coming? But HG himself in the same exposition immediately explained how one enemy was related to another, how he started to unravel another burning mystery. He examined for himself how Plato guided him to Shelley. Here, too, was a road which he found for himself, and the intellectual link became indissoluble.

So by way of Plato, I got my vision of the Age of Reason that was just about to begin. Never did anyone believe more firmly in the promptitude of progress than I. And then, to add to the excitement, as my mind filled up and broadened out at Midhurst, I began to resent the state of sexual deprivation in which I was living, more and more explicitly. All over Europe and America youths and maidens fretted under the same deprivation. Not only were their minds being afflicted by that nightmare story of the Ogre-God and his Hell, not only were they being caught helplessly young and jammed for life into laborious, tedious, uninteresting and hopeless employments, but they were being denied the most healthy and delightful of freedoms of mutual entertainment. They were being driven down to concealed and debilitating practices and shameful suppressions. Every year the age of marriage was rising and the percentage of marriages was falling, and the gap of stress and vexation between desire and reasonable fulfilment was widening. In that newspaper shop on the way to Landport where I saw and sometimes bought the *Freethinker*, I also found the *Malthusian* displayed, and one or two numbers had been the subject of a lively discussion with Platt and Ross. The Bradlaugh–Besant trial had occurred in 1876 and the light of sanity was gradually breaking into the dark places of English sexual life. There was perhaps a stronger belief current then that births were completely controllable than the actual facts warranted. Now under the stimulus of Plato's Utopianism and my quickening desires I began to ask my imagination what it was I desired in women.

I desired and needed their embraces and so far as I could understand it they needed and desired the embraces of men. It came to me as the discovery of a fresh preposterousness in life as it was being lived about me, that there were endless millions of young people in the world in the same state of sexual suspense and unrest as myself, quite unable to free themselves sweetly and honestly from these entangling preoccupations. Quite enough, there was, of either sex to go round. But I did not want an epidemic of marriages. I had not the slightest wish for household or offspring at that time; my ambition was all for unencumbered study and free movement in pursuit of my own ends, and my mind had not the slightest fixation upon any particular individual or type of individual. I was entirely out of accord with the sentimental patterns and focused devotions adopted by most people about me. In the free lives and free loves of the guardians of the *Republic* I found the encouragement I needed to give my wishes a systematic form. Presently I discovered a fresh support for these tentative projects in Shelley. Regardless of every visible reality about me, of law, custom, social usage, economic necessities and the un-explored psychology of womanhood, I developed my adolescent fantasy of free, ambitious, self-reliant women who would mate with me and go their way, as I desired to go my way. I had never in fact seen or heard of any such women; I had evolved them from my inner consciousness.

He often wrote, as he had done here in his autobiography, of what he called 'the chances by which one meets or escapes books'. How he met Plato and how he escaped Marx were matters of great significance for him in his understanding of Communism; how he heard the reverberations from the Bradlaugh–Besant trial, how he first met Shelley, how he had met Jonathan Swift even earlier, so that he seemed to preside over so many of these proceedings. He thought he was thinking it all out for himself and then he discovered that multitudes of minds had been moving in the same direction.

He pictured himself making his own way at the age of 18, but he pictured also the influence of his father. Glimpses of that portrait would appear often in his own novels, but the portrait in his autobiography should not be missed:

One bank holiday, Whit-Monday no doubt, he took advantage of a cheap fare to go back with me to his boyhood at Penshurst. We walked across the park from Tonbridge. He wanted me to see and feel the open life he had led before the shop and failure had caught him. He wanted to see and feel it again himself. 'We used to play cricket here – well it was just about here anyhow – until we lost sight of the ball in the twilight . . . There's more bracken and less turf about here now.' He talked of a vanished generation of our cousins, the Dukes, and of a half-sister I had never heard of before. She and he had gone fishing together through the dew-wet grass between sunrise and the beginning of the day's work. She was a tall strong girl who could run almost as fast as he could. He repeated that. So I guess his first dreams of women were not so very unlike mine. He showed me where she sat in Penshurst Church. Also he discoursed very learnedly on the growing of willows to make cricket bats and how long it took for a man to learn to make a first-class cricket bat. That was a great day for my father and me.

He won his way, almost entirely by his own efforts and decisions, to the holiest sanctum of the Normal School of Science, South Kensington, where the great Professor Huxley taught. He might have transformed this achievement into some personal conceit; instead he filled his lungs with the collective spirit of the times and translated his scientific discoveries into a broader understanding. He studied physics, chemistry, geology, astronomy and biology. Especially the period he spent under Huxley, studying comparative anatomy, he saw as, beyond all question, 'the most educational year of my life'. * He had traced the whole process of man's evolution, and had measured man's place in the universe by the scale of the stars. But he was attracted also, if not yet captivated, by the political life he saw all around him. He attended Socialist gatherings at the house of William Morris in Hammersmith; strayed into meetings of the Fabian Society – and strayed out again; had his first meetings with some of the leading lights of the Society – Bernard Shaw and Graham Wallas – and, more important, still found time for his own literary discoveries: Thomas Carlyle's *French Revolution*, William Blake's prophecies, and a host more of varied masters of his own choosing. He started writing himself for the *Science Schools Journal* on topics even more various. Maybe at first such a variety of pursuits injured his studies; he failed his first final examination. But next year, in October 1890, he took a Bachelor of Science degree with first-class honours at the University of London.

Against all the odds, he had escaped from the penitential rigours of the shop floor and acquired a first-class scientific

* *Experiment in Autobiography*, vol. 1, p.186.

training. Unconsciously almost, but none the less instruc-
tively, he had turned from one set of authors, selecting his own
favourites in a manner which no school or authority could have
prescribed. He might have broken himself altogether by such
scholastic exertions, especially since most of his physical
weaknesses showed signs of recurring. Yet all this dedicated
labour was not allowed to subdue his natural charm, a kind of
excitement which he spread wherever he went and, most
unforgettably of all, with his restless darting blue eyes. Not
merely did he make a deep impression at the Science School;
he formed some friendships which he kept all his life. One of
these was Elizabeth Healey, who was there with him and
throughout the years 1884–7.

> Mr Wells was slender and pale when I first met him with
> remarkable blue eyes – and thick tumbled brown hair. He was very
> popular with his fellow students for he was sociable, amusing,
> friendly and a most brilliant talker – who was refreshing and
> stimulating – without ever showing malice or ill-nature. As a
> speaker in the Debating Society, he never had an equal in my
> time. His wit was keen and swift – his sarcasm never wounded the
> victims of it – for it was tempered with humour and truth. He
> attacked conventions, shams and humbugs with all that courage of
> youth – which has never failed him throughout his later life. He
> loved 'cockshies' and smashing popular beliefs. *

Sadly, no photograph gives a proper impression of the young
HG, which is one reason why he disliked posing for them, then
and thereafter. His own 'picshuas' convey his spirit better.

Where would his renewed zest and high spirits guide him
next? But then, through no fault of his own, he was struck
down again, and the blow was almost literally mortal. The
accident happened on the football field where he was knocked
down and trampled upon; but it was the subsequent treatment,
or lack of it, which caused the real trouble. One collapse

* J. R. Hammond (ed.), *H. G. Wells: Interviews and Recollections* (1980), p. 1.

followed another. One diagnosis suggested consumption, and within a few weeks he was restored to the care of his mother and the upper-room library at Up Park, and with something like a relentless pressure to look for a new way of earning his livelihood since he appeared to have no capacity or no luck in earning it as a teacher. He must look to his own writing more than ever before. The letters he wrote from his sickbed, most of them to truly loving friends, male and female, whom he had made at the science college, show the Wellsian valour at its best and how truly formidable were the forces ranged against him: 'I have a faint idea that God has sent all this to chasten me. If so, he has certainly mistaken his man. I have learnt some wholesome lessons in human charity, but I repudiate God more than ever. He's a beggar, he is.'*

He had to try and try again to make himself a writer, and another letter to another of his science college friends put the point still more graphically:

Item 1	Short Story	Sold £1. 0. 0d.
Item 1	Novel, 35,000 words	Burnt 0 0 0d
Item 1	Novel unfinished 25,000	" 0 0 0d
Item	Much comic poetry	Lost 0 0 0
Item	Some comic prose	Sent away, never returned
Item	Humorous Essay	*Globe*, did not return
Item	Sundry Stories	Burnt
Item	1 Story	Wandering
Item	A Poem	Burnt
		etc. etc.

Total income (untaxed) £1. 0. 0d

Some day I shall succeed, I really believe, but it is a weary game.

* This letter and several more written in the same honourable, rebellious sense are taken not from HG's own *Autobiography*, but from Geoffrey West's *H. G. Wells: A Sketch for a Portrait* (1930), which appeared just before HG started writing his autobiography. Quoted by himself, they might have been dismissed as too egotistical. Selected by West, they offer indispensable evidence, especially for this period, of how strong was the heart which beat in that weak body.

Love and work, work and love, the young HG, or the man as he grew older, found himself constantly torn between the two operations. Both were necessary for his peace of mind, his enjoyment of living, his survival even. But he had to find all this out for himself, or so he thought in his young days. How he learned so much from his wayward father and his repressed mother is not easy to determine, but of course he did, much more than he might acknowledge; and, in any case, he never held them responsible for these deficiencies in his upbringing. When the occasional, odd, real teacher did happen to cross his path, he was thrilled and unfeignedly thankful. He knew later, even if he did not see at the time, what he owed to such priceless benefactions. HG learned from what he was taught and what he was not taught, and the combined recollection, happy or bitter, gave him his lifelong absorption in questions of education.

His love affairs with women, like those with his mother and father, were conducted in the same spirit of experiment. He could not imagine that his skinny, feeble body, so often afflicted by fresh unexpected ailments, could be anything other than repulsive to women. His mother, of course, could not talk to him on these sacred matters, and even his jovial father was inhibited. He and his cousin, Isabel Mary, were not designed for each other at all. It was just the proximity combined with these unexplained sexual stirrings which pushed the affair forward; yet it was in the London of the 1880s, and HG would never forget those sudden excitements and discoveries. He had to find everything out for himself; nobody told him anything worth knowing. How the HG of the 1870s and 1880s could have made such good use of a Marie Stopes or Bertrand Russell guidebook, but nothing remotely to be compared with these classic expositions was available. What he really needed with his beautiful, high-spirited, good-natured cousin, Isabel Mary, was a period of companionate marriage such as Bertrand Russell would daringly advocate fifty years later. 'My nature', HG wrote in his autobiography, 'protested at having to wait for her so long, protested at having to marry her in church instead of at a registry office. I didn't believe in marriage anyhow, I insisted. The great thing was not marriage, but love. I invoked Godwin, Shelley, Socialism.' Instead they were properly married at Wandsworth parish church on 31 October 1891. And she lived unhappily ever afterwards, or almost so; but it was certainly not her fault, and not exactly his.

Everyone who knew Isabel – headed by HG himself – testified to her beauty and her charm, and a 'quick humour' equal to his own. It should have been a perfect match, and HG would constantly recall the thrill of their first meetings in the London he was also starting to explore and extol. Maybe the shifts and unsettlements and suffocations of London lodgings contributed to the trouble, but Regent's Park could restore their spirits. 'Their marriage soon broke down,' wrote one expert witness (if there can be such observers in such matters), 'and for reasons which happen even in quite conventional upper- and middle-class families and, even at that time, could have led to a quiet termination by one or other legal procedures. But in Wells's world there was not a single soul with a grain of worldly wisdom. So he stayed with Isabel till he fell in love with a student in one of his science classes.'* HG had discovered sooner than Isabel that it would not work. Even though he did everything he could to help her, his conscience was scarred. The wound which he had inflicted on her intensified the hatred he felt for the whole apparatus of Victorian marriage and morals. The worldly wisdom of that age still offered no reprieves, no mitigations.

His love for Isabel, however short and sharp the actual marriage, was real, and he never ceased to celebrate it in one way or another. He had been captivated ever since he first set eyes on her at her home in 181 Euston Road one bright morning in 1886. 'I tethered my sexual and romantic imagination to her,' he wrote much later. Tethered may seem a strange term to use in the circumstances but a host of Wellsian-

---

* Rebecca West's review in the *Sunday Telegraph*, 17 June 1973, of Norman and Jeanne Mackenzie's *The Time Traveller* (1973).

trained lovers in the first decade of this century or later became her devotees too.

Jane was something quite different. He found in her, as he said, 'the embodiment of all the understanding and quality he desired in life' – not all at once, of course, but very soon. He had met Amy Catherine Robbins in 1893; she was a pupil at the place where he was teaching. 'We were the most desperate of lovers; we launched ourselves upon our life together with less than fifty pounds between us and absolute disaster, and we pulled through.'* For the next year or two they lived together in 7 Mornington Place and 12 Mornington Road in the neighbourhood of Primrose Hill. Both hated the name Amy, and he called her Jane. She loved him – and she knew how he wanted to work, and maybe, in that particular, she knew him better than he knew himself. He had many fits and starts in his attempt to learn his trade as an author. Even with Jane safely ensconced at his side, the setbacks and the blockages seemed to get worse. He almost gave up.

Such moods were no part of his normal temperament. He never forgot the sense of cockney exhilaration and insolence in which he had wooed both Isabel and Jane. He could see around him a whole generation of young men and women whose voices had never been heard in the England of his time. Even the language they talked was not exactly English, but it had a pith and rhythm and resonance of its own. The only place on the planet about which HG had any real practical knowledge was London; deep in his heart he would never forget, but the seedy lodging-houses of Camden Town offered him no guidance about how to make his fortune, how to keep his head above water even – and Jane's head and his mother's and his father's, and Isabel's too. All of them looked more and more to him, and at one stage the rising pressures threatened to overwhelm him altogether. Thus he wrote to his mother and father on 5 February 1895, a year which was to be fateful for him, but he did not know as much then: 'However hard up you were when I

---

* *The Book of Catherine Wells* (1928), p. 11.

was a youngster, you let me have paper and pencils, books from the Institute and so forth, and if I haven't my mother to thank for my imagination and my father for skill, where do I get these qualities?' They could not quite approve his divorce from Isabel which went through in the first months of 1895; but they could never doubt the love of such a son. *

How the frail, ill-educated, ill-conditioned HG transformed himself into a writer is a heroic story. He told it himself again and again but without self-glorification. How, a few years later, the self-taught writer also transformed himself into one who could not merely face the world but was determined to change it was hardly less heroic. And the whole combined, miraculous transformation was compressed into the short period of a single decade. A little while later he would look for a way of translating this experience into a literary form, but he was not ready for that yet. His was the story of love, London and the end of one epoch and the birth of a new one, and a genuine modesty in the face of all these accumulated confrontations.

The London of the 1890s, where he wanted to make his mark and where he had to struggle so hard to win a meagre livelihood, was not at first sight the kind of place he could be expected to accept readily. Some aspects of it, and the most glaring, intensified the hatred already instilled in him against the injustice of it all. The poverty, the shoddiness, the squalor, the ugliness – young HG never ceased to rail against all these horrors which the London of his time paraded. He soon acquired a contempt for those who sought excuses for the continuance of such infamies or, worse still, sought to proclaim that they were ordained by a benevolent Providence. The English ruling class, like his mother's God Almighty, had recruited a new and formidable enemy.

How that rule with all its insufferable manifestations was to be challenged and overthrown was one argument in which he found himself engaged. He heard the case for what was called Socialism in lecture-halls and at street-corners and on bicycle

* *Experiment in Autobiography*, vol. 1, p. 400.

expeditions. His acquisition of a bicycle was a truly momentous event; he himself was one of the first to discover its double use – for preaching the new Socialism or approaching the new Woman. However, his most important explorations were in London itself. Necessity or choice pushed him from one avenue of exploration to another, and each of them might soon be granted the distinction of a place in his writing: Mornington Place, Brompton Road, Euston Road, Camden Town, Primrose Hill and a host more, familiar places, familiar names, and his odyssey became part of him. He loved London, and this emotional attachment remained for ever an essential element of his own charm. He made the place part of his being more than any writer since Dickens, and could not allow his precious allocation of patriotism to be wantonly dispensed anywhere else. Most important of all in these moves, enforced or otherwise, was the consolidation of his cockney pride and independence. And yet he still had to deal with a London where the old society survived and, more especially, where the opportunity for would-be writers, especially self-made ones from the suburbs, was blocked by convention and snobbery. Successful writers did not easily come from his class or his particular layer within it: he was an upstart who had to fight every inch of his own way, an outsider who was never told any of the rules, an infant prodigy in the library who had shaped his own Gothic-Gulliver specimens to suit his own taste.

One special moment in the transition from defeat to victory stood out in HG's own mind and also in the mind of his benefactor. One among his huge stack of unpublished articles was called 'The Rediscovery of the Unique', and he had sent it to a journal called the *Fortnightly Review*, at one time edited by the Liberal historian and statesman John Morley, and later by Frank Harris. HG had a special liking for the piece; that didn't help much. But, when the great Frank Harris did send him a message, HG, who was living at the time with his aunt Mary in Fitzroy Road, Camden Town, was not exactly prepared for such an occasion.

I found the summons disconcerting. My below-stairs training reinforced the spirit of the times on me, and insisted that I should visit him in proper formal costume. I imagined I must wear a morning coat and a silk hat and carry an umbrella. It was impossible I should enter the presence of a Great Editor in any other guise. My aunt Mary and I inspected these vitally important articles. The umbrella, tightly rolled and with a new elastic band, was not so bad, provided it had not to be opened; but the silk hat was extremely discouraging. It was very fluffy and defaced and, as I now perceived for the first time, a little brownish in places. The summons was urgent and there was no time to get it ironed. We brushed it with a hard brush and then with a soft one and wiped it round again and again with a silk handkerchief. The hat remained unsubdued. Then, against the remonstrations of my aunt Mary, I wetted it with a sponge and then brushed. That seemed to do the trick. My aunt's attempt to restrain me had ruffled and delayed me a little, but I hurried out, damply glossy, to the great encounter, my début in the world of letters.

Harris kept me waiting in the packing office downstairs for nearly half an hour before he would see me. This ruffled me still more. At last I was shown up to a room that seemed to me enormous, in the midst of which was a long table at which the great man was sitting. At the ends were a young man, whom I was afterwards to know as Blanchamp, and a very refined-looking old gentleman named Silk who was Harris's private secretary. Harris silently motioned me to a chair opposite himself. He was a square-headed individual with very black hair parted in the middle and brushed fiercely back. His eyes as they met my shabby and shrinking form became intimidatory. He had a blunt nose over a vast black upturned moustache, from beneath which came a deep voice of exceptional power. He seemed to me to be of extra-ordinary size, though that was a mere illusion; but he was certainly formidable. 'And it was *you* sent me this Universe R. R. Rigid!' he roared.

I got across to the table somehow, sat down and disposed myself for a conversation. I was depleted and breathless. I placed my umbrella and hat on the table before me and realised then for the first time that my aunt Mary had been right about the wetting. It had become a disgraceful hat, an insult. The damp gloss had gone. The nap was drying irregularly and standing up in little tufts all over. It was not simply a shabby top hat; it was an improper top hat. I stared at it. Harris stared at it. Blanchamp and Silk had evidently never seen such a hat. With an effort we came to the business in hand.

'You sent me this Universe Gur-R-R-Rigid,' said Harris, picking up his cue after the pause. He caught up a proof beside him and tossed it across the table. 'Dear Gahd! I can't understand six words of it. What do you *mean* by it? For Gahd's sake tell me what it is about? What's the sense of it? What are you trying to say?' I couldn't stand up to him – and my hat. I couldn't for a moment adopt the tone and style of a bright young man of science. There was my hat tacitly revealing the sort of chap I was. I couldn't find words. Blanchamp and Silk with their chins resting on their hands, turned back from the hat to me, in gloomy silent accusation.

'Tell me what you think it's about?' roared Harris, growing more merciless with my embarrassment, and rapping the proof with the back of his considerable hand. He was enjoying himself.

'Well, you see . . .' I said.

'I don't see,' said Harris. 'That's just what I don't do.'

'The idea,' I said, 'the idea . . .'

Harris became menacingly silent, patiently attentive.

'If you consider time is space like, then . . . I mean if you treat it like a fourth dimension like, well then you see . . .'

'*Gahd*, the way I've been let in!', injected Harris in an aside to Gahd.

'I can't use it,' said Harris at the culmination of the interview. 'We'll have to disperse the type again.' And the vision I had had of a series of profound but brilliant articles about fundamental ideas, that would make a reputation for me, vanished. My departure from that room has been mercifully obliterated from my memory. But as soon as I got alone with it in my bedroom in Fitzroy Road, I smashed up that hat finally. To the great distress of my aunt Mary.

It might be thought that this brilliant and touching account of the confrontation was in some way fanciful. But not at all. Frank Harris's own account of the same scene confirmed it. His description of the young Wells rings true in every particular. He claimed that he had come across the piece by Wells, left by John Morley, and had thought it was charmingly written, the style simple, easy, rhythmic, the architecture faultless. 'I had expected some well-known name: H. G. Wells.' No-one had heard of him, neither Harris's associates nor anybody else.

'You will hear of him,' ventured Harris – perhaps the only piece of embroidery added to this particular tale. For when the actual interview occurred a few days later Harris was no longer impressed. He had even forgotten the hat.

> A few days afterwards Wells called and I asked him to take a seat. I told him of his article and how greatly I admired it, all the while studying him. A man of middle height, well-made, with shapely head, thick chestnut hair, regular features; chin and brow both good; nothing arresting or peculiar in the face, save his eyes; eyes that grew on one. They were of ordinary size, a grayish blue in colour, but intent, shadowed, suggesting depth like water in a half-covered spring; observant eyes too, that asked questions, but reflection, meditation, the note of them; eyes almost pathetic in the patience of their scrutiny.
>
> His manner was timid; he spoke very little and only in response; his accent that of a Cockney. He professed himself a student of science.
>
> 'I've written some things for science papers, for *Nature*. I scarcely hoped to have this paper accepted it has been so long since I sent it in. I'm glad you like it . . .'
>
> He was so effaced, so colourless, so withdrawn, that he wiped out the effect his paper had made on me. I lost sight of him for some time, but knew his value. [*]

Yet the mysterious confrontation ended happily, thanks chiefly to the intervention of another contributor to Frank

[*] Frank Harris's *Contemporary Portraits* (1920), p. 5.

Harris's paper who was quite ready to profess himself impressed by 'The Rediscovery of the Unique' by the unknown H. G. Wells. How HG discovered that it was Oscar Wilde who had come to his rescue is still not clear, but HG honoured him thereafter whenever he got the chance.

What to write and how to write – apart from his love affairs with Isabel and Jane, apart also, as we should constantly insist, from his mission to restore some happiness to his mother and father: this became the dominant pressure upon him. His first attempts – a *Textbook of Biology* and his *Honours Physiography*, written with his friend R. A. Gregory, however worthy, opened no real future in that direction. All through the anxious years at the beginning of the decade he had tried his hand at different ideas. On 21 June 1894 a short story entitled 'The Stolen Bacillus', signed H. G. Wells, appeared in the *Pall Mall Budget*; it was the first to appear over his name. He had published much before anonymously, and the wise editor of the *Budget* was eager to publish everything else he submitted that year. HG himself had a natural liking for the piece. Authors do love their firstborn, especially if the delivery has been so lengthy and painful as it had been for HG. He was a hard-pressed, hard-working young man of 27. Several authors from homes where they have not had to fight for their existence and survival have had the chance to start and make their blundering entry into the literary world much earlier than that. He was just trying his hand at these various forms of expression, but he could not afford too many failures. A good description of what HG's mood must have been was written by his son Frank: 'These stories were written during the few years from 1894. They were written by a professional earning a living. They were written by an exuberantly creative mind and by the shadow of an empty till.'* Just about this time he himself recalled that he

---

* Frank Wells wrote introductions to several of his father's books when they were published by Collins in the 1950s. He is often a very good guide indeed to those rare readers who read introductions. He called them 'ordinary H. G. Wells', by which he meant no slight, and when HG himself made selections of his best stories he included several of these.

had taken 'a cleansing course of Swift and Sterne'.* Those two together, in mighty alliance, should be given the chief credit for the next stage.

The London of the 1890s was not provincial in any sense; it was constantly influenced by the wider intellectual world which embraced the stirrings or the lamentations across the Channel or across the Atlantic. The end of the century seemed to prompt apocalyptic forebodings, partly indicated in the writings of Friedrich Nietzsche but not by him alone. HG absorbed these moods, too, as he sought to find his way round the new London. A later definition which seemed to fit was the Age of Oscar Wilde. At the turn of the decade, he published his brilliant series of essays headed by 'The Soul of Man under Socialism' in which Wilde illustrated how confidence in the old order had been intellectually shaken. Wilde's plays captivated London – the still-gauche, impecunious H. G. Wells attended the first nights of *An Ideal Husband* and *The Importance of Being Earnest*. These were his first commissions as a theatre critic: his reviews were intelligent, but not ecstatic, and at least as favourable as those of Bernard Shaw, with whom he now talked for the first time. When the terrible trial of Oscar Wilde followed three months later, HG was naturally horrified. He was also naturally obsessed by his own activities, and he had as yet no inkling that this was to be the year of his deliverance.

He must make his livelihood as a writer, but how the deed was to be done and what precisely he should write were still not clear at all. He had made a long series of false starts and accumulated a prodigious collection of rejection slips. Time was slipping by; the pressure became overbearing. 'The writer', as he himself recorded, 'was living from hand to mouth as a journalist. There came a lean month when scarcely an article of his was published or paid for in any of the papers to which he was accustomed to contribute and since all the offices in

* This quotation comes from one of the prefaces to the Atlantic Edition of his works (1924–7).

London that would tolerate him were already amply supplied with still unused articles, it seemed hopeless to write more until the block was moved.'* So he set about rewriting, in desperation, the idea that had already been printed in another form in Henley's *National Observer* a year before. He had moved with Jane to lodgings at Tusculum Villa, Sevenoaks, in August 1894. She did everything to help him, but his Sevenoaks landlady was not so co-operative. As he wrote late one summer night by an open window, she grumbled about the excessive use of her lamp. So he wrote on more hectically than ever; it was the last part of the book which had to be finished in these adverse conditions, and HG himself would make no special claims for the final product.

But the London of 1895 and the rest of the literary world beyond would soon offer a remedy. *The Time Machine* was published in book form in May 1895, and became one of the most instant successes in publishing history. How and why and with what justification it received so much acclaim for its literary qualities are questions we must still examine. But henceforth HG's own fortune was transformed. He still thought that this piece of writing which had brought his relief was 'the work of an inexperienced writer', but he could always recall the thought of 'that needy and cheerful namesake' of his who lived 'back along the time dimensions', and who now had his own first real taste of success.

Who in the outside world was the very first to hail *The Time Machine* as a masterpiece? Competing claims were made. It was W. T. Stead, editor and founder of the *Review of Reviews*, who wrote the piece first appearing in the *New Review* which included the term 'a man of genius'; but Grant Richards, his assistant, who later became an adventurous editor and publisher in his own right, insisted that he had written the actual words. An anonymous writer in the *Daily Chronicle*, on 7 July 1895, said that a hitherto unknown author had produced in the

* H. G. Wells's own new introduction to the Random House edition of *The Time Machine* (1931).

form of fiction that rarity which Solomon declared to be not merely rare but nonexistent – 'a new thing under the sun'. Israel Zangwill in the *Pall Mall Magazine* said the writer was responsible for 'a fine imaginative creation worthy of Swift, and possibly not devoid of satirical reference to "the present discontents" '. This verdict must have gladdened HG's heart on every count. Despite his truly severe struggle to get a real start as a writer, he had the good luck to live in an age of great editors. Three who certainly qualified for that title – Henley, Harris and Stead – had each given him some essential encouragement. Stead's appreciation of *The Time Machine*'s qualities came at the most advantageous moment, as HG was eager to acknowledge.* And if there were doubts about who might first have the honour of acclaiming his recognition, no doubt was possible about the people with whom he most wished to share the moment: 'My dear Mother . . . My last book seems a hit . . . It's rather pleasant . . . to find oneself something in the world after all the years of trying and disappointment.'†

One part of *The Time Machine*'s satire arising from the tumults of the time portrayed what could happen if the war between the classes was allowed to develop and intensify. Civilized values would perish altogether. But the prophylactic warnings had a larger context still. What might not have happened to men? What if cruelty had grown into a common passion? What if, in this interval, the race had lost its manliness and had developed into something inhuman, unsympathetic and overwhelmingly powerful? This was the greatest Swiftian theme adapted to modern conditions, with the question left open whether mankind and womankind – they had a special role for Wells, as for Swift – would have the combined nerve and intelligence to turn back from the path which led to horrific catastrophe. One reason for the sudden,

* HG's relationship with W. T. Stead was fully and fairly examined by Joseph O. Blaylen in an article which appeared in the *Huntingdon Library Quarterly*, November 1974. HG himself always acknowledged his debt to Stead, although they had some fierce quarrels later about *Ann Veronica* and *The New Machiavelli*.
† *Experiment in Autobiography*, vol. 2, p. 400.

stunning success of *The Time Machine* was that it did touch the Nietzschean chord in the spirit of the age: the mood which rejected absolutely Victorian triumphalism, the still-prevalent view that the England of that time deserved to spread its empire wider and wider. The prophecies of *The Time Machine* stripped bare these delusions.

V. S. Pritchett, HG's most perceptive modern critic, offered this judgement on *The Time Machine*: 'Without question it is the best piece of writing. It will take its place among the great stories of our language.'* Then he continued with this emphasis: 'Like all excellent work, it has meanings within meanings' – and he underlined especially the moment when the Time Traveller reveals the foundation of slime and horror on which the pretty life of his Arcadians is precariously and fearfully resting. Some interpreters saw the contest between the Eloi and the Morlocks as Wells's prophecy about the outcome of the class war defined by the Marxists, and since he later became known for his deep-seated opposition to Marxism the implication of *The Time Machine* was cited as evidence against him. But Wells's own intention was surely plainer and more fundamental. This part of the argument derived from his refusal to accept any élitist doctrine. His insistence was that any élitist culture, the general system so uncritically accepted by the English ruling class in the 1890s, was the enemy of civilization and of culture itself, for the profound reason that it made the people loathe everything which seemed to be in any way associated with it. Altogether, the Wells of the 1890s, according to Pritchett, comprehended the pain and the horrors which human beings might inflict upon one another. The great question of human or inhuman cruelty was already present in his writings in those times. 'We turn back to our Swift,' wrote Pritchett, 'there we see a mad world dominated by the sober figure of the great Gulliver, that plain, humane figure.' HG cherished that particular Jonathan Swift no less than Pritchett

* Bernard Bergonzi (ed.), *H. G. Wells: A Collection of Critical Essays* (1976).

himself. He would never allow the Swiftian presence to be long removed from his thinking; he would be cited at every turn.

Thus the greatness of *The Time Machine* is properly and incontestably assessed. But even the perfectly sympathetic Pritchett can raise other doubts. He poses questions about what he calls 'the faint squirms of idyllic petting', presumably the appearance of Weena, the one enduringly sympathetic character whom the Time Traveller encounters in the whole of his voyage, and the one whom he enlists as his last word to restore some faith for the future – 'and I have by me, for my comfort, two strange white flowers, shrivelled now and brown and flat and brittle, to witness that even when mind and strength had gone, gratitude and a mutual tenderness still lived on in the heart of man'. How much HG loved flowers, we should never forget; he had been taught by his beloved father.

Doubtless several of HG's enemies with full ferocity – and even the kindly Pritchett – would still dismiss these last words, and indeed the whole Weena intrusion, as a piece of un-conscionable sentimentality. And yet, if Weena is to be dismissed altogether on these or other grounds, what is to be substituted as the climax of the story? The love of Weena, the love of womankind, however transient, redeems the whole prospect. And something not so different, we may recall, occurs in *Gulliver's Travels*: 'My master and his friends continued on the shore till I was almost out of sight; and often I heard the sorrel nag (who always loved me), crying out Hnnyillanyhamajah Yahoo, Take care of thyself, gentle Yahoo.' If the astringent Gulliver was to be allowed his sentimental Sorrel Nag, HG should not be denied his Weena. And, in any case, to remove her altogether would be to destroy the balance which the hard-pressed author of *The Time Machine* had so carefully drawn. And, if the all-consuming cruelty which mankind could be incited to inflict was one governing moral which had to be deduced, it was no less worth noting how gentleness and compassion could still reappear.

Within that feeble frame (he still weighed less than eight stone), there was another HG struggling to find expression; and the triumph of *The Time Machine* helped to liberate him, too. The pilgrim of eternity would never be content to leave this matter at the wayside. The contrast might be defined as the case of the two bicycles, and HG himself would usually be ready to prick any trend towards pomposity. He himself wrote thirty years later: 'So *The Time Machine* has lasted as long as the diamond-framed safety bicycle which came in at about the date of its first publication.' The birth of Socialism in our country was also the age of the bicycle, and HG was, despite many rival claimants for the title, the writer-laureate of the new cult. Dangle of the *Clarion*, alias Alexander Thompson, the joint editor of that journal which owed so much to the cycling revolution and more than paid its debt, summed up one part of the position: 'The man of the day is the Cyclist, the press, the public, the pulpit, the faculty all discuss him. They discuss his health, his feet, his shoes, his speed, his cap, his knickers, his handlebars, his axle, his ballbearings, his tyres, his rims and everything that is his, down unto his shirt. He is the man of Fin de Cycle – I mean Siècle. He is the King of the Road.' But what of the female of the species, the Queen of the Road? Obviously the liberation for her and the spectacle for trained observers must be even more sensational. HG, ever alert to the allure of the female body and the latest swish of fashion, applied another part of his mind to the investigation. Bloomers were better even than Boadicea.

His first creation in this role was Hoopdriver in *The Wheels of Chance*. It is, as Bernard Bergonzi remarks, 'a book of the open road, full of fresh air and sunshine', but full, too, of passing references to such shockingly avant-garde figures as Beardsley and Ibsen and Shaw – H. G. Wells had one of his eyes fixed on them. He himself justly remarked at the time: 'The cycle is one of the greatest blessings which the nineteenth century has brought us. Its value is simply inestimable to nervous men, and I think all writers are more or else troubled with their nerves . . . All the cobwebs are brushed away from the brain, and you return to your work really refreshed.'

Thanks to the bicycle, thanks to *The Time Machine*, HG

himself helped to shape the spirit of the age; he was a child of the *fin de siècle*, and one of its creators. He worked for three of the great editors of that decade – Frank Harris, W. E. Henley and W. T. Stead – and impressed them all with his touch of modernity. He read the novels of Thomas Hardy and Joseph Conrad, and gave them a discriminatory welcome. His review of *Almayer's Folly* was one of the most perceptive; his outburst against the attempted suppression of *Jude the Obscure* the most furious. Unforgettably, it might be thought, although it was forgotten, he wrote of the attempted suppression of *Jude* that he had claimed to hear 'the voice of the educated proletarian speaking more distinctly than it has ever done before in English literature'. But more important than these excursions into criticism, which were not his natural bent, was the extraordinary range of his own imaginative work, a series of varied and innovating books which might have been enough for another author's whole output in a lifetime.

Since HG himself had looked back with critical pride over a perspective of some thirty years to greet the creator of *The Time Machine* in his defiance of all the principalities and powers, and not least the landladies of Sevenoaks and all the rest of their tribe, a biographer may follow his example. This was the H. G. Wells who first became known to the wider world, and a most striking phenomenon it was. The year 1895 was for sure his *annus mirabilis*, the moment when the outside judgement about his work and his own self-confidence were suddenly transformed. But then several other miraculous years followed – five, to be precise – when he presented something no less original. Some part of this tremendous overflowing output was due to the pent-up ideas or actual writings which he stored in his mind before the entirely unsuspected success of *The Time Machine*. Maybe that applied to a few of the short stories, but most of these were of the highest quality, too. And several of his other works produced in that golden period would have shaken the world, even if there had been no *Time Machine*. One most significant and creditable feature of them was that they did not seek to repeat the *Time Machine* formula in any sense whatever. The only exception to this rule was *The Sleeper Awakes* which, along with some other similarities, did seem to create at one stage the class-war crisis of *The Time Machine*, and this proved to be the only failure. All the other six major novels, treating their different subjects in six different manners, were works of art which could not have been written before the age of H. G. Wells, before he started spreading the sensational news from the science colleges to the Socialist seminars, from South Kensington to Hyde Park Corner, across all the famous London streets which HG helped to make more famous still. He was never vain about his writings – at least, not in these early days when he still knew he had so much to learn, and when he had so deliberately taken as his masters the best in the English tradition. But he did not like to be called a second Jules Verne, or a second Edgar Allan Poe, or a second Charles Dickens, when one of his primary aims was to look with fresh scientific, Swiftian eyes at the world all around him, and especially *his* London which he wanted to hear *his* Socialist message.

One practical achievement of *The Time Machine* was to make an end to his financial worries; Jane and the whole family could soon share his success. Editors would be chasing him instead of the other way round. Never again would he have to face poverty and defeat. Such a transformation in his fortunes might have insidiously undermined the purpose and calibre of his writing. Nothing of the sort is detectable in his conduct or his character or his treatment of his own ideas. Rather, in choosing his new fields of operation, he was much more likely to select topics which would give higher offence still in the proper quarters or make new explorations which would invite a renewal of his own past failures. It was supposed to be the true artist who followed his star wherever it led; the suddenly liberated author of *The Time Machine* did so more recklessly than ever before.

Both *The Wonderful Visit* and *The Island of Dr Moreau* owed much to the Swiftian guidance to which HG said he had reverted in the first years of the decade. The second is often accepted as more Swiftian than the first, but Swift in all his moods could influence HG. He could capture the polite or impolite conversation of his contemporaries as Swift had taught him. One critic saw 'such a pure jet of romantic as that which Mr. Wells refreshes our spirits'. Even his friendly angels start to worry about the problem of pain. His mind was moving in that direction, but nothing prepared his readers for the ferocity of *The Island of Dr Moreau*. 'There is nothing', wrote another critic, 'in Swift's grim conceptions of animalised man and rationalised animals more powerfully conceived than Mr. Wells's description of these deformed and malformed creations of Dr Moreau, repeating the litany in which they abase themselves before the physiological demigod by whom they have been endowed with their new powers of speech, their new servility to a human master, and their profound dread of that "house of pain" in which they have been made and fashioned into half baked men.' Dr Moreau should have been enough all on his own to kill the idea that Wells shut his eyes to the possibility of human depravity; there was the peril indelibly and blasphemously described. When the book was attacked, he found himself defending it as 'the best work I have done'. Whenever he spoke in such terms of his own work, his case should be respectfully examined. Like all authors he could misjudge his own work; but since he had made such elaborate efforts to ensure that every argument, every theme was weighed and balanced he was the more outraged when his fiercest, most apoplectic critics presented their criticism as if he had attempted nothing of the sort. He would have to accustom himself to that form of criticism: maybe this was his first taste of it. A whole argument was proceeding in that England of his time, thanks to Darwin and others, about the nature of human cruelty. Wells's *Dr Moreau* examined it with a new comprehension of man's origins and man's history. No other writer of the time struggled so boldly to weave together the new knowledge and the old.

His constant readiness to tackle the most awkward questions, his recently fortified confidence in himself, his artistic genius helped him to dicover new forms. *The Invisible Man* soon became as well known as *The Time Machine*. Apart from all its other strange attributes, his new machine had a heart. 'To HG', wrote his son Frank,

> it was the effect that scientific progress would have on the world, and the way in which people would react to the coming wonders that was of the greatest importance. In *The Invisible Man* he goes even deeper by studying the effect on the individual. He restates the sad and relentless cruelty of the mob to the unusual, to the hunchback, the cross-eyed, the monster or the pathetic simple-ton. He lays before us the despair and loneliness of the mob's victim, the schism between the desperate frightened individual, out of joint, and the close unthinking mutually protective herd. *

Yet the herd also states its case or offers a fresh portrait in this new setting. Several individual characters and some happy East Enders make their contribution. The reader's sympathy sways back and forth until the very last moment when he may suddenly ask himself how at last he has been affected. The 'double-take' was supposed to be an invention of the cinema screen, but it may be traced also to the ironic last twist which Swift might give to tales or poems, leaving his most devoted follower reeling from the exposure. HG did not always keep his balance so well, but *The Invisible Man*, presented so boldly to a world recovering from his *Dr Moreau*, was just another example of how he would exert himself to the limit to serve his community and his generation. It is especially odious that the title he made world famous should have been purloined by one of his modern detractors, and a Christian one at that, to suggest that the real HG himself had no heart at all.

If not a second Jules Verne, what about a second Daniel Defoe? The suggestion was made, not quite in these terms, but in a manner which must have won HG's unstinting accept-ance, in a full-scale, unsigned review in *The Spectator* in

* Another of Frank's most engaging introductions, written in 1953.

January 1898, of *The War of the Worlds*. Defoe's *Journal of the Plague Year* was, as the *Spectator* writer said, 'an immortal book', and he quoted the precedent to suggest not that the author was imitating the previous one, but that there was so much likeness in 'two very acute and sincere intelligences'. Both were engaged in the primary task of persuading their readers that something extraordinary had actually happened. Defoe's readers had been amazed to discover later that his story was fiction, and so were Wells's readers of his new volume. 'One reads and reads with an interest so unflagging that it is positively exhausting. *The War of the Worlds* stands in fact the final test of fiction.' It did indeed, and stood every test. Moreover, if anyone supposed the storyteller was content with his story, the whole was overcast with the doom which might await imperial Britain if she imagined that her pretentious, vainglorious claims to greatness were not soon dramatically remedied. The idea of the book had come, as HG later explained, in a conversation with his brother Frank, when they had talked of 'the discovery of Tasmania by the Europeans – a very frightful disaster for the native Tasmanians!' Not so different from the 'war of extermination' which threatened to destroy London. 'Are we such apostles of mercy as to complain if the Martians warred in the same spirit?' It was touch and go; London, 'the Mother of Cities', had to be evacuated (as it so nearly was, in another war in another century). Several readers were naturally reminded of the denunciations of imperial pride which appear in HG's old favourite *Gulliver*. And one particular friend, R. A. Gregory, who, of course, was most familiar with HG's Swiftian interest, added a particular touch which clinched the association more exactly than ever before.

A remarkable case of the fulfilment of fiction is furnished by the history of the satellites of Mars. When Dean Swift wrote *Gulliver's Travels* (published in 1726), he made the astronomers on the island of Laputa not only observe two satellites, but caused many of these to move round the planet in less time than the planet itself takes to rotate on its axis. As every student of astronomy

38

knows, the satellites were not discovered until 1877, and one of them actually does revolve round Mars three times while the planet makes a rotation. The coincidence is remarkable; but it is to be hoped, for the sake of peace of mind of terrestrial inhabitants, that Mr. Wells does not possess the prophetic insight vouchsafed to Swift. *

Altogether, a new triumph to give a special delight to his closest friends. His brother Frank had set his mind moving in that direction; his scientific friends who had watched his advance from Kensington days were naturally excited.

He had had such success with his own brand of the new scientific romances that he was likely to return there with fresh vigour and new departures. *When the Sleeper Awakes* was not such a success. If any of his writings at that time could be dismissed as derivative, this was it. But, if any doubts were sowed about his capacity, they were dismissed by the appearance of *The First Men in the Moon*. Others had attempted that journey before HG, but he added an ingredient of his own which no-one else could match. According to the true Wellsian doctrine, the first man on the moon – or, rather, his bosom spheroid companion – was not some contrived scientific superman but an authentic ne'er-do-well London East Ender who, despite all his natural fears and alarms, still knows what's what and can pluck up his courage to stride across the universe.

Again, it might have been supposed that the young Wells should stick to his line of renewed success; that must always have been the temptation. But the fact was that this same HG was quite prepared – at the drop of a hat, it might be said – to contemplate fresh adventures into unexplained regions in time or place, in the country of the blind or heaven knows where else. Almost all these voyages into forbidden territories were undertaken between 1895 and 1900; but, as the old century seemed to lose some of its glamour and impetus, the still young HG turned to open a new vein of writing altogether or what

* Patrick Parrinder (ed.), *H. G. Wells: The Critical Heritage* (1972), p. 74.

might seem new to those who had taken insufficient notice of the Hoopdriver odyssey.

How does genius flower and fade? No-one knows; no prevailing rules are easily unravelled and the real possessors of the supreme quality may be the least capable of defining their claim. William Hazlitt in a famous essay offered one definition which must apply. 'A really great man', he said, 'has always an idea of something greater than himself.' The H. G. Wells of the 1890s would certainly pass that test, and not only because of the tremendous themes he had tackled in *The War of the Worlds* and so many others, headed, of course, by *The Time Machine* itself. His pursuit of larger realities was no less evident when he described the ambitions of Mr Hoopdriver or the long list of those who figured in the short stories. Much of this work covering such an extraordinarily vast range was required to keep the wolf from the Mornington Place or Sevenoaks door. Still, the astonishing fact remained: he had written in that first decade of his writing life a huge amount of inspired work. None of it was trash; most of it had a creative exuberance of its own, to use Frank's phrase; and, taken altogether, it did conform to the Hazlitt requirement. The new phenomenon on the literary scene was not at all concerned with some egotistical display: he had a world to save, and he never lost sight of that vision. Thanks to a combination of factors, his upbringing, the class from which he rose, his own choice of literary models, HG's genius followed no accepted pattern. After a series of setbacks which would have broken most men's spirits, his *Time Machine* had suddenly opened for him a whole new world as sensational almost as that which the Time Traveller himself had discovered. All the lovely things he had dreamed of in all those seedy London lodging-houses had suddenly fallen into his lap. He could do what he wanted, write what he wanted – although suddenly here, after a while, he stumbled on an unforeseen obstacle. Several of his readers, some of his best friends or dearest admirers, believed that *The Time Machine* was his masterpiece, and that nothing could ever touch it. The temptation to try to repeat such a triumph might have been overwhelming, and occasionally HG did fall for it. *The Sleeper Awakes* was the clearest case in point; and, a good while later, HG himself acknowledged his weakness. However, much more remarkable in those circumstances was his refusal to follow the easier course, his respect for his own creative instinct, his devotion, according to the Hazlitt principle, to great ideas greater than himself. Possibly he was assisted by his own estimate of *The Time Machine*. He never praised it himself in quite the terms that others did; he had several other pent-up ideas which he wanted to unleash, and later he wanted to attempt something greater still.

He applied his talent more directly than ever before to produce a work of art – he would not call it that, but Henry James would – a work which would present the truth, a hopeful truth, but none the less an unmistakably honest one, about a young man from a new and disinherited class in society who would arrive in London to meet the accumulated challenge of learning and love in the last days of Queen Victoria and the first days of the triumph of science and Socialism, and how courage and hope won in the end. Among the new friends whom he had won by his *Time Machine* triumph, varying verdicts were offered: Henry James acclaimed a work of art; Arnold Bennett thought that he should stick to his earlier modes. HG himself knew how he had worked and reworked it, how he had polished the presentation more carefully or scrupulously than he always did. He thought that with *Love and Mr Lewisham* he had succeeded, and he summoned to the witness-box his most valued tutor, Jonathan Swift, a witness more obviously available to help sustain some other of his writings.

Not only the lovers make the new novel: Mr Chaffery at Home is a truly Swiftian character; he is an arguer who knows that irony is one of the most effective weapons of debate, for the simple reason that it may delude the reader and make him convict himself when he discovers the truth. Mr Chaffery had exposed himself – at least, to Mr Lewisham – as one of the most well-known frauds of that period: dabblers in spiritualism who faked the evidence from their seances. But Mr Chaffery is barely even discomforted by the exposure; he compares his minor and venial deceit with the whole vast conspiracy of fraud and pillage against the poor which is Victorian capitalism, and not least that last *fin de siècle* in which the Victorians themselves started to lose their self-confidence. Or, for those who had not reached even that moment of enlightenment, Chaffery had his own sensational means of exposing 'the ghastly truth of things . . . What a lie and sham all civility is, all good breeding, all culture and refinement, while one poor ragged wretch drags hungry on the earth.' And in fact there were millions of them: 'To think that men who preside over such horrors should dare to use the word *pride*.' That was Swift's complaint; and HG through the mouth of Chaffery, offered his variation. 'A much viler swindle than my facetious rappings', was what he saw all around him: 'Self-deception and self-righteousness. That is the essential danger. That is the thing I always guard against. Heed that. It is the master sin, self-righteousness.'

So Mr Chaffery could hold his own in that company and so could some others and not only the young lovers – the rival woman, for example: 'To be frank in self-criticism, there is more than a touch of the New Woman about me, and I feel I still have to live my own life. What a beautiful phrase that is – to live one's own life – redolent of honest scorn for moral plagiarism. No *Imitatio Christi* in that . . .' And at one moment Mr Lewisham was accepting the challenge of the whole world around him – 'We're all in the same boat'; and then in the next he was laughing – 'His laugh marked an epoch. Never before had Lewisham laughed at any fix in which he had found himself. The enormous seriousness of adolescence was coming to an end, the days of his growing were numbered. It was a laugh of infinite admissions.'

HG's own adolescence had ended a little earlier. He had truly loved Isabel, and the happy ending of *Love and Mr Lewisham* was an acknowledgement of it. But Jane had offered more, an example of the New Woman, and something else as well. Some of the new admirers whom he had won with *The Time Machine* and the sudden, sustained display of genius in the next few crowded years thought that he should never have turned aside along this supposedly more conventional path. Fortunately for the gaiety of mankind and womankind, he made up his own mind. * He had no patience with the idea that artists or lovers should be allowed to desert the battlefield.

* Much the most important critical work on this period of Wells's life is Bernard Bergonzi's *The Early H. G. Wells: A Study of the Scientific Romances* (1961). No reader of this volume is likely to question the greatness of Wells's achievement, and how HG himself would have been excited by such an appraisal. However, Bernard Bergonzi does also seem to accept the view that somehow thereafter Wells deserted his high artistic calling. HG himself would strongly dissent from such a judgement, as he explained in his own new introduction to *The Scientific Romances*, published in 1933 and 1934:

> My early, profound and lifelong admiration for Swift appears again and again in this Collection, and it is particularly evident in a predisposition to make the stories reflect upon contemporary political and social discussions. It is an incurable habit with literary critics to lament some lost artistry and innocence in my early work and to accuse me of having become polemical in my later years. That habit is of such old standing that my first book, *The Time Machine*, concerned itself with 'our present discontents'.

It did indeed.

THREE

A Hannibal at Large

> She went down to the poor as the saints do; I
> came up from the poor in a state of flaming
> rebellion, most blasphemous and ungainly.
> Beatrice wanted to socialize the ruling classes,
> and make them do their duty. I wanted to destroy
> them . . .
> H. G. Wells, in *An essay on the Passing of Beatrice
> Webb* (30 April 1943)

H. G. Wells declared war on the century of his birth; the sweep
and intensity of his antagonism should never be underestimated.
He had seen with his own eyes and felt in his own fragile bones
the poverty which still prevailed and sometimes seemed to cut
even deeper in the England of the 1870s and 1880s and 1890s.
And yet this Britain was supposed to be the richest and most
powerful country in the world, blest for so long with the most
sophisticated political institutions. So, if the poverty persisted,
these claims of the political leaders became all the more
irrelevant and insulting.

Much the most hopeful harbinger of a new world for HG
himself was what he had learned from the scientists. They
seemed to speak a simpler, bolder truth than the politicians; and
when several of the politicians, to protect their own interest,
pious or otherwise, looked to the means of suppression or
distortion of what they were saying he was all the more outraged.

He derived no impression from his experience that Britain's unique political institutions were somehow paving the way for a general amelioration. Nothing of the sort: conventional politics looked like a fraud and an imposture. Many Socialist speakers or writers arrived at this conclusion, from different points of view. And the cure for this state of affairs was to make enough converts to secure a real revolution – a Socialist revolution. He was serious about the proposition and, by the turn of the century, he wanted to see it more robustly presented than ever before, both to the English people and the world at large.

Even after his series of trumphs as a writer in the late 1890s, he did not feel secure or relaxed. His health was still pitifully precarious, which was one reason why he and Jane moved to a cottage in Sandgate, near Folkestone, and soon to Spade House nearby which he was able to design for his own purpose. Here he began to make friends with several fellow writers, some already famous and some soon to be so: George Gissing, Arnold Bennett, Joseph Conrad, Ford Madox Ford, J. M. Barrie, Stephen Crane and Henry James. But the bare list may give a false impression. He would spend time and effort on his friendships, and these would be among the most important for him.

With all of them, and with anyone else when he had the chance, he would renew the argument about the roles of the artist and the propagandist. The men ranged against him were all giants – or, at least, soon became successful in their own spheres. He listened but would not yield: even in his adventurous youth, he was an unshakeable disciple of his Swiftian creed. The most important friend with whom he argued most agreeably was Arnold Bennett: 'We both had a natural zest for life and we both came out of a good old English radical tradition. We were liberal, sceptical, and republican. But beyond this we were very different animals indeed.* One part of the difference between them did concern the great question of the pre-eminence of the artist, but nothing could alter the significance

*Experiment in Autobiography, vol. 2, p. 227.

for both of them of their lifelong friendship. They both loved their new breed of readers, male and female; and, artists or journalists, they could address them in a new accent.

However, from this galaxy of literary talent, it was with George Gissing, the one whose capacities were still least appreciated, that HG at first struck his closest chord of comradeship. Both were outsiders; neither in the ordering of British society nor in the universe at large did they see much reason to respect the decrees of authority. It was Gissing who persuaded HG, with Jane, to come on their first excursion, abroad: a journey, first of all, to Rome and then an extensive tour of southern Italy. HG by now could afford to do most of the paying while Gissing did most of the expounding. He was a devoted pupil of Gibbon – as, indeed, HG was proud to claim that he was also. He might have been content to unloose what he called 'my youthful prejudices' against the Scarlet Woman. Instead, he saw for himself that Protestantism had not done justice to Renaissance Rome. But that was just a glimpse. He was starting to acquire his sense of history in the city which had plenty to teach. Great empires could collapse with precious little warning from the most revered authorities; new beginnings might be unearthed in the strangest places. History might take wrong turnings altogether; if the proper warnings were neglected, the catastrophe could be impossible to remedy. How near had his hated, complacent nineteenth century come to that. How mighty must be the exertion to find a different way.

His main production, and one which first established his reputation as a prophet, was called *Anticipations*. His friend, and certainly a true one, Arnold Bennett called them 'Uncle's dissipations'. But, then, also, Bennett had thought *Love and Mr Lewisham* a diversion. HG himself took the whole affair seriously; when the turn of the century made so many writers look back, when the *fin de siècle*, on the brand-new bicycles or not, looked like the end of something, he gazed with a magnificent presumption to the future: to what the world in general and Britain in particular might be in the year 2000.

Within a few months, he had a success on his hands to match the popular novels of the period, a new reputation altogether.

Prophecy was the trade in which he was engaged; but, as with the prophets in the past, exposure of present evils could not be avoided. The old methods would have to go: Liberalism itself and its means of exposition could not survive.

> It is improbable that ever again will any flushed undignified man, with a vast voice, a muscular face in incessant operation, collar crumpled, hair disordered, and arms in wild activity, talking, talking, talking actively, copiously, out of the windows of railway carriages, talking from hotel balconies, talking on tubs, barrels, scaffolding, pulpits – tireless and undammable – rise to be the most powerful thing in any democratic state in the world. Continually the individual vocal demagogue dwindles and the element of bands and buttons, the organisation of the press and procession, the share of the machine, grows.

That was how he saw the passing of Mr Gladstone, but he soon treated Mr Alfred Harmsworth, the owner of the London *Daily Mail*, the director of the machine, with equal despatch. The new newspaper proprietors were already bowdlerizing the news in their own interests.

> It is upon the cultivation and rapid succession of inflammatory topics that the modern newspaper expends its capital and trusts to recover its reward. Its general news sinks steadily into a subordinate position: criticism, discussion, and high responsibility pass out of journalism, and the power of the press becomes more and more to be a dramatic and emotional power, the power to cry 'Fire!' in the theatre, the power to give enormous value for a limited time to some personality, some event, some aspect, true or false, without any power of giving a specific direction to the forces this distortion may set going.

Not such a bad definition of the millionaire press when it was hardly out of the womb. And, of course, this servile instrument would play an essential part in the drum-beating which would lead to war. 'Patriotism is not a thing which flourishes in the void – one needs a foreigner. A national and patriotic party is an anti-foreign party: the altar of the modern god, Democracy, will cry aloud for the stronger men.' Thus HG heard the campaign which was drumming in his ears over South Africa and which would be repeated so often in the coming century – until all competing nationalisms, whether democratic or not, escaped from the confusion 'into the higher stage, into the higher organism, the world-state of the coming years'. This was Wells's own first statement about the world state; and, whatever else it was, in the teeth of the howling nationalist tempests of the time, it was a brave and potent vision.

To give a sharper outline to his forecast, he found it necessary still to renew the attack on the institutions, especially the British institutions, which blocked the path. The British ruling class could not even comprehend the advantages of the English language: it was part of their general hatred of real education.

Of the few ideas possessed by the British governing class, the destruction and disencouragement of schools and colleges is unfortunately one of the chief, and there is an absolute incapacity to understand the political significance of the language question. The Hindoo who is at pains to learn and use English encounters something uncommonly like hatred disguised in a facetious form. He will certainly read little about himself in English that is not grossly contemptuous to reward him for his labour. The possibilities that have existed, and that do still in a dwindling degree exist, for resolute statesmen to make English the common language of communication for all Asia South and East of the Himalayas will have to develop of their own force or dwindle and pass away.

Quite a vision indeed, and HG's precise prophecy did nearly come true. The English language conquered, even after the English conquerors had made such a mess of it.

Several of his other prophecies deserved attention then, and secured it.

There can be no doubt that at present the Germans, with the doubtful exception of the United States, have the most efficient middle class in the world, their rapid economic progress is to a very large extent, indeed, a triumph of intelligence, and their political and probably their military and naval services are still conducted with a capacity and breadth of view that find no parallel in the world. But the very efficiency of the German as a German to-day and the habits and traditions of victory he has accumulated for nearly forty years, may prove in the end, a very doubtful blessing to Europe as a whole, or even to his own grandchildren.

HG himself foretold, as others had done, the coming unification of all Western Europe, but that would not mean 'Germanisation'. Then, a little later, he also foretold: 'Before Germany can unify to the East, she must fight the Russian, and to unify to the West, she must fight the French and perhaps the English, and she may have to fight a combination of these powers.' This brand of forecasting was common at the time, but HG's own application of it had a peculiar appositeness. He gave a proper weight to the new Germany, saw how she might overreach herself but how she could play a better part in a new twentieth-century Europe.

But even when he looked to the larger world canvas he could not escape his understanding of where the British state was failing.

Government by the elect of the first families of Great Britain has in the last hundred years made Ireland and South Africa two open sores of irreconcilable wrong. These two English-speaking communities will never rest and never emerge from wretchedness under the vacillating, vote-catching incapacity of British Imperialism, and it is impossible that the British power, having embittered them, should ever dare to set them free. But within such an ampler synthesis as the New Republic will seek, these states could emerge to an equal fellowship that would take all the bitterness from their unforgettable past.

Often these prophecies of the future would merge with the exposures of the past, and the effect could be doubly over-powering. Thanks to his own experience, and to the even harsher experience of his own parents, he thought there ought to be far-reaching changes in the way the State treated the family.

I am inclined to think that when the New Republic emerges on the other side of this disorder, there will be a great number of marriage contracts possible between men and women, and that the strong arm of the State will insist only upon one thing – the security and welfare of the child. The inevitable removal of births from the sphere of an uncontrollable Providence to the category of deliberate acts, will enormously enhance the responsibility of the parent – and of the State that has failed to adequately discourage the philo-progenitiveness of the parent towards the child. Having permitted the child to come into existence, public policy and the older standard of justice alike demand, under the new conditions, that it must be fed, cherished, and educated not merely up to a respectable minimum but to the full height of its possibilities. The State will, therefore, be the reserve guardian of all children. If they are being under-nourished, if their education is being neglected, the State will step in, take over the responsibility of their management, and enforce their charge upon the parents. The first liability of a parent will be to his child, and for his child; even the dues of that darling of our current law, the landlord, will stand second to that. This conception of the responsibility of the parents and the State to the child and the future runs quite counter to the general ideas of to-day. These general ideas distort grim realities. Under the most pious and amiable professions, all the Christian states of to-day are, as a matter of fact, engaged in slave-breeding. The chief result, though of course not the intention, of the activities of priest and moralist to-day in these matters, is to lure a vast multitude of little souls into this world, for whom there is neither sufficient food nor love nor schools, nor any prospect at all in life but the insufficient bread of servitude. It is a result that endears religion and purity to the sweating employer, and leads unimaginative bishops, who have never missed a meal in their lives and who know nothing of the

50

indescribable bitterness of a handicapped entry into this world, to draw a complacent contrast with irreligious France. It is a result that must necessarily be recognised in its reality, and faced by these men who will presently emerge to rule the world; men who will have neither the plea of ignorance, nor moral stupidity, nor dogmatic revelation to excuse such elaborate cruelty.

And having set themselves in these ways to raise the quality of human birth, the New Republicans will see to it that the children who do at last effectually get born come into a world of spacious opportunity. The half-educated, unskilled pretenders, professing impossible creeds and propounding ridiculous curricula, to whom the unhappy parents of today must needs entrust the intelligences of their children; these heavy-handed barber-surgeons of the mind, these schoolmasters with their ragtag and bobtail of sweated and unqualified assistants, will be succeeded by capable, self-respecting men and women, constituting the most important profession of the world. *

All or almost all these anticipations had a collectivist or Socialist tinge to them, all seemed to be influenced by the death of Liberalism which he also detected; but, if the Liberal state (with the capital L which HG himself had used throughout this dissertation) vanished, what was to take its place and how would the transformation be accomplished? HG thought that he was giving a definite answer, certainly more so than most thinkers or practitioners in the same field. However, since he himself looked forward with greater knowledge and precision at these matters, we may do the same. It was alleged against him – hardly at all by readers at the time but by hostile critics decades later – that some passages at the end of *Anticipations* expose him both as an anti-Semite and a racist of the breed which produced Hitler later in the century. If either of these accusations had been proved or, worse still, both together, it would indeed have been a terrible indictment, and, whatever H. G. Wells's other virtues, he would not have deserved to live to prophesy another

* *Anticipations* (1901), pp. 268–9.

day. He was deeply concerned, as many other writers were at the time, about the huge projected increase in the world's population and what could be done to check it. Some of the things he said were clumsy and ill phrased, but all of his projected remedies seemed to be governed by the answer to the question how the races should be dealt with: 'Certainly not as races at all.'* That was his emphasis, governing everything else.

It would have been strange if Wells had fallen into such a racist trap so soon after, in the same *Anticipations*, as we have seen, he expressed his horror at the insult British white men could inflict upon Hindus in India or black men in South Africa. As for the charge of anti-Semitism, it was sometimes levelled against him in his lifetime, and he would answer it. But, curiously, the alleged anti-Semitism in this passage can be seen to have been written by him with exactly the opposite purpose. Of the particular vices alleged against the Jews, he wrote:

> I really do not understand the exceptional attitude people take against the Jews. . . The Jew is mentally and physically precocious and he ages and dies sooner than the average European; but in that and in a certain disingenuousness he is simply on all fours with the short, dark Welsh. He foregathers with those of his own nation and favours them against the stranger, but so do the Scotch. I see nothing in his curious, dispersed nationality to dread or dislike. He is a remnant and legacy of Medievalism, a sentimentalist perhaps, but no furtive plotter against the present progress of things. He was the medieval Liberal; his persistent existence gave the lie to Catholic pretensions all through the days of their ascendancy, and today he gives the lie to all our yapping 'nationalisms', and sketches in his dispersed sympathies the coming of the world state . . . Much of his moral tradition will, I hope, never die.

---

* It may seem incredible, but Michael Coren, who has recently revived the charge of racism against Wells in his book *The Invisible Man* (1992), omits this sentence altogether; and so, I am sorry to say, does John Carey in his more serious essay in *The Intellectuals and the Masses*.

Not exactly the language of Hitler: no fair-minded reader could brand the writer of *Anticipations* an anti-Semite.

All the heroes and most of the heroines in HG's novels called themselves Socialists; they were not afraid of the word or the idea. However, if he himself might question the effectiveness of the Liberals by calling them 'not so much a party as a "multitudinous assembly" ', the same must apply, in retrospect at least, to the growing number and variety of Socialist organizations. Some saw the future, and a not too distant one, in terms of Robert Blatchford's *Merrie England*; others, influenced by Continental models of one form or another, recognized that any Socialism worthy of the name must be international in character. Blatchford himself, of course, would not dissent from that ideal but he was determined to speak a language which every man and, in his case especially, every woman could understand. That happened to be the language of Swift and Paine and Cobbett, which was Wells's language, too. Moreover, within the rapidly growing Socialist 'assemblage', if the same Wellsian word is applied to them, there seemed, outwardly at least, to be a greater cohesion: all of them thought the future was theirs. The great question was the pace at which the change in society could be achieved. It was often a tense debate but, from the start, a reputable one.

HG's temperament alone, it might be supposed, would have been enough to deter him from joining a society called the Fabians. He was much more, in his conception of tactics or strategy, a natural Hannibal. After so many false starts, he had taken the London of the 1890s by storm with his *Time Machine* and his *War of the Worlds*, and then, such a little time later, with something quite different, his grandiose but still comprehensive *Anticipations*. He did not appear as an obvious ally for the leading Fabians. Sidney and Beatrice Webb could explain to him the nature of the British governing Establishment and how it might be infiltrated and remodelled and converted to beneficent causes; they were soon inviting HG to their dinner-parties. Anyone from the Tory Prime Minister, A. J. Balfour, downwards might be present. HG was impressed but not dazzled; he could try to turn all experience to good account in his writing. But he could muster no respect for this monstrous apparatus of government. It was not a means of deliverance; more a lion across the path which would have to be slain. He would recognize readily enough that some effective new administrative organization must be preserved or created – he went on arguing with others and with himself on this awkward, maybe insoluble, topic until his dying day – to discharge the duties of the new Socialist state. It could not happen without anyone ever having thought of it. But still the real enemy, the British state which condemned a great mass of the English people to such poverty or England itself to such peril among the nations, must be frontally challenged. HG never had any doubts about that proposition, least of all in those first exhilarating years of the century before any true challenge to the central citadel had even been delivered. He understood the impatience of the young men and the even younger women who were marching, or, more usually, cycling on their latest recruiting campaigns. How long would they have to wait for their elders to catch up?

The other leading Fabian who might have been expected to welcome and share HG's buoyant declaration of hopes for the future was Bernard Shaw. He was ten years older than Wells, and had taken the trouble to give himself a real training as a Socialist, reading Karl Marx in the British Museum or brilliantly carrying the campaign, on platforms and soapboxes, across the country. He had played a leading part in founding the Fabian Society in the early 1880s. Apart from his other gifts, still to be developed as a dramatist of genius, he had trained himself to be a devastating debater. HG could never match him, and was usually not foolish enough to try. But the power of debate was not everything; HG could invoke his own imaginative under-standing of his own age. By coincidence, they had both been there on the first night of Oscar Wilde's *The Importance of Being Earnest*. Shaw was already a practised dramatic critic; HG was making his very first attempt at the task. Both were great admirers of Wilde, but Wells wrote the more appreciative notice. They walked home together that night from the Strand Theatre. It was the beginning of a long and often boisterously interrupted friendship which, however, lasted two lifetimes. Shaw could keep cool and deadly in argument when HG was at his most intemperate. Maybe Shaw was more assured of his cause and his genius, and he could certainly cite on his side the long service which he and the Webbs had given to the Fabians; they had the right and duty to protect their society from impertinent upstarts, who might not appreciate what qualities were needed to sustain real enthusiasm. But HG knew better – better than anybody – the impatience of the young.

At first, the new partnership worked smoothly. Fabius and Hannibal kept to their appointed methods. If the Webbs had all the learning and authority, and Shaw the eloquent charm which could attract audiences, large and small, HG had something else which he exercised quite unconsciously: a happy, guileless, infectious gift of high spirits, a radiant hopefulness. The effervescence worked best in small companies. Even though his physical attractions were not obvious, women fell in love with him easily, and even those who didn't could find themselves captivated. Two first impressions recorded in Beatrice's diary may be quoted in full:

> Wells's *Anticipations*. The most remarkable book of the year; a powerful imagination furnished with the data and methods of a physical science working on social problems. The weak part of Wells's outfit is his lack of any detailed knowledge of social organisations, and this, I think, vitiates his capacity for foreseeing the future machinery of government and the relation of the classes. But his work is full of luminous hypotheses and worth careful study by those who are trying to look forward. Clever phrases abound, and by-the-way proposals on all sorts of questions from the future direction of religious thought to the exact curve of the skirting round the wall of middle-class abodes. *

* *The Diary of Beatrice Webb, 1892–1905*, ed. Norman and Jeanne Mackenzie, vol. 2, p. 226.

A little later (February 1902), she elaborated:

We have seen something lately of H. G. Wells and his wife. Wells is an interesting, though somewhat unattractive personality except for his agreeable disposition and intellectual vivacity. His mother was the housekeeper to a great establishment of forty servants, his father the professional cricketer attached to the place. The early associations with the menial side of the great man's establishment has left Wells with a hatred of that class and of its attitude towards the 'lower orders'. His apprenticeship to a draper, his subsequent career as an assistant master at a private venture school, as a 'government student' at South Kensington living on £1 a week, as an 'army' crammer, as a journalist and, in these last years, as a most successful writer of fiction, has given him a great knowledge of the lower-middle class and their habits and thoughts and an immense respect for science and its methods. But he is totally ignorant of the manual worker, on the one hand, and of the big administrator and aristocrat on the other. This ignorance is betrayed in certain crudities of criticism in his *Anticipations*. He ignores the necessity for maintaining the standard of life of the manual working population; he does not appreciate the need for a wide experience of men and affairs in administration. A world run by the physical-science-man straight from his laboratory is his ideal; he does not see that specialized faculty and knowledge are needed for administration exactly as they are needed for the manipulations of machinery or [natural] forces. But he is extraordinarily quick in his apprehensions, and took in all the points we gave him in our forty-eight hours' talk with him, first at his own house and then here. He is a good instrument for popularizing ideas, and he gives as many ideas as he receives. His notion of modern society as 'the grey' – not because it is made of uniform atoms of that shade, but because of the very variety of its colours, all mixed together and in formless mass; his forecast of the segregation of like to like, until the community will become extraordinarily variegated and diverse in its component parts, seems to us a brilliant and true conception. Again, democracy as a method of dealing with men in a wholesale way, every man treated in the bulk and not in detail, the probability that we shall become more detailed and less wholesale in our provision for men's needs, that again is a clever illumination. Altogether, it is refreshing to talk to a man who has shaken himself loose from so many of the current assumptions, and is looking at life as an explorer of a new world. He has no great faith in government by the 'man in the street', and, I think, has hardly realized the function of the representative as a 'foolometer' for the expert.

His wife is a pretty little person with a strong will, mediocre intelligence and somewhat small nature. She has carefully moulded herself in dress, manners and even accent to take her place in any society her husband's talents may lead them into. But it is all rather artificial, from the sweetness of her smile to her interest in public affairs. However, she provides him with a charming well-ordered home, though I should imagine her constant companionship was somewhat stifling. They are both of them well-bred in their pleasant tempers, careful consideration of the feelings of others, quick apprehension of new conventions and requirements, but they both of them lack ease and repose, and she has an ugly absence of spontaneity of thought and feeling. *

For quite a while, relations between them prospered. Beatrice recorded, three years later:

H. G. Wells came for the night: he had sent us his *Utopia*. 'The chapters on the Samurai will pander to all your worst instincts,' he laughingly remarked when I congratulated him. He is full of intellectual courage and initiative, and is now settling down to psychological novels – I fancy somewhat inspired by Henry James's late success. †

A long talk with H. G. Wells at Sandgate. Two articles of our social faith are really repulsive to him: the collective provision of anything bordering on religious or emotional training and the collective regulation of the behaviour of the adult. As to the latter

---

* *The Diary of Beatrice Webb*, vol. 2, pp. 239–41.
† *The Diary of Beatrice Webb*, vol. 2, p. 342.

we are not really at variance, for we would willingly accept his limitation of this intervention to all such behaviour as impinges on the non-adult (heaven knows that little scheme would give us enough regulation of the adult and to spare). But he is obdurate as to education: no form of training must be provided out of common funds that he personally objects to. My plea for variety and experiment for leaving the door open for new religions or morality by permitting those who believe in the old to have it provided for their children – [as well as] Sidney's plea for tolerance strikes a deaf ear. 'The child is not fit for emotional training until after adolescence,' he [Wells] dogmatically asserts; 'there is no justice in not giving one form of training,' he insists. But he went further than this. 'I don't believe in tolerance; you have got to fight against anything being taught anybody which seems to you harmful, you have got to struggle to get your own creed taught.' We all got hot and exaggerated in our arguments and were no nearer agreement when we parted.

I suppose it is inevitable that we who believe in extending the functions of the state in all directions should be keenly desirous of making this activity as catholic as possible; of safeguarding each new departure by deliberate provision for dissenters from the established view. Clearly the whole of liberalism in England is swinging into rigid conformity, both in the structure and formations of the social organism. As you cannot have each individual separately provided for according to his needs, therefore you must give identical treatment to all – seems their present dogma. *

Most of the introductions which opened a new world for the Wellses seemed to come via the Webbs. One was the prestigious Co-Efficients Club which brought together, as HG justly said, 'the queerest diversity of brains' – Liberal cabinet ministers like Sir Edward Grey and Haldane, Tory imperialists, young and old, like Milner or L. S. Amery, and rising radicals like Josiah Wedgwood or C. F. G. Masterman. Not even Haldane did HG find sympathetic: 'He was a self-indulgent man with a large

* The Diary of Beatrice Webb, vol. 2, p. 344.

white face and an urbane voice that carried its words as it were on a salver.' But worse, much worse, 'the shadow of Joseph Chamberlain lay dark across our dinner table, the Chamberlain who had either a sunstroke or a Pauline conversion in South Africa, and had returned still intending to shape British politics in his own image'. HG wrote: 'He had no long views. He began a struggle to impose the crude common sense and hard methods of a monopolistic Birmingham hardware manufacturer upon international relations.' HG saw something deeply menacing in these developments: 'I was in at the very beginning of the English recoil from our pretensions –and with many they were more than pretensions – to exceptional national generosity, courage, and world leadership.'*

Among the nondescript company at the Co-Efficients, 'the most untried and irresponsible', like himself, was Bertrand Russell. He defined a little more sharply than HG the cause of the break-up of the whole company:

> All the members except Wells and myself were imperialists and looked forward without too much apprehension to a war with Germany. I was drawn to Wells by a common antipathy to this point of view. He was a Socialist and at that time although not later considered great wars a folly. Matters came to a head when Sir Edward Grey, then in opposition, advocated what became the policy of the Entente with France and Russia, which was adopted by the Conservative Government some two years later, and solidified by Sir Edward Grey when he became Foreign Secretary. I spoke vehemently against this policy, which I felt led straight to World War, but no-one except Wells agreed with me.†

If the company of the Co-Efficients proved uncongenial, one of the Fabian households offered something much happier, both for HG himself and at first for Jane. When they first heard the name E. Nesbit, he thought she must be a man, and he would always address her thereafter playfully as Ernest. She was later to win fame for that name as a writer, almost the first writer, of

* *Experiment in Autobiography*, vol. 2, p. 763.
† Bertrand Russell, *Portraits from Memory* (1956), p 77.

children's stories, but at the time when the Wellses first met her she had not yet discovered that gift. She was the most spirited of Fabian hostesses, planning one great easy-going hospitable Bohemian household at Well Hall, Eltham, and then another at Dymchurch, just a few miles from the newly established Wells home at Sandgate. Several visitors there achieved a later glory, even if not so grand as that of the Co-Efficients: the Chesterton brothers, Enid Bagnold, Berta Ruck, Jack Squire, a happy, talkative multitude of young writers and actors. Presiding over them all was this 'tall, engaging, restless, moody, humorous woman'. Not so 'inviting' was her husband, Hubert Bland, who was, however, a big figure in the Fabian Society, next only to the Webbs or Shaw. What made him a Socialist or a Fabian or any other variety was less clear. He liked to present himself as a man of the world, a businessman, although, as HG insisted, 'he had no gleam of business ability'. * However, his unwanted presence was more than compensated for by Edith's dazzling perfor-mances. And HG could appreciate not only her appearance, but also some of her particular writings. What writer would not be overwhelmed by such a letter as he sent her in December 1904:

Steamed Lady,
I never told you how we like the *Phoenix and the Carpet* and how extraordinarily more than the late Mrs. Ewing who was once first we now esteem you. The Phoenix is a great creation; he is the best character you ever invented – or anybody ever invented in this line. It is the best larking I ever saw. Your destiny is plain. You go on every Xmas never missing a Xmas, with a book like this, and you will become a British Institution in six years from now. Nothing can stop it. Every self-respecting family will buy you automatically and you will be rich beyond the dreams of avarice, and I knock my forehead on the ground at your feet in the vigour of my admiration of your easy artistry.

* Julia Briggs, A *Woman of Passion: The Life of E. B. Nesbit* (1987). Julia Briggs writes that this letter 'was one of Wells' prophecies that, exceptionally, came true', and that he had later told Doris Langley Moore how much he did admire Nesbit's children's books.

So, for a while, HG charmed Beatrice and her fellow Fabians, and she and they had a powerful effect on him. They did not take over his whole intellectual life; no-one could do that. But their influence was none the less extensive and lasting. He wrote a series of books which were suffused with Fabian arguments, even if none of them implied a full surrender to the Fabian thesis. His output during the period was colossal. None was a masterpiece; but all were provoked by the real controversies of the time. Here is the bare list, enough for a normal man's lifetime: *The Discovery of the Future* (1902); *Mankind in the Making* (1903); *A Modern Utopia* (1905);* *Kipps* (1905); *The Misery of Boots* (1906); *Socialism*

---

* *A Modern Utopia* looked afresh at the argument he never wished to dodge. An accusation frequently made against him, although often in the most contradictory terms, was that he had once advocated, and thereafter consistently favoured, a ruthless programme of eugenic action to check the menace of the ever-increasing world population. He had set out his views in *Anticipations* and in several other of his early publications. He certainly did believe that, without effective action in this field, all hopes of improvement in the human condition would be frustrated. All hopes of creating a society worthy of the name of Utopia – and he invented several of them – would have to be postponed for ever, if this challenge was not tackled by one means or another. Several other writers of the period described the problem in similar if not such graphic terms as HG employed, but when he saw that some critics were interpreting what he had written in *Anticipations* in what might be called racist terms – despite his specific disavowal – he took precautions in his *A Modern Utopia* to try to ensure that he would guard against any such misplaced and even malicious misinterpretation. That hope was vain. The topic itself was much too exciting. HG himself would constantly define how these ideas could not be divorced from his conception of Socialism, his idea of freedom. A later exposition of true Utopian ideal was given in *Men Like Gods*, published in 1923 and discussed below in Chapter 8. A brilliant exposition of these charges and counter-charges was given by Patrick Parrinder in the *London Review of Books*, 8 April 1993, when he was reviewing Michael Coren's biography. Parrinder also cites in the review the claim made by Peter Morton in *The Vital Science* (1984) which shows how Wells, following such precursors as Alfred Russel Wallace and Grant Allen, soon became 'the champion of a "social reformist eugenics" looking to female emancipation, birth control, and the Welfare State, to improve the species, and rejecting the policies of the human stud-farm'. My claim in this volume is that he was the pioneer in advocating the combination between social reformist eugenics and sexual liberation for men and women. I must ask the impatient reader to await the appearance of such specimens as Ann Veronica or the less-celebrated Mr Barnstaple of *Men Like Gods*.

and the Family (1906); *The Future of America* (1906); *In the Days of the Comet* (1906); *New Worlds for Old* (1908). Periodically, throughout his literary career, his friends or his enemies might plead with him to control the flood. But he wanted to say what he wanted to say next so urgently that nothing and no-one could stop him. No writer could keep up such a flow and not weaken. In his case, the miracle was how often and persistently he sustained his standard of the highest class of journalism, verging every now and again upon a true artistic achievement.

Each of these pieces had something of a Fabian inspiration, but the one which caused the most trouble – for a start, at least – was *The Misery of Boots*. HG himself reckoned that he was doing his duty to show how the case for Socialism should be presented. Some readers at the time thought it was the very best simple statement of the Socialist case ever written, and readers today may concur. The argument is compulsive and overwhelming; it is Wells at his polemical best. No better statement of the case, at least, was available in those first years of the century when the eagerness to learn, especially among the young, was so evident and when what was needed was that rare combination: simple reasoning, a passionate faith and a sophisticated political conclusion. That was *The Misery of Boots*, first presented by HG as a lecture in 1905 and published as a pamphlet in the first weeks of 1906. It was a classic, say, like Swift's *Drapier's Letters* or Paine's *Rights of Man*. But it also contained an implied criticism of the Fabian leadership for the pace or lack of pace at which it was moving. HG was asked to modify these offending passages, but he saw no need to comply. Was *The Misery of Boots* further evidence of his incorrigible mischief-making or was it the proof of his pamphleteering genius? The Fabian old guard denied the first conclusion; most of the rest of the world accepted the second. And that was HG, the direct propagandist; he could also turn his hand elsewhere.

Artie Kipps might not strike any observer, casual or attentive, as a likely recruit for the Socialist cause, less still an active proselytizer in his own right, but he became both. At his first appearance on the scene, in the latter months of 1905, he was first and foremost the draper's assistant who clambered up the ladder of English middle-class snobbery and met with a series of frustrations and indignities on the way. He had, most monstrously, left his young true love for higher things; but eventually they came together again, and she seemed able to teach him some real Socialist lessons. After several other adventures, Artie had had his mind changed by his Mecca-like visit to one of Wells's own favourite parts of London. Artie raised the question: 'I've never rightly got the 'ang of this Socialism; what's it going to do, like?' And the answer came in a flood.

'Collectively the rich today have not the heart nor imagination. No! They own machinery; they have knowledge and instruments and powers beyond all previous dreaming, and what are they doing with them, think what they are doing with them Kipps, and think what they might do . . . How they have wasted and are still wasting all that the new science and the new world could offer. How they were wasting the brains of our people. I did think knowledge would do it . . . I did think that. I've fought for knowledge as other men fight for bread. I've starved for knowledge. I've thrown my life away to make myself too good for use in this huckster's scramble.'

The old Socialist's frustration could be unbearable, but the purpose was to strip aside all concealments and help young Artie Kipps to think for himself. He could do it – with Ann's essential assistance. A whole chapter was devoted to 'The Housing Problem' – how they could get a house or build a house fit for them and their rising family to live in.

'They build these 'ouses', said Ann, 'as though girls wasn't human beings. It's having all these 'ouses built by men, I believe, makes all the work and trouble . . .' The Kippses, you see, thought they were looking at a reasonably simple little contemporary house, but they were looking for dreamland in 1975 AD or thereabouts, and it hadn't come.

That was HG writing in 1905 or a few years earlier. He had started writing a major new novel soon after the completion of *Lewisham*. It was originally called 'The Wealth of Mr Waddy', Mr Waddy being the malevolent benefactor whose legacy changed the fortunes of Artie and Ann. But HG lost his own original manuscript and, when he returned to the theme, in his own words, 'out of it walked Kipps with a life of his own'. Indeed; but out of it also stepped Ann at his side. The idea that, in the Wellsian world, the men always instruct the women was just not true. It was not so in the notable case of Artie Kipps and Ann. *
Several readers thought that *Kipps* was his best book: Henry James wrote especially to congratulate him on the irony of the whole conception.

But turn to the Fabians in Kipps's London, who thought they could instruct him. The actual lecture, 'Faults of the Fabians', was read by HG at a private meeting of the Society in their shabby old rooms in Essex Hall on 9 February 1906. He had a few teasing, ineffectual references to Edward Pease, the secretary, to Bernard Shaw's jocular methods, and to the drawing-rooms of the Webbs, this last feature being part of the real indictment. No doubt also his own faltering speech added to the discomfiture and helped to unloose the sustained counter-attack. But, still, when all this and everything else that could be said against HG himself and his method of operating is noted, nothing could alter the fact that the indictment was devastating. He was not engaged in some petty intrigue or vendetta; he had given his whole liberating mind to the subject. He knew what he meant by Socialism; he thought it was shared by growing numbers of people throughout the country, especially those whom he defined as 'the whole generous multitude of the educated young'. But the Fabian Society – or, at least, the leading Fabians – no longer offered, if they had ever done, a true guide to the way

* The discovery about the 'Wealth of Mr Waddy' manuscript was made public in 1969 by the Southern Illinois University. Henry T. Moore contributed a preface and Harris Wilson an excellent introduction and notes. No doubt is possible about the authenticity of the document, but it is not easy to guess what HG himself would have done to *Kipps* if he had had another chance.

Socialism could be achieved. They hardly even dared use the word. 'We don't advertise, thank you, it's not quite our style. We cry Socialism as the reduced gentlewoman cried oranges – I do hope no-one will hear me.' The Wellsian wit could be constantly invoked; and he offered, too, detailed criticisms and detailed remedies. But the major assault, it must be constantly insisted, was an exposure of the way the Fabian method could betray Socialism.

I find in our society, cropping up sometimes in the speech of this member, and sometimes in the speech of that, a curious conceit of cunning, something like a belief that the world may be manoeuvred into socialism without knowing it; that by being very slim and lively and subtle we shall presently be able to confront the world with a delighted, 'But you are socialists! We chalked it on your backs when you weren't looking.' We in this society, I say this with doubtings and regret, have tended more and more to become the exponents of a masked socialism that I fear and dread, that in the end may, quite conceivably, not leave one shred of the true socialist spirit alive in us. This society is to keep like it is, all existing institutions are to keep as they are, there is still to be a House of Lords, an established Church, bishops – they'll not believe in Christianity, but still bishops – Tories – they won't believe in property in land, but they will still be Tories – and yet socialism will be soaking through it all, changing without a sign of change. It is a quite fantastic idea, this dream of an undisturbed surface, of an ostensibly stagnant order in the world, while really we are burrowing underground, burrowing feverishly underground – a quite novel way of getting there – to the New Jersusalem . . .

You know this cryptic socialism is not a little reminiscent of the mouse that set out to kill the cat; violent methods were deprecated; an organisation of all the available mice, and the old crude tactics of attack in multitude that extinguished Bishop Hatto, were especially discouraged. The mouse decided to adopt indirect and inconspicuous methods, not to complicate its proceedings by too many associates, to win over and attract the cat by friendly advances rather than frighten her by a sudden attack. It is believed that in the end the mouse did succeed in permeating the cat, but the cat is still living and the mouse can't be found.

Then we are to invade municipal bodies, bring about the millennium by tempting the local builder on the town council with socialist projects for the housing of the working classes, and by luring incompetent urban district boards administering impossible areas into the establishment of electric power stations they are about as well equipped to control as they are the destinies of this empire. Perhaps I go too far with this again. No doubt it is quite possible to achieve all sorts of good purposes through existing organisations and institutions, only – it isn't the way to socialism. Make socialists and you will achieve socialism; there is no other way; democratic socialism is the only possible sane and living socialism. The only possible socialistic state is a state which is understood, upheld, willingly and cheerfully lived, by the great mass of its people. Even were it possible to achieve really socialist institutions in our insidious way, what would it all amount to? We should have the body of socialism without its spirit, we should have won our Utopia with labour and stress – and behold it would be stillborn!*

For good measure, he added the further thrust that the original Roman Fabius had never won a battle anyhow; he waited for the day so long that the chance faded. Maybe this was the stroke which hurt most; ridicule – the only weapon, according to Byron, which the English climate would not rust. HG was rarely a match for Shaw in direct polemical combat. But this time – as posterity may judge – he more than held his own.

Beatrice's own response to both the January and the February lecture was noted in her diary:

1 March – 41 Grosvenor Road: H. G. Wells has broken out in a quite unexpectedly unpleasant manner. The occasion has been a movement to reform the Fabian Society. The details are un-

---

* 'The Faults of the Fabians', reprinted in Samuel Hynes, *The Edwardian Turn of Mind* (1968), p.400.

important, for I doubt whether he has the skill and the persistence and the real desire to carry a new departure. But what is interesting is that he has shown in his dealing with the Executive, and with his close personal friends on it – Shaw, Bland, and Webb – an odd mixture of underhand manoeuvres and insolent bluster, when his manoeuvres were not successful. The explanation is, I think, that this is absolutely the first time he has tried to co-operate with his fellow men – and he has neither tradition nor training to fit him to do it. It is a case of 'Kipps' in matters more important than table manners. It is strange for so frank a man that his dealings have been far from straight – a series of naive little lies which were bound to be found out. When at last he forced the Executive to oppose him he became a bully and remained so until he found they were big enough to knock him down. I tell Sidney not to be too hard upon him, and to remember there was a time when 'the Webbs' were thought not too straight and not too courteous in their dealings (and that after a dozen years of mixing with men and affairs). But we have shown our displeasure by slight coolness; GBS has expressed himself with his usual scathing frankness, and it is more than likely that HGW, with his intelligent sensitiveness, will feel he has taken false steps into semi-public affairs and retire into his own world of the artist. It is more for 'copy' than for reform that he has stepped out of his study; when he has got his 'copy' he will step back again. *

Two other events in that crowded, momentous 1906 contributed to the growing tension between HG and the Webbs. Having launched the assault as they thought, he went off for two critical months on a visit to America. At some moments Beatrice seemed to imply that his awkwardly contrived visit was just another example of his exhibitionism. If so, that was most unfair, as readers of *The Future of America* may judge for themselves. He wanted to broaden his own mind; and he thought that his fellow Fabians could profit from a little broadening, too. His journey and the book were truly an attempt to lift the case for Socialism on to a higher international plateau.

* *The Diary of Beatrice Webb*, vol. 2, p. 31.

He knew or had freshly discovered how various American writers of a Socialist or at least secular outlook were challenging the old capitalist complacencies in terms brasher or more brilliant than their English counterparts. Wherever he went he would honour or defend his own trade as a writer, especially when some of its practitioners were made to suffer from the unthinking intolerance and persecution which the Americans could inflict. Two particular cases came to a head during the period of his visit, and he did his best to speak out and offer practical assistance to the victims. One was the case of William MacQueen, a young English student from Leeds, a fellow reader along with HG himself of William Morris, Tolstoy and Blatchford's *Clarion* who called himself an anarchist: 'Such an anarchist was Emerson among other dead Americans whose names are better treasured than their thoughts.' Somehow the anarchist MacQueen, falsely equipped by the press with a full police record, brought from England, found himself held responsible and jailed for five years for participation in the notorious Paterson strike riots. HG went and saw him in his Trenton jail and confirmed every detail in his own mind: MacQueen was the victim of a monstrous, continuing injustice. He continued to raise the case at every available opportunity and he collected a fine miscellany of excuses from judges and politicians, liberal and otherwise, who could adduce their own reasons why the property-owners of Paterson must be protected. Otherwise the whole system at the mercy of the same violence would collapse.

Even more startling in its revelation of American manners and morals was the fate of a new friend whose visit to America coincided with his own. Maxim Gorky was better-known as a writer – or, at least, better-known for his political message – than the H. G. Wells of that period. 'The American nation', wrote HG, 'seemed concentrated upon one great and ennobling idea, the freedom of Russia, and upon Gorky as the embodiment of that idea. A protest was to be made against cruelty and violence and massacre; the reception to be given to Gorky was to be the sign of how all America largely joined the liberating cause.' Gorky could not speak a word of English; HG could not speak Russian, but he was already starting to share the liberating momentum of ideas which seemed to be breeding in the Russia of that time and which Gorky especially expressed. He and HG were kindred spirits, and the ease of communication between them was quickly assisted by the interpreter Gorky had brought with him: Madame Andresieva, 'who has been now for years in everything but the severest legal sense his wife'. The sudden explosion of outrage against the two of them passed all comprehension. 'It was like a summer thunderstorm. At one moment, Gorky was in an immense plenipotentiary from oppression to liberty, at the next he was almost literally pelted through the streets.' Nothing could save him. Boston and Chicago swiftly matched the ostracisms of New York City. Every hotel in the country was forced to slam its doors in their immoral faces. At last, he and Madame Andresieva awaited removal from the country on Staten Island, and HG spent his last evening on American soil in their company.

> He had come – the Russian peasant in person, out of a terrific confusion of bloodshed, squalor and injustice – to tell America, the land of light and achieved freedom, of all these evil things . . . MacQueen in jail, Gorky with his reputation wantonly bludgeoned and flung aside: they are just two specimens of the myriads who have come up this great waterway bearing hope and gifts.

It was his hope and fear for the America which would dominate the coming century – he himself had little doubt about that proposition, although it was by no means a judgement generally shared – which was the subject of his book, but two other individual meetings appeared to be the most memorable. One was with Booker T. Washington, the negro leader of his time, who would not repudiate the clear right of the black man to every educational facility, to equal citizenship and equal respect. But Mr Washington, HG recorded, was a leader who calculated 'what he could win and what he might lose'; his statesmanship could 'grasp the situation and destinies of a people'. He still kept open the option that his people might retain their separate culture, like the Jewish communities in New York. HG argued with him about that, but his general response was one of overflowing understanding and goodwill. 'The Welsh, the Irish, the Poles, the white South, the indefatigable Jews may cherish grievances and rail aloud . . . And none of all the races upon earth which have suffered such wrongs as this negro blood that is still imputed to him as a sin. These people who disdain him, who have no sense of reparation towards him, have sinned against him beyond all measure . . .' Yet HG still believed there could be for them 'finer understandings and a nobler time'. He would summon to his aid all his highest eloquence to put the black man's case. It must seem barely credible that in the next breath he might be accused of being a racist.

The other big man he met in America was the President himself, a quite different kind of politician from the breed he was accustomed to dealing with in Britain. Theodore Roosevelt reflected the mighty changes which were shaking his country, and he was not afraid of them. 'Day by day he changes with the big world about him – contradicts himself.' Very well, Walt Whitman had recommended that resort. HG was not finally convinced that this versatile, adventure-loving President would 'declare for Socialism', as Fabians in England might use the phrase, but the fact that he could pose the question at all showed how broad was the ground which he and the President had traversed: collective action to tame the forces of anarchical capitalism would not be abjured. Besides, he and the President quickly discovered that they could talk about books. HG had been proud to note the part played by his profession in challenging the current orthodoxies. He could not exactly contrast the President's performance here with what happened in Edwardian England. Prime Ministers there might read real books – the age of Jeffrey Archer and John Major had not yet arrived. But Teddy Roosevelt was a real reader. Not merely had he studied HG's own *Time Machine*; he turned literary critic and happily explored its double meanings. If the final moral was one of despair, he and the rest of humanity must act as if the whole cause could still be saved.

No such acclaim greeted him on his return home, where prophets still had to contend with old agendas and endless committee meetings. He had been greatly impressed by his meeting in the White House with Theodore Roosevelt. No-one, not even the Webbs, could imply that he was a likely recruit for some 'great man' adulation. He opposed that kind of weakness all his life, both the theory preached, say, by Carlyle, and any other lapse in that direction. But no doubt he himself liked to be lionized, and this was his first real taste of it. Beatrice suggested in her diary that he was suffering from a swelled head; and, if he was, he had some excuse. Just to look back, say, to the last days of his hated nineteenth century when he was starting on *Kipps*, what wondrous fresh worlds had opened before him. He had been invited to lecture at Oxford and he treated them to his own original ideas, on logic and philosophy. He had designed afresh his own Modern Utopia, and joked with Beatrice about how it must appeal to her worst instincts. It was not true that everything he touched turned to literary gold, but compared with the successive setbacks of the early 1890s what a transformation had been achieved. It was the more extraordinary that the swelling did not become chronic or incurable. His own boast was that he had a surer grip on what the youth of the country thought Socialism meant or could mean than the others engaged in the controversy, and that grip he never lost -- at least, in those heady Edwardian times when the prospect could still be painted in such blazing colours or the peril could be defined so starkly. He could do both. Even in America he had never been willing to forfeit that claim. 'We are a young people', he would maintain, speaking for the Socialists, 'We are a new generation.'

The other fresh cause of the clash among the Fabians was both more delicate and explosive. Even before the Fabian Executive meeting when his proposition about the Society's future was to be determined, he approached – as he thought, quite tactfully – the great sexual question of *Socialism and the Family*, as his own pamphlet was called, or 'Socialism and the Middle Classes',

71

which was the title of his first lecture on the subject to the Fabians in October. He thought his views on the subject and his kind of Socialism could have an especial appeal to fairly well-to-do people who had only rarely been invited to think on these matters before. They might suppose that Socialism was solely concerned with property relationships between master and man; of course, that was no small part of the problem, but what about the property-owners who thought they owned their women, the husbands who enslaved their wives, and the children? No-one who heard HG deliver this lecture – or, rather, no Socialist – could doubt his sincerity. He talked of the Socialism in which he believed as being 'a very great thing indeed, the form and substance of my ideal life, and all the religion I possess'. No-one else had put it quite in those terms, and maybe he should have recognized how sharp would be the shock both among his Fabian audience and further afield.

His second lecture, hastily arranged in an attempt to mitigate some of the damage, described how surprised he himself had been by the reaction. 'Nothing', he insisted, 'could have brought this out more clearly than the comical attempt made recently by the *Daily Express* to suggest that Mr. Keir Hardie and the party he leads was mysteriously involved with my unfortunate self in teaching Free Love to respectable working men.' The accusation had to be repudiated in those respectable days, and HG did so partly by contrasting the modern Fabian attitude to these tender subjects with his recollections of some other disputes:

> . . . my mind drifted back to the days – it is a hazy period to me – when Godwin and Mary Wolstonecraft were alive, when Shelley explained his views to Harriet. These people were in a sort of way Socialist; Paleon-Socialists. They professed also very distinctly that uncovenanted freedom of activity in sexual matters which is, I suppose, Free Love.

HG's knowledge of Shelley's attitudes was a good deal less hazy than he implied, but in the circumstances the apologia was venial enough. If the Free Love label had been made to stick, much damage would have been done to the Socialist cause, Keir Hardie included. To permit that, if it could be avoided, would have been foolish and unfair. But on this issue HG was forced on to the defensive, and his influence was impaired in the larger Fabian controversy.

He always took trouble with his lectures; he knew his weakness. On these last two ocasions he had spoken from his eloquent heart but – ironically, in view of the accusations made against him – he would turn ever more readily to his own art. Over the past year, he had been completing a new novel – some parts of it were written in the congenial atmosphere of the Nesbit garden. If any doubt ever existed about Kipps's allegiance, no similar questioning was possible about the hero and indeed the heroine of the novel he was writing throughout most of the tempestuous year 1906. Willie Leadford was a more devoted and younger recruit to the cause than any of his predecessors, and so was his Nettie, we may emphasize, although she strayed from the fold and his arms at an early stage, too; women exercised such outrageous rights in the world of Wellsian fiction sooner than is usually appreciated. Willie was a worker born in the Potteries; his desire to escape from the dirt and the poverty became desperate. The most pitiful victim of the system which prevailed there, no less than in London, was his mother. When he had the chance to make the contrast with those who had not had to work with them, HG could not forget her gnarled hands.

If anyone could ever doubt the quality of *In the Days of the Comet* or the implacable inspiration of his Socialism, they can heed the passage written just after the death of his mother.

After our midday dinner – it was a potato-pie, mostly potato with some scraps of cabbage and bacon – I put on my overcoat and got it (my watch) out of the house while my mother was in the scullery at the back.

A scullery in the old world was, in the case of such houses as ours, a damp, unsavoury, mainly subterranean region behind the dark living room kitchen, that was rendered more than typically dirty in our case by the fact that into it the coal-cellar, a yawning pit of black uncleanness, opened, and diffused small crunchable particles about the uneven brick floor. It was the region of the 'washing up', that greasy, damp function that followed every meal; its atmosphere had ever a cooling steaminess and the memory of boiled cabbage, and the sooty black stains where saucepan or kettle had been put down for a minute, scraps of potato-peel caught in the strainer of the escape-pipe and rags of a quite indescribable horribleness of acquisition, called 'dish-clouts', rise in my memory at the name. The altar of this place was the 'sink', a tank of stone, revolting to a refined touch, grease-filmed and unpleasant to see, and above this was a tap of cold water, so arranged that when the water descended it splashed and wetted whoever had turned it on. This tap was our water supply. And in such a place you must fancy a little old woman, rather incompetent and very gentle, a soul of unselfishness and sacrifice, in dirty clothes, all come from their original colours to a common dusty dark grey, in worn, ill-fitting boots, with hands distorted by ill use, and untidy greying hair – my mother. In the winter her hands would be 'chapped', and she would have a cough. And while she washes up I go out, to sell my overcoat and watch in order that I may desert her. *

However, when *The Comet* hit the earth, everything was transformed. The great change, the Socialist change, came overnight. Even the words of the Socialist International were fulfilled: 'We'll change *forthwith* the old conditions!' Of course, it was a fantasy, a device to show what real Socialist aspirations could achieve, if Socialists were loyal to them when they had the power. It was another attempt by HG to describe his Utopia. He invented so many, and not only in the book which bore the specific title *A Modern Utopia*. A few of them had features which Socialists might not approve; so that it might be excusable to

* Brian Aldiss admirably quotes this passage in his 'Wells and the Leopard Lady' lecture delivered in 1988, reprinted in Patrick Parrinder and Christopher Rolfe (eds), *H. G. Wells under Revision: Proceedings of the H. G. Wells Symposium*, London, July 1986 (1986); and it is not difficult to imagine how multitudes of *Clarion* readers read it eighty years before. *The Comet* was their favourite before modern critics moved to the same conclusion.

overlook this one; but any such neglect would be a pity, for this was one of his best. Eyebrows might be raised, say in Grosvenor Road, but everywhere the *Clarion* campaigners toured the welcome was ecstatic. He carried all before him with the sheer force of his invention and eloquence. 'And through all the world go our children, our sons the old world have made into servile clerks and shopmen, plough drudges and servants; our daughters who were erst anaemic drudges, prostitutes, sluts, anxiety- racked mothers, or sere, repining failures; they go about this world glad and brave, learning, living, doing, happy and rejoicing, brave and free.'*

One part of the prophecy which seemed to give special offence in both Liberal and Conservative circles was the satirical description of the pretentious Cabinet Council which was supposed to direct these events but which was much more obviously just catching up with the Clarionites. Since this was 1906, this might have been a satire directed at the new Liberal government, but HG subtly altered the indictment by suggesting that several of the grandees from *both* parties might sit in the same ineffectual controlling body. A few years later it became a common question of public debate why the new Liberal Cabinet with such a large majority in Parliament achieved so little. HG's answer was:

> There was no common idea. The great empire over which they presided was no more than a thing adrift, an aimless thing that ate and drank and slept and bore arms and was inordinately proud of itself because it had chanced to happen. It had no plan, no intention, it meant nothing at all. And they ruled and influenced the lives of nearly a quarter of mankind, these politicians, their clownish conflicts swayed the world, made mirth perhaps and made excitement and permitted – infinite misery. †

* *In the Days of the Comet* (1906), p. 460.
† Readers of Samuel Hynes's book *The Edwardian Turn of Mind* may see how much I have relied on it. It is the best book on the period, although I feel he too often sides with the Webbs against Wells. But I quote this pregnant sentence with which he opens one of his chapters: 'The question of why the Liberals, possessed of such unusual power, and with such clear occasions for the beneficent use of it, did not act to correct flagrant social wrongs is one of the crucial questions of the Edwardian era.' Wells in *The Comet* was posing that question right at the beginning.

And some of those who sat round that table were the same who had met around Beatrice's dinner-table. 'There was Carton, the Lord Chancellor, a white-faced man with understanding; he had a heavy, shaven face that might have stood among the busts of the Caesars, a slow elaborating voice, with self-indulgent, slightly oblique, and triumphant lisp, and a momentary, voluntary, humourous twinkle; "We have to forgive – even ourselves." '

But none of these figures, comic or imposing, could match the newly liberated Nettie. 'She stepped into the centre of that dream of world reconstruction that filled my mind and took possession of it all. A little wisp of hair had blown across her cheek, her lips fell apart in that sweet smile of hers; her eyes were full of wonder, of a welcoming scrutiny, of an infinitely courageous friendliness.' And Nettie held her own until the end of the story, as well she might with such a smile, even if it was not reserved for him. One part of that Utopia was a recognition of free love or at least the right of men and women to choose for themselves; not a lust for promiscuity but a hymn to something higher altogether, like Blake's *Jerusalem*.

His relations with Beatrice, as her diary shows, although slightly strained, were still good. Public appearances could give way to private badinage. Just after the two lectures and the publication of *The Comet*, he came to stay at Grosvenor Road and she recorded how he had sought to justify his novel as a work of art and that therefore it should not be criticized on grounds of morality.

'When Michaelangelo displayed groups of such nude figures in stone or colour, it does not follow that he desired to see all his acquaintances sprawling about without clothes.' A specious retort to my criticism. However he afterwards admitted that he thought 'free-er love' would be the further relation of the sexes when we got over the sordid stage of the masculine proprietorship of the women. 'At present any attempt to attempt that free-er love means a network of low intrigue – assumes and therefore creates an atmosphere of gross physical desire – but this is only an incident of a morality based on the notion of private property in women. No decent person has a chance of experimenting in free-er love today: the relations between men and women are so hemmed in by law and convention. To experiment you must be base; hence to experiment starts with being damned.'

And Beatrice did not altogether object to this formulation. She could see the truth in his argument although she still craved a higher morality in which man – and presumably woman, too – would be able 'to subordinate his physical desires and appetites to the intellectual and spiritual side of his nature'. And yet this was the aspect of the argument in which, despite outward appearances, she retained her sympathy for him. 'There are fine qualities in the man – of heart and intellect – but he has no manners in the broadest meaning of the word.' He had never been anywhere to be taught that, and maybe he *had* taught her something.

Leaving morals and manners aside – and she could hardly insist that the one was as important as the other – maybe this was the nearest point when he and Beatrice came to explaining each other's view on the great sexual question. Neither had said everything which was in his or her mind, neither could be accused of reticence. HG did believe in a form of free love, and he was ashamed of himself later for having appeared to qualify his doctrine. Beatrice also had been reticent in a way that only she could understand but which was surely the reason why she could not condemn his views in private in the terms which she later used in public. In her own diaries, years before – but unknown to anybody but herself at the time or anyone else until the diaries were published in full in the 1980s – she had described her own illicit love-fantasies and what an agony her own celibacy had been. It could be as intolerable for a woman as for a man. She knew that, and she had described the condition in those unforgettable and unprintable parts of her diary. And, if she had confessed these truths to him there and then, the beginning of a common Fabian policy on these high matters might have been designed. It still would not have been easy to shape a full philosophy, if the word is not too portentous in this context, but HG himself might have been kept out of some of his scrapes, and the Fabians themselves might have devised a less hypocritical approach to the subject; some of the sexual liberations, say, of the 1960s or 1980s might have been achieved much earlier, and an infinity of human suffering, male and female, might have been avoided. Altogether, what a moment it would have been if he had known that Beatrice, too, was one of those passionate daughters who would long so much for love and happiness.

Several of these were matters which HG had raised in *The Comet* and which got him into trouble on all sides. His new friend Bertrand Russell invited him and Jane over to Badley Wood near Oxford where he lived, but the visit was not an unqualified success. When the earth is hit by the Comet the victory of good sense, according to Russell, was shown in two ways: a war between England and Germany was stopped and everybody took to free love. Wells was assailed in the press, not for his pacifism but for his advocacy of free love. When Wells sought to deflect the charge, Russell still pressed the point: 'Why did you first advocate free love and then say you hadn't?' Wells replied, according to Russell, that he had not yet saved enough money to do so. Russell acknowledged: 'I was perhaps in those days too strict and this answer displeased me.' Too strict indeed: Bertrand Russell himself had had no comparable experience of earning his own living, and of how awkward and expensive the expression of free ideas on this subject might be.

Even as HG reopened or intensified his quarrel with the old gang, Beatrice in her diary could show how she sometimes appreciated his worth and his intentions better than the others, better for sure than Sidney, better also at this period than Shaw. She did read *The Comet* seriously. It did not convert her to free love or anything like it, but it did provoke a transformation in her views hardly less remarkable. Surprisingly, she had never supported the campaign for Women's Suffrage. Indeed, she had once added her prestigious name to the list of women, headed by Mrs Humphry Ward, who had published a document opposing the whole idea. But somehow the new controversy of 1906 made her think afresh on these great questions, and clearly she must have had some arguments with HG and with Jane. At the beginning of November she wrote a long letter to Millicent Fawcett explaining her change of mind; it was published prominently in *The Times* a few days later. And she wrote privately to HG: 'Mrs. Wells will rejoice that I have at last thrown in my lot with Women's Suffrage. See what you have accomplished by your Propaganda! Far more important than converting the whole of the Fabian Society.' In fact, *The Comet* was not primarily directed at the question of the vote for women. HG had not placed that demand at the head of his list. Jane must have emphasized the point more strongly. Beatrice showed afresh the magnanimous side of her nature. It would have been tragic indeed if, just at the time when the suffrage campaign was rising to its climax, such a great national woman reformer as Beatrice had continued to use her influence against it. HG had helped save her from that.

The rest of HG's campaign seemed to lose its momentum. Two crowded meetings of the full Society in Essex Hall that December were required to see his main proposition defeated. He had really been no match for the organizing skills of the Webbs and the Blands and, above all, for Bernard Shaw's debating prowess. At one of the last meetings Shaw taunted him into an acceptance of the proposal that, whatever the verdict, he would not resign from the Society. 'Wells was squelched by a joke,' was one verdict. But it had been quite a near thing. Beatrice concluded that, if he had avoided his personal attacks on the old gang, if he had concentrated on what she called his fervid enthusiasm for vague and big ideas, he would have succeeded. Probably that was true; she would know better than anybody else. So it seems that HG had thrown away a wonderful opportunity to advance his cause through his swelled head and his hot temper. Maybe – and the charge has been frequently renewed, with the citation of the Webb diaries as the most clinching piece of evidence. He would never learn how to curb his rebellious temperament to suit sedate committees; Beatrice was certainly right about that. But still he understood better than they the mood of the times and how it could be mobilized. The year 1906 was a near-revolutionary one in English political history. It saw the expulsion of the Tories, after twenty years of office, the chance for a real Liberal revival, and the arrival at Westminster of a new party dedicated to the proposition that fundamental social change was necessary. In such a climate, even Fabians might be forgiven for moving a little faster.

HG did believe in free love, and he practised it. It was subsequently held against him that this was the primary, even the sole, cause of his row with the Fabian leadership. But the dates and details tell a quite different and more revealing story. It should not have been so difficult for readers of *Lewisham* or *The Comet* and much else in his early writing to discern what a passionate man HG was, how in the end the passion might take command, how this might contrast, we may note in passing, with the conduct of the philanderer Bernard Shaw, who would arouse emotions and then not bring them to a climax. Anyhow, HG had not sought to hide this aspect of his nature from Beatrice Webb, and she had seemed to understand better than the others.

How soon the others in his life came to perform their different roles is a significant question. Nettie, the heroine of *The Comet*, was a real woman in his life; or, rather, there were several Netties. He was constantly caught by the infinite charm of a woman's smile. He was often falling in love, and the passion was reciprocated. To live, and to work, and to love were for him all part of the same process of finding out what the modern world was about, and he could not easily imagine how he could dispense with any of the three. He might often be quoted against himself, relegating the love-obsession to a lower category, and maybe it was these ill-considered, clumsy asides which provoked the inept accusation that he was in some sense a misogynist. One rebuttal for the charge is supplied by comparing the periods in his life when his inspiration was strongest and best-sustained.

Nettie's smile did not win conquests in every quarter, although devoted admirers of *The Comet* may find the qualification difficult to accept, especially since it came from a quarter for which HG was showing a growing respect and fascination.

Dorothy Richardson was a friend and contemporary of Jane who happened to be the first critic who wrote about Wells's writing from a woman's point of view. Some time in that crowded, memorable year, he started an affair with her, or maybe even in this instance it was the other way round. Anyhow, neither one nor the other felt any sense of guilt or recrimination. She had a tendency to lapse into what he called 'a vein of ego-centred mysticism'; but the irritations were not serious and, as in the case of so many of his relationships, they remained friends after they had been lovers. What she wrote about *The Comet* there and then illustrates how he could take criticisms from lovers more profitably than from presiding Fabians. Maybe he also learned from her how to improve on the already adorable Nettie. 'One hopes for a book', wrote Richardson in the November 1906 issue of *The Crank*,

> where womanhood shall be as well presented as manhood. So far he has not achieved the portrayal of a woman with the one exception of Leadford's mother. His women are all one specimen, carried away from some biological museum of his student days, dressed up in various trappings, with different shades of hair and proportions of freckles, with neatly tabulated instincts and one vague smile between them all.

Much too severe a verdict for sure on poor Nettie, and maybe there was just a twinge of jealousy, but all would be forgiven by HG as he read the glowing tribute to Leadford's mother. That was his own mother, and he would make the world love her as he loved her himself. Dorothy must have known her, too, and may have been able to see for herself what happiness and honour her son restored to her in the place of the horror which providence had ordained.

He must have made the awkward but delightful discovery about the way his love affairs affected his work some time after he and Jane had settled in at Sandgate, and after the two boys were born. He was a wonderful father; no-one ever doubted that. But how soon exactly Jane learned of his other activities is not clear. Her correspondence with Edith Nesbit suggests that nothing developed in 1906, the year when the political row proceeded. Soon he must have discussed some of his free love doctrines with her. And it must often have been an agony for her, then and thereafter. However, to use the horrible word, she did show herself a complaisant wife as well as a brilliant organizer of his various homes and his business affairs, and he quickly made the most of it. And he took some terrible risks, the most perilous of all in the year or two which followed the Fabian row. It was a true passion; perhaps the truest he ever felt.

FOUR

Love and Mr Polly

But a propaganda of more and franker and
healthier love-making was not, I found – as Plato
found before me – a simple proposition.
Experiment in Autobiography, vol. 2, p. 475

Amber Reeves had a rare combination of qualities: beauty,
brains, passion, an irrepressible and truly feminist independence
of spirit, and, most important of all, a strong reciprocal dose of
the overflowing good humour which HG himself brought to
such affairs, having wrested it by his own application from so
many setbacks and tribulations. Together, they would make the
world anew; everything else could be held in suspense. And the
journey to that promised land need not follow some vale of tears;
it could be a glorious adventure.

Exactly when they first set eyes on each other is not clear: it
must have been at one of those 1906 Fabian lectures where the
HG on the platform could often stumble or stutter but where the
man's invincible courage would still win through in the end, and
where the youngest members of the audience were most likely to
be captivated. The whole Reeves family were Fabians. Her
father, William Pember Reeves, was a New Zealander with

leftish politics who had been sent over to act as agent-general in London. Her mother, Maud, had suffered 'matrimonial flattening', according to HG, but soon showed signs of independent recovery. She may have fallen beneath HG's spell even before her daughter. The two families became friends, including Amber and her younger sisters: 'Tell Mr. Wells', wrote Maud to Jane, 'that if Mr. Henry James ought to have been a nursery maid, H. G. Wells ought to have been a finishing governess; how those girls revelled in him, and how excellent was his influence.' In the autumn of 1907, Amber went up to Newnham College, Cambridge, as a science student; women in those days had to be very clever indeed to do that. HG, of course, did nothing to discourage or disturb the process. As the affair developed, he became as proud of her as she was of him. How soon their mutual attraction was transformed into an exclusive, overpowering interest is not clear also. It seems to have covered the whole of the period at Newnham, and must have influenced his other reactions to the events of the time.

The suspicion in some Fabian circles, widely disseminated long before his association with Amber was known, was that he had offered his care and protection and something more to Rosamund, the daughter of Hubert Bland and Edith Nesbit. She was not actually Edith's daughter, although HG could not have known that at the time. He certainly showed real sympathy and friendship for Rosamund, although the evidence that it went much further seems slight.

HG is supposed to have absconded with her until Bland overtook him at Paddington Station with a horsewhip. But neither at the time nor later did HG accept this account of what had happened. His sympathy for Rosamund was justified. She had certainly poured out her heart to him and, indeed, professed a love for him till her dying day. That was the effect he could have on women, young and old; and this was the time, maybe, when this side of his personality had reached its highest development. We may pause here to quote a passage from his autobiography, written about this particular period, but not necessarily referring to Rosamund or Amber:

I found nothing for self-reproach in my private conduct. I did not know that the imaginations of the back benches of the Fabian Society and the riff-raff of the literary world were adorning my unwitting and undeserving head with a rakish halo. I did not realise how readily my simple questionings could be interpreted as the half confessions of a sort of Fabian Casanova, an inky Lovelace, the satyr-Cupid of Socialism. *

Just about that time also, although the exact date cannot be fixed, he had a furious exchange with Bernard Shaw on these sexual questions. His own letter refers to Bland and Rosamund, but it is difficult not to believe that it was his own knowledge of his relationship with Amber which stirred his real fury.

The more I think you over the more it comes home to me what an unmitigated middle Victorian ass you are. You play about with the ideas like a daring garrulous maiden aunt, but when it comes to an affair like the Bland affair you show the instincts of conscious gentility and the judgement of a hen. You write of Bland in a strain of sentimental exaltation, you explain his beautiful romantic character to me – as though I don't know the man to his bones. You might be dear Mrs. Bland herself in a paroxysm of romantic invention. And all this twaddle about 'the innocent little person'. If she is innocent it isn't her parents' fault anyhow.

The fact is you're a flimsy intellectual, acquisitive of mind, adrift and chattering brightly in a world you don't understand. You don't know, as I do, in blood and substance, lust, failure, shame, hate, love and creative passion. You don't understand and you can't understand the rights or wrongs of the case into which you stick your maiden judgement – any more than you can understand the aims of the Fabian Society that your vanity has wrecked. Now go on being amusing. †

It is hard to see how any friendship or even a political association could survive such a barrage which, however, did

* *Experiment in Autobiography*, vol. 2, p. 474.
† Briggs, *A Woman of Passion*, p. 312.

continue for weeks, months, years – indeed, for the rest of their respective lives. Both were masters of invective; each believed that some flippancy or lack of dedication on the part of the other could injure the Socialist cause in which they both believed; each could accuse the other of retreating behind some barricade of incorrigible egotism when they ought to be together on the same battlefield ranged against the common enemy. Each could discern the weakness in the character of the other or, more temptingly still, that of their closest allies. Moreover, the Old Gang feared that HG was no gentleman; he did not seem to have been taught the rules of any game. In the last resort or at the moment of crisis, he would just look after his own interest and nobody else's. That, at least, was how he conducted his love-affairs or, rather, that is how the matter appeared to the sedate, established Fabian leaders, the Shaws no less than the Webbs. An irony which did not escape HG's attention was that Shaw took natural pride in the daring success of his play *Getting Married* in which many marital conventions were mocked and both the *ménage à trois* and other convenient arrangements were properly considered. The New Woman was also coming into her own, and HG's Jane certainly considered herself to be one of that distinguished company. In 1908 she was elected to the Fabian Executive and soon became active with the Women's Group.

The debate among the Fabians is sometimes presented as if the Shaw–Webb victory combined with the Wellsian defeat at the meeting in December was decisive. But none of the leading combatants treated it quite that way: they all lived to fight another day and to offer a different aspect to the outside world. HG produced three new books, none of which, whatever their other virtues or vices, offered a challenge to the Fabian leadership. One was an attempted philosophical work, *First and Last Things*, the next a new novel, *The War in the Air*, and the third a new book on Socialism, *New Worlds for Old*. The first was an attempt, and by no means a derisory one, to face meta-physical problems: 'No such thing as a man without a philosophy, even though he doesn't know he has got one . . .

My beliefs, my dogmas, my rules, they are made for my campaigning needs, like the knapsack and water bottle of a Cockney soldier invading some stupendous mountain gorge.' The second book, which, as implied in the title, did make the prophecy that flying planes would transform future warfare, still offered as its chief character another little Wellsian hero on the make. Bert Smallways held his own against the odds and the Gods, even if he didn't quite know what he was doing: he, too, devised his own philosophy. But the most substantial volume of the three was his *New Worlds for Old: A Plain Account of Modern Socialism*, in which he sought to present a case which could retain its appeal for all. Here he had continued or initiated several arguments with his fellow Fabians, but it was done in a most charitable tone, and only after he had sought to pay full tribute to the Webbite achievements: 'He – that is Sidney – dreams of the most foxy and wonderful digging by means of boxlids, table-spoons, dish-covers – anything but spades designed and made for the job in hand – just as he dreams of an extensive expropriation of landlords by a legislature that includes the present unreformed House of Lords . . .'

But even more significant, in the light of later developments, was the stress which he laid – in the year 1908, be it emphasized – on the need for a Socialism which was both international and libertarian. Mostly, on these matters, he had both the Webbs and the Shavians on his side but not always in the emphasis which he attached to the argument. On the first issue, he insisted:

> The Socialist movement is from this point of view, no less than the development of the collective self-consciousness of humanity. Necessarily, therefore, it must be international as well as out-spoken, making no truce with prejudices against race and colour. These national and racial collective consciousnesses of to-day are things as vague, as fluctuating as mists or clouds, they melt, dissolve into one another, they coalesce, they split. No clear isolated national mind can ever maintain itself under modern conditions; even the mind of Japan now comes into the common melting-pot of

thought. We Socialists take up to-day the assertion the early Christians were the first to make, that mankind is of one household and one substance; the Samaritan who stoops to the wounded stranger by the wayside our brother rather than the Levite . . .*

Then, again, he warned of the danger which could come from a Socialism which neglected freedom.

We must insure the continuity of the collective mind; that is manifestly a primary necessity for Socialism. The attempt to realise the Marxist idea of a democratic Socialism without that might easily fall into the abortive birth of an acephalous monster, the secular development of administrative Socialism gives the world over to a bureaucratic mandarinate, self-satisfied, interfering and unteachable, with whom wisdom would die. And yet we Socialists can produce in our plans no absolute bar to these possibilities. Here I can suggest only in the most general terms methods and certain principles. They need to be laid down as virtually necessary to Socialism, and so far they have not been laid down. They have still to be incorporated in the Socialist creed. They are essentially principles of that Liberalism out of whose generous aspirations Socialism sprang, but they are principles that even to-day, unhappily, do not figure in the fundamental professions of any Socialist body.†

We may accustom ourselves to the idea that the Wellsian mind could find itself tugged in opposite directions by Plato and Swift; neither of them was ready to loosen the hold each established in his early reading. Plato could feed these grand, comprehensive, even totalitarian themes which Beatrice might approve, but then Swift would intervene to restore his humanity. These were major political questions to which he gave his full mind, but he was often much less wise on lesser political matters. When Winston Churchill was a candidate as a

*New Worlds for Old (1908), p. 291.
†New Worlds for Old, p. 293.

left-wing Liberal at a Manchester by-election, HG, thinking
him a likely lad for the future, sent him a letter of support. But a
Socialist candidate was standing at the same election, and all the
Fabians, left and right, regarded the Wellsian lapse as one of
folly or worse.

However, one subject which *New Worlds* did not explore with
his usual candour and audacity – writing in his autobiography
twenty years later, he expressed shame for his reticence – was the
question of free love, which he was alleged to have launched so
boldly or brashly in *The Comet*. He had an excuse: his affair with
Amber was rising to its climax or, rather, moving apace through
its series of climaxes.

What the outside world saw and overheard was, of course,
very different from what HG and Amber felt themselves. It was
the clash between the two which produced the crisis, one of such
proportions that it came near to wrecking HG's life altogether
or, at least, catapulting it into a quite different field of
operations. He did, very nearly, sacrifice everything for her; she
was ready to do so for him. No kind of pretence existed on either
side; it was touch-and-go on a whole series of occasions. Even
the most horrified observer had to admit that. One of these, and
perhaps the best-informed, was Beatrice Webb, who wrote in
her diary for early August 1909:

> The end of our friendship with H. G. Wells. A sordid intrigue with
> poor little Amber Reeves – the coming of a baby, and the run to
> cover of marriage with another man, a clever and charming young
> Fabian (Blanco White), who married her, knowing the facts, out of
> devoted chivalry. The story got about owing to Amber's own
> confidence to a Cambridge don's wife, and owing to H. G. Wells's
> own indiscretions. Moreover, after the hurried marriage, without
> the Reeves' knowledge, of Amber and Blanco, Amber and H. G.
> Wells insist on remaining friends – a sort of *Day of the Comet* affair.
> We hear of it late in the day and feel ourselves obliged to warn
> Sydney Olivier, who was over on a holiday, against letting his four
> handsome daughters run about with H. G. Wells. (Apparently
> H.G. tried to seduce Rosamund Bland. If the Reeves had only

known of that, they would not have allowed Amber to stay with him [at his Sandgate home] for a month at a time.) So I think we were right to tell Sydney Olivier. But as a matter of fact H.G. had already told him that Amber was going to have a baby, that he was supplying the rent of the house, and that he had been madly in love with Amber and that 'we were much too timid about these things.'

For some reason that we do not understand, Sydney Olivier quoted us as his authority, and so we got these letters from H. G. Wells as well as a pathetic one from Reeves. It is a horrid affair and has cost us much. If Amber will let us, we shall stand by her as Blanco's wife and drop H. G. Wells, once and for all, as he no doubt will drop us. He will doubtless drift into other circles – probably the only person of his own *ménage* who will suffer is his patient and all-enduring little wife, who, having entered into that position illicitly herself at the cost of another woman, cannot complain.

But the whole case, and the misery that seems likely to follow, is a striking example of the tangle into which we have got on the sex question. We accepted Wells, in spite of his earlier divorce case, on grounds of tolerance. He and his wife were happy – the other wife has married again, and there seemed no reason on ordinary enlightened principles, for us to hold back or object. The Reeves knowing all these facts, and Mrs. Reeves claiming to be 'advanced' in her opinions (she did not object to In the Days of the Comet), were very intimate with him and allowed him to become Amber's guide, philosopher and friend. Amber being a little heathen, and H.G. being a sensualist, they both let themselves go, and start a surreptitious liaison. At first, both of them think that they will stand it out. But Amber gets into a panic, and married the first faithful swain who will let himself be married to a lady with a 'past' of an imminent character. But apparently there is no breach; and the household goes on being of a very mixed sort – the Reeves parents looking on in tragic sorrow, and Reeves calling H.G. a 'vile impudent blackguard'.

And all this arises because we none of us know what exactly is the sexual code we believe in, approving of many things on paper which we violently object to when they are practised by those we care about. Of course, the inevitable condition today of any 'sexual experiments' is deceit and secrecy – it is this that makes any divergence from the conventional morality so sordid and lowering.

That is why upright minds are careful not to experiment, except in the 'accustomed way' (ie. with prostitutes). It is hardly fair to become intimate with a young girl, fresh from college, on the assumption that you believe in monogamy, and then suddenly to propose a polygamous relationship without giving her guardians and friends any kind of notice. That is not playing the game of sexual irregularity even according to the rules of a game full of hazards, at any rate for the woman.

Oddly enough, Sidney had long had a settled aversion to H. G. Wells, thought him a purely selfish creature, with no redeeming motive, nothing but his cleverness to recommend him.

What we regret is the possibility of adding to W. P. Reeves's grief, of doing anything to lessen the bare chance of a happy marriage between Amber and Blanco. If either of us is to blame, it is I, and it is Sidney who seems likely to get the blame from Reeves and others. *

HG himself wrote an account of the affair in which he claimed that he had done 'my best not to exculpate myself'. He insisted: 'I was, by twists and turns, two entirely different people, the man for whom Jane's security and pride and our children and my work were the most precious things in life, and the man for whom Amber had become the most maddeningly necessary thing in life.'† His plea for his own honesty in this particular respect will hardly be disputed. The one person who lived through the whole experience was Amber, and he could see what she felt, too. Indeed, when the recollection was still hot in his mind, he described the scene. He did it in a novel written a year later. Ann Veronica was not Amber Reeves; he had to devise several dissimilarities to protect himself and her. But a parallel much too close to be accidental was the description of the cruel perils she would run if she chose to go off with him. This was Amber's

---

* The Diary of Beatrice Webb, ed. Norman and Jeanne Mackenzie, vol. 3 (1984), pp. 120–2.
†G. P. Wells (ed.), H. G. Wells in Love (1984), p. 80.

declaration no less than Ann's: 'As you will, dear lover. But for me it doesn't matter. Nothing is wrong that you do. I am quite clear about this. I know exactly what I am doing. I give myself to you.' Ann Veronica did go off with her hero – and they had a wonderful honeymoon in the mountains, and came home to live happily ever after. Amber was not able to do that, and since she obviously shared Ann Veronica's beauty, and most of her other qualities, it was for her a hard dispensation. But for all of them, Ann Veronica and her man, Amber and HG, it was nothing like the sordid tale enshrined in Beatrice's diary. It was a real love, and their child, Anne, came to love both her mother and her father. *

For HG, love was rarely a distraction or, if it was, it wasn't really love. Almost always for him, it was an incitement to action, often a development of his writing which he had not attempted before. Ever since *Kipps*, ever since *Mr Lewisham*, ever since his startling exploration of the Up Park attic, he wanted to try his hand at a more ambitious novel. He made the effort quite consciously. Nothing like the same acclaim given to *Kipps* had been given to *The Comet*: a mistaken depreciation, as he himself judged. But he must try again, as he always did.

He poured his full heart and mind and the experience of a lifetime into *Tono-Bungay*. He exerted his artistic gifts more consciously and continuously than ever before. Every separate interest which had figured in his other writings found its special place here. He thought his own treatment of the novel could be elaborated to cover all his own requirements and, maybe, to achieve something new, not only in his political thinking but in the form of the novel itself. He was directly encouraged by the discovery of a particular inspiration. It is not certain when he

---

* Several of the other implications of *Ann Veronica* will be discussed a little later; they are of first importance for HG's relationship with the feminists. But what I have sought to emphasize here is that part of the story which illustrates the quality of Amber which distinguishes her from the Beatrice Webb caricature. The best edition of *Ann Veronica* is the one recently published by Everyman (1993) and edited by Sylvia Hardy. Indeed, she presents the whole Wellsian saga in a new, enlivening context.

had made his first acquaintance with Laurence Sterne. As far as we know, there had been no copy of *Tristram Shandy* alongside *Gulliver's Travels* in that upper-loft library at Up Park, where the eighteenth century exercised such a sway that later blundering intrusions would be treated with deep suspicion. Yet the moment was decisive for HG's future. Gradually or not so gradually, Sterne established an unshakeable hold on his mind. He could not displace Swift from his pre-eminence; but no such dislocation was necessary since Sterne, too, was a pupil of Swift's, if a wayward or self-willed one. HG's own reading of novels had become varied and vast. He had to make up for lost time with his famous contemporaries or with the French or Russian masters, whom they had followed. But somehow he made his own discovery of Laurence Sterne whom he patriotically hailed as greater than any of them. He put his imprint on *Tono-Bungay* in a way which could never be effaced.

The charge was often made against HG's writing generally and against *Tono-Bungay* in particular that he would elaborate his grand ideas with unfailing zest but then leave the final dilemma unresolved or insoluble. Maybe that was true, but *Tono-Bungay* was not the artistic failure which was often also another part of the accusation. He might be portrayed as a hare-brained, science-worshipping optimist or an incurable humanity-hating pessimist. He was neither, and the balance he sought to sustain in such an ambitious, comprehensive work as *Tono-Bungay* should have been enough on its own to refute the interpretation. A much more apposite way of describing the point was offered, as so often, by V. S. Pritchett, the most sympathetic of his critics. 'Wells as an artist thrived on keeping the seeds of his self-contradiction alive,' and that was truer of *Tono-Bungay* than of any other of his writings. If it was a fault, he had done it on purpose. He was seeking to describe how the money-grubbing, empire-grabbing, decent-value-mocking society of late-Victorian, Edwardian England had betrayed every ideal of the England he loved: an older England he may have idealized out of all recognition and yet it was something in the best English tradition – the England of Thomas Paine and David

Hume and Edward Gibbon and, yes, a little earlier, the England of his own original master, Jonathan Swift. Let us quote what was written of the Swift constantly accused of committing the same misdemeanour as HG: 'For all his elusiveness and indirection, his readiness to compromise or change his ground, few writers have been more consistent than Swift, but for him consistency could be sustained only by such methods, as these. Balance in the state or the individual mind could be kept only by an agile shifting of weights.'* Never did HG himself shift those weights more deliberately and skilfully than in *Tono-Bungay*.

What even the most friendly critics might fail to appreciate was the scale of his assault, both the intention and the achievement; it was his *Dunciad*. He directed his full fire against the stupidity, the waste, the ugliness, above all, the injustice of the Great Anarch of his time: British capitalism at the peak of its power and glory and the deadly disease which it unloosed. 'Light dies before thy uncreating word.' He wanted the reality of that great line to be understood, and the reality of a new kind of politics. Multitudes of readers did understand, and most readily the young ones. They could feel, especially, the injustice of the system, as did George Ponderevo. That curious name deserved to become as famous as Tristram or Gulliver or any other of HG's own creations.

Tono-Bungay was the book in which, in the person of George Ponderevo, he told more movingly and ambitiously than ever before the story of his own arrival in Edwardian London, which claimed to be the most powerful and prestigious city in the world and which still presumed through its ruling cliques to dictate the economics, the politics and the morals of the rest of the community. He carried his adventures and researches into every corner of the city. He explored the whole place as it had never been explored before. He weighed it all in the balance and found it wanting, but this biblical judgement was not enough. He gave some hint of the Socialist dream which guided him at

---

* Kathleen Williams, *Jonathan Swift and the Age of Compromise* (1958), p. 211.

the start and to which he would return after every setback and calamity.

George Ponderevo had an extra dose of the secret Wellsian charm – not that HG claimed it for himself. He could turn aside awkward moments with his good humour and prick the first signs of pretentiousness in the company. He could show this form best in the presence of another soul, if any could be found, with the same gift of raillery. His Aunt Susan in *Tono-Bungay* is such a creation – together with his uncle, the two characters which most surely justify the comparison between HG and Dickens. How much either was based on a character in HG's real life it is hard or unprofitable to guess. Her love for George was a mother's love, and the moments when she shows it must touch any heart, as they did George's, especially when he was dealing with such monstrous ineptitude with poor Marion. Her role partly fits the fiasco of HG's own marriage with his cousin Isabel. At first, it looks as if the portrait drawn in *Tono-Bungay* is being grossly unfair to her, but then all such mistaken judgements are set aside by an indictment of the rules and regulations or non-existent access to knowledge which condemned the whole rising generation to find out for itself. The Beatrice who reappears to take Marion's place, for all George's glowing endearments and her aristocratic bearing – not a match, as we shall see, for some of his later heroines – is not touched by any sense of liberation. She is as much the victim of cruel, Mrs Grundyish convention as poor Marion. Neither of them could share the exuberant hopes which the young George brought with him.

London! I came up to it, young and without advisers, rather priggish, rather dangerously open-minded and very open-eyed and with something – it is I think the common gift of imaginative youth, and I claim it unblushingly – fine in me, finer than the world, and seeking fine responses. I did not want simply to live or simply to live happily or well. I wanted to serve and do and make – with some nobility. It was in me. It is in half the youth of the world.

George had that spirit of youth, which his creator understood better than anyone else, knocked out of him, not only by his uncle's antics in the exploitation of *Tono-Bungay*. He saw 'a great deal of the great world' during those eventful years.

> I saw the statesmen without their orders and the bishops with but a little purple silk left over from their canonicals, inhaling, not incense but cigar smoke. I could look at them all the better because for the most part they were not looking at me but at my uncle and calculating consciously or unconsciously how they might use him and assimilate him to their system, the most unpremeditated, subtle, successful plutocracy that ever encumbered the destinies of mankind. Not one of them, so far as I can see, until disaster overtook him, resented his lies, his almost naked dishonesty of method, the disorderly disturbance of this trade and that, caused by his spasmodic operations.

Nothing counted but the pursuit of money: everything else was now subordinate. It was the futility of it all even more than the indecency which most outraged George. He knew there was a better way, and he knew what it was called.

> 'Glad to think you're a Socialist, Sir,' said one of his old scientific student companions: 'It's the only civilised state. I've been a Socialist some years – off the *Clarion*. It's a rotten scramble, this world. It takes the things we make and invent and it plays the silly fool with them. We scientific people, we'll have to take things over and stop all this financing and advertisement and that. It's too silly.'

For a while all such voices of sanity were swept aside. The life of plutocratic London was supposed to be the ideal for which all men strove with their sycophantic, subordinate women at their side. (Only the ever discriminating Aunt Susan insisted on a preference for the flowers. She always had a special eye for the Michaelmas daisies and the perennial sunflowers.) Otherwise, the life of the *nouveau riche* was everything.

For this the armies drilled, for this the Law was administered and the prisons did their duty; for this the millions toiled and perished in suffering, in order that a few of us should build palaces we never finished, make billiard rooms under ponds, run imbecile walls round irrational estates, scorch about the world in motor cars, devise flying machines, play golf and a dozen other foolish games, crowd into chattering dinner parties, gamble and make our lives one vast dismal spectacle of witless waste! So it struck me then, and for a time I could think of no other interpretation. This was Life! It came to me like a revelation at once incredible and indisputable of the abysmal folly of our being!

Sometimes the picture was painted in such black colours, the imminence of the catastrophe so near, that no relief was possible. But somehow George himself never allowed his exuberant humanity to vanish altogether. When he and Aunt Susan suddenly found themselves in each other's company, the old companionship could instantly revive. It was often critically alleged against several of H. G. Wells's novels that he had not resolved his own philosophical contradictions. True enough; but he often thought that life itself contained the contradiction, too.

Tono-Bungay ended with a torrent of eloquence poured over the head of his benighted, beloved London. He was often accused of accepting weak, irresolute conclusions for novels which he had embarked upon with confident audacity. The accusation can be made against many writers, but it was much less true of Wells than is commonly supposed. It was certainly not true of *Tono-Bungay*. He may not have contemplated such an ending when young George was reading Swift and Paine in the upper rooms in Bladesover, which was of course his truest representation of the library at Up Park. Within a few years he had learned as much about that London as anyone had ever learned, the evil and the good, the true traditions and the modern infamies, the aspirations which might inspire him on the heights of Highgate and Hampstead; but still he would not deny how he would allow himself to be 'demoralised by the immense effect of London'. If London could demoralize, it could also inspire. No reader could truthfully claim that this was the final note of the *Tono-Bungay* peroration, but nor could the other verdict be dismissed. 'Sometimes I call this reality science, sometimes I call it truth. But it is something we draw by pain and effort out of the heart of life, that we disentangle and make clear.' And nor was that even the final word.

Since no-one knew better than HG himself what exertions he had made to produce *Tono-Bungay*, he must have been especially abashed by its reception. Only a few of his closest friends, with Arnold Bennett at their head,* seemed to appreciate it properly. Bennett first hailed *Tono-Bungay* as Wells's most distinguished and most powerful book, and showed also that he fully understood the author's own ambitions and intentions. It was the arraignment of a whole epoch at the bar of the conscience of a man who was both intellectually honest and

---

*A year later Bennett wrote about HG's *The New Machiavelli*: 'But where in fiction, ancient or modern, will you find another philosophical picture of a whole epoch and society as brilliant and as honest as *The New Machiavelli*? Well, I will tell you where you will find it. You'll find it in *Tono-Bungay*.' Bennett's judgement about *Tono-Bungay* was denounced at the time but it seems still more valid today. And we may note that it was HG's honesty which so many of his contemporaries most wished to celebrate. Bennett's articles first appeared in the *New Age* and were later included in *Books and Persons* (1917). I reread *Tono-Bungay* in the Everyman edition (1994), with its new introduction by John Hammond. No-one better-fitted for the task or, rather, the adventure; he was among the first modern critics, or maybe was the very first, to recognize the 'modernism' in *Tono-Bungay* or to see *Tono-Bungay* as the ambitious work which HG himself saw it. Authors often misjudge the comparative value of their own writings, but HG's own affection for *Tono-Bungay* had a substantial basis, as I hope I have sufficiently indicated. Probably the most important individual criticism of *Tono-Bungay* was David Lodge's piece which appeared in his *Language of Fiction* (1966). He called his chapter '*Tono-Bungay* and the Condition of England', and he quoted HG's own definition of the enemy. The whole essay must be read; it needed a good modern novelist to put several of the others in their place. Sometimes philosophers could understand, too. As I finished rereading *Tono-Bungay*, I received a note from my friend Professor Ted Honderich who had just read the new edition of *Tono-Bungay* to his Jane, as I once read an earlier edition (before either of them were born) to Jill. He fully supports the John Hammond–Patrick Parrinder–David Lodge thesis. Let all sceptics, if there are any left, try the *Tono-Bungay* remedy themselves.

powerfully intellectual. George Ponderevo transgresses most of the current codes, but he also shatters them.

HG's enemies, old and new, made no attempt to understand what he was attempting and how, at the worst, his tremendous exertion should be judged. His aim was, as he himself said later, 'to give a view of the contemporary social and political system in Great Britain, an old and degenerating system, tried and strained by new inventions and new ideas and invaded by a growing multitude of mere adventurers'. He thought he had in the same act raised the level of political debate and the status of the novel. Defenders of the old system had every right to receive warily so formidable an assailant. Many Fabians, especially the young ones, hailed this latest exertion from their champion. But the Old Guard could not suppress their suspicion and their malice. Beatrice insisted that she had 'the bad taste' to prefer Wells's *War in the Air* to his *Tono-Bungay*, especially since she claimed that 'he had taken from her and caricatured the workings of the capitalist system'. Bernard Shaw could only lament amid some other controversy 'that he had no time to spare to insult *Tono-Bungay*'. Hubert Bland was more specifically vindictive. 'Mr. Wells's habit of letting his pen wander at large is growing upon him. Presently the artist who gave us *Love and Mr. Lewisham* will be no more. We shall have only a greatly inferior Sterne.'

If George Ponderevo did not become a household name, as HG himself may have hoped and expected, Ann Veronica immediately stepped forward to take his place. Anyhow he must have been contemplating them both if not actually writing about them at the same time. She was the most daring character he had ever drawn, and she got him into most trouble. The essential part of the book was inspired by Amber; without her, he might never have written in this manner, with the woman seeming to be in full command from the beginning to the end. And yet the book also sought to examine the real arguments about the women's cause which rose to one particular climax in that same year of 1909 with one of the main suffragette invasions of the House of Commons, duly chronicled in these pages when

Ann Veronica joined the invaders. But was Ann Veronica a true exponent of the women's cause? Was HG himself? Candid and intricate answers to these questions must be sought and supplied; they touch upon important aspects of his character and general political judgement. He would have liked to believe – and so no doubt would Amber – that he was leading Socialist thought on these great questions, as on so many others. Yet several of his particular references and perhaps the general theme seem to tell against him. Some of the most prominent suffrage campaign leaders are presented as caricatures in his pages whereas some of the real ones were raging beauties who could have held their own in any normal Wellsian gallery. He did not share Bernard Shaw's taste for commanding Amazonian goddesses but, contrary to the common later accusation, few of his women characters ever lacked a genuine individuality. Still, whatever part the women's movement played in her story, Ann Veronica did return finally and contentedly to a state of orthodox domestic happiness. This end of her tale might have been constructed – and so it was in suffrage circles of the time and later – as the final surrender.

However, the argument is a good deal more entrancing and complicated. *Ann Veronica* had two heroines, Ann Veronica herself and the place where she was educated, the Imperial College where she fought for the right to study biology. Her college was given a slightly different situation on the London map, which HG knew so well, than the real one in the Cromwell Road where he himself had taught and where, indeed, he had originally met Jane. Perhaps it was this coincidence which helped reconcile Jane to the story. HG did greatly honour the few places which both taught him properly and allowed women to be taught properly at the same time. *Love* is not too strong a word to apply to these rare institutions. By the same token, Veronica's outrageous father was seeking to deny her access to higher education altogether: 'he had met and argued with a Somerville girl at a friend's dinner table, and he thought that sort of thing unsexed a woman' – a favourite Victorian anti-feminist taunt. Moreover, it was there that Veronica met the man she wanted and eventually secured even though he was several years older than herself and already mysteriously married. Of course, he bore a likeness to HG himself, and the occasional critical views on the women's movements bore some resemblance to HG's views, too, but much more evident than any such resemblance was the exposure of his position – and hers – to the scandalous prejudice of the age. If they decided to go off together, both their respective lives could be wrecked, his career at the Imperial College and her hopes of acceptance in any quarter, the straight-laced family she had deserted or her new-found Fabian friends in London. Everything was at stake for them – but still they did it. For all his superior knowledge of the world, she was the one who made the tremendous choice. This was the part of Ann Veronica which most resembled Amber Reeves, and this was the sequence of events which most shocked public opinion at the time. Ann Veronica was not afraid of her own sexuality; she was proud of it. She thought no-one should be allowed to prevent her from expressing it in her own style. She thought she had the right to choose the man she wanted. If he was prepared to respond to her, she thought no-one and nothing had the right to stand across their path. She believed in free love for the woman as well as the man. That, of course, was HG's view, and this expression of it was the real cause of the outcry. No-one had said this before, especially since the unrepentant Ann Veronica, with her adulterous husband, went on to live happily ever after.*

HG knew he was attempting something original; he would have been ashamed of himself in the circumstances if he had not. 'The youthful heroine', he wrote years later, 'was allowed a frankness of desire and sexual enterprise hitherto unknown in English popular fiction.' And she was real. 'It was held to be an unspeakable offence that an adolescent female should be sex-conscious before this thought was forced upon her attention.' What he described was only a faint reflection of what had

* HG acknowledged, with his typical honesty, in his autobiography, twenty-five years later, that he did owe something to Grant Allen who had written several books on these sexual themes in the 1890s. He said he owed a 'certain mental indebtedness to him. Better twenty-five years late than never.'

happened, but still she appeared convincing; 'from the outset, Ann Veronica was assailed as though she was an actual living person'.

And, if Ann Veronica was real, the row about her was real, too. It was not some morality play contrived by interested clergymen or cantankerous Fabians. It was an explosion of shock and anger showing how powerful were the forces which HG was challenging and how much they felt they had the right and duty to stop him in his tracks before the contamination was allowed to spread. First of all, Macmillan, his publisher, refused to publish the book on the grounds that sections of it would be exceedingly distasteful 'to the readers who normally read their books'. He soon got another publisher, but a few days after publication a lengthy letter from Edmund Gosse, the leading critic of the day, one of the acquaintances he had made at Sandgate, gave further indication of how delicate was the ground on which he was treading. Then came the thunderbolt, designed to finish the argument for ever. 'The Wellsian world consisted of this and nothing more: If an animal yearning or lust is only sufficiently absorbing it is to be obeyed. Self-sacrifice is a dream and self-restraint delusion. Such things have no place in the muddy world of Mr. Wells's imagining. His is a community of scuffling stoats and ferrets, unenlightened by a view of duty or abnegation.'* But even this was not the final word. Ann Veronica must be consigned to the flames, too. 'Boswell tells us of a conversation in which he defended with sophisticated excuses a woman who had betrayed her husband. Dr. Johnson cut him short with his immortal – "My dear Sir, never accustom your mind to mingle virtue and vice. The woman's a —, and there's an end of it." '

It was HG's turn to be outraged, and his responses in such arguments were not always as effective as they might have been: 'I do not make a good or dignified martyr,' he confessed later, when he recalled the immediate aftermath. But surely he did win in the end. After *Ann Veronica*, things were never quite the

* Unsigned review, 'A Poisonous Book', *Spectator*, 20 November 1909.

same: 'in the world of popular English fiction, young heroines
with a temperamental zest for illicit love-making, and no sense
of an inevitable Nemesis, increased and multiplied not only in
novels, but in real life.*

The peril still was, in those innocent times of 1909, that the
Amber-Veronica scandal could destroy the whole family. If the
judgement of Beatrice's diaries had become public, he could
have been overwhelmed. But Jane as well as Amber came to his
rescue – *Ann Veronica* seemed to carry a dedication to them
both. First, they contrived a family tour to the Continent,
and then the discovery of a new home in London. Jane and he
installed themselves at 17 Church Row, Hampstead, and he
soon had a Pisgah of his own from which to plan fresh conquests
of the London he could not help both hating and loving. A full-
scale Wellsian map of London showing all the highways and
byways which he explored for his novels and short stories would
emphasize another side of his character. Hampstead, maybe, was
a little too sedate for him, and he took at the same time what he
called a minute flat in Camden Street. He remained an
incurable cockney who would not be stopped from saying what
he thought in any accent or style he might choose.

He wrote or finished at Church Row two novels, *The History
of Mr Polly* and *The New Machiavelli*, and several short stories
including 'The Country of the Blind'. He was discovering a new
overt interest in what the novel could be or should be, and he
stated his views in an essay or lecture, entitled 'The
Contemporary Novel', which showed how deeply and fruitfully
he had tackled the subject. He wanted to establish, above all, in
his own words, 'the right to roam', and he put the claim thus.

But if Flaubert is really the continental emancipator of the novel
from the restrictions of form, the master to whom we of the English
persuasion, we of the discursive school, must for ever recur is he
whom I will maintain against all comers to be the subtlest and
greatest *artist* – lay stress upon that word artist – that Great Britain

* *Experiment in Autobiography*, vol. 2, p. 472.

103

has ever produced in all that is essentially the novel, Laurence
Sterne . . .*

Alas, the whole of that dazzling essay cannot be reprinted
here, but he did give notice there and then – long before the
modern suppressions of the Joyces and the Rushdies – how grand
the comprehension of the modern novelist was to be and how
crucial it was to forbid all forms of suppression.

> We are going to write about it all. We are going to write about
> business and finance, and politics and precedence and pretentions
> and decorum and indecorum, until a thousand pretences and the
> thousand impostures shrivel in the cold, clean air of our elucida-
> tions. We are going to write of waste or opportunities and latent
> beauties until a thousand new ways of living open to man and
> woman. We are going to appeal to the young and the hopeful and
> the curious against the established, the dignified and defensive.
> Before we have done, we will have all life within the novel.

At least, he had picked a good model. He had a Sterne to add to
his Swift, and as usual he was overflowing in his acknowledgements.

Established in his new vantage-point over his beloved
London, having just escaped disaster by the skin of his teeth,
precariously balanced on his Hampstead stile, like his new hero,
he gave a faultless exhibition of cockney impudence. He
invented a new hero of his own for the purpose and, try as they
will, his enemies, past and present, cannot take him from us. At
one glance, *The History of Mr Polly* may seem a lop-sided affair,
quite inadequate for the purpose. For, most monstrously, and
contrary to his normal method, as we have seen, the women are
given no place at all or swiftly despatched to the back seats or the
kitchen sinks. No real woman in his own life proved as pitifully
incapable or hateful in the habits she developed as Miriam unless
it was his own mother; and instead, as we have seen, he loved

---

An Englishman Looks at the World (1914), p. 155.

her. Jane, the truly admirable Jane, makes no appearance and nor even does Amber unless she is the romantic schoolgirl who fleetingly mocks Mr Polly from the garden wall. Wellsian experts might detect in the landlady at the Potwell Inn a premonition of his own Moura – 'she seemed, as it were, to embrace herself with infinite confidence and kindliness, as one who knew herself good in substance, good in essence'. Indeed, she does help to adjust the balance, as do a few others – for example, the militant suffragette who on this occasion comes to the aid of the militant Mr Polly, facing male aggression in all its naked horror with a nonchalant air which neither he nor we seemed to know he had. However, all these examples lumped together are no more than incidental. It is still the case that in no other of HG's novels, before or after, are the women reduced to such a subordinate role. That might be a hopeless, incurable defect. And yet *who does not love Mr Polly?* If there are such specimens, they merely acknowledge their own inhumanity. All his tastes and idiosyncrasies, his waywardness, his dreaming, his true love of the language he mangles, the way he piles up his books and knowledge, his refusal to conceal his hatreds from himself, the whole character being not, by any reckoning, a replica of HG himself, but rather an original creation of his own comic genius – like Shakespeare's Falstaff, or Cervantes' Don Quixote, or Fielding's Tom Jones, or Charle Chaplin's Little Man: the incarnation of the Wellsian assurance that, if you don't like the way the world is ordered, you can change it. All you have to do is, having studied the matter properly, to show the same courage as Mr Polly, the same contempt for the way other people try to tell you how to behave when their methods have been exposed as being useless or dangerous. And maybe also we should add that there is a touch of Swift's Gulliver in him, too – the Gulliver who could expose human antics with such a straight face, or at least the Gulliver of the Pritchett interpretation who was always master of the plot. Once he has made up his mind, our Mr Polly never loses his poise; and we, too, should share his confidence. It is HG's masterpiece. Here he said more simply than ever before what he wanted to say. Of course, simplicity is not the only virtue, and he had plenty of other things to say, and he felt within himself the driving requirement to provide all the ignorant aspiring Mr Pollys with the education they craved and had been so scandalously denied. But after Mr Polly how should the world deny the goodness of HG, as clear as that of the Potwell landlady? And where would she have been without Mr Polly?

If everyone in his or her senses could not help loving Mr Polly, nothing of the sort could be said of the next hero delineated by HG and sufficiently satisfactory from his point of view to be revived in varying guises later: Richard Remington, philosopher, prophet, politician, a fitting candidate for the Samurai order, Member of Parliament indeed. Richard himself was truly loved as we shall see: maybe that became his only surviving role, but in *The New Machiavelli* he was supposed to be a political thinker and actor of major significance; hence the citation of Machiavelli himself, who certainly presented that combination in the highest degree. Richard Remington does not fit that bill. He seems to view the Edwardian political scene with patronage or condescension. Possibly HG himself *was* suffering from the swelled head which Beatrice Webb had attributed to him.

The mention of Beatrice can remind us that *The New Machiavelli* was chiefly noticed or remembered because of the satirical passages which refer to Beatrice and Sidney Webb and the representation of the whole Wellsian–Webbian clash in the Fabian Society. These are incisive, unforgettable individual portraits. They showed that HG had a gift for political satire even if he was hopelessly ill-fitted for political intrigue himself. And the portraits of the Webbs are by no means merely hostile: Beatrice at least comes out of the whole book, as she herself was able to discern, as a real character with a first-class political brain. Beatrice and Sidney are reported to have joked to one another as they read the offending volume. 'I'm in it,' said Beatrice. 'I'm the woman whose voice is described as a "strangulated contralto" – but you are not, Sidney.' 'Oh! yes, I am, I'm described as "one of those supplementary males often found among the lower crustaceans".' Maybe HG himself did not wish these portraits, however skilfully drawn, to bulk so large in the minds of his readers. He thought he was posing much larger moral-cum-political questions. His new hero had been better-trained than his Wellsian predecessors; he came from a higher class; he had been educated at public school and university. That did not mean that he had been well educated, according to the Wellsian requirement. But it did mean that he could argue, in Fabian or other circles, with a new assurance. And one part of his argument which he revealed in what he said or what he did or what he failed to do was the chronic inadequacy of British parliamentary institutions. Could the great changes which the times demanded be achieved by the age-old contest between the parties? And, if the suffrages of the men had failed to achieve what they wanted, would the suffrage of the women change everything so much? Many Socialists, many Fabians, offered conflicting answers to these awkward, insistent questions. HG himself had never shown himself an unqualified enthusiast for any English Parliament – except, maybe, the one which his friend Oliver Cromwell and the Levellers had operated in the seventeenth century. But he could form his own sound judgement on the modern Liberals or the modern Tories or, worse still, anyone calling themselves Socialists who talked as if any good new wine could be drawn from those old bottles. So when the young, upstanding Richard Remington played the game according to all the proper rules – chose his party with some care, got adopted in a good constituency, acquired a highly satisfactory wife, won a thumping victory in the general Liberal triumph of 1906 – it was not so surprising when the great hopes of the time so quickly faded. 'We Liberals know as a matter of fact – nowadays everybody knows – that the monster that brought us into power has, among other deficiencies, no head – we've got to give it one – if possible with brains and a will.' That was from one of Remington's closest allies, and he drove home the charge: 'But of all the damned things that ever were damned, your damned, shirking, temperate, sham-efficient, self-satisfied, respectable, make-believe, Fabian-spirited Young Liberal is the utterly damnedest.'

Or they would suddenly find themselves confronted with the political leadership of the last century which HG himself had often defined: 'He was full of that old middle Victorian persuasion that whatever is inconvenient or disagreeable to the English mind could be annihilated by not thinking about it.' And he could apply these astringent views to the question of British rule where he supposed it to be the most effective:

> Our functions in India are absurd. We English do not own that country, do not even rule it. We make nothing happen; at the most we prevent things happening. We suppress our own literature there . . . The sum total of our policy is to arrest any discussion, any conferences that would enable the Indians to work out a tolerable scheme of the future for themselves. But that does not arrest the resentment of men held back from life. Consider what it must be for the educated Indian sitting at the feast of contemporary possibilities with his mouth gagged and his hands bound behind him. In some manner we shall have to come out of India. We have had our chance, and we have demonstrated nothing but the appalling dullness of our national imagination.

And that prophecy was written in the early years of the century in which India did achieve her independence. On HG's recommendation, it could have been done much earlier, much more honourably, and with much less shedding of blood or proscription of our literature. Several of the books which the young HG discovered at Up Park in his teens were forbidden reading throughout the Raj, at least for those who qualified to complete their education in the English universities of the time.

Some events nearer home also he believed could be transacted much better, if some of his Wellsian doctrines were studied more carefully. *The New Machiavelli* contained, like *Ann Veronica*, a description of how the suffragist and suffragette campaigns were rising to a fresh climax – most notably an account in both novels of the scenes in Parliament Square, when the challenge was made most directly. Ann Veronica, in almost every move she makes, seems to have the full-hearted feminist backing of her creator. Yet questions were asked, then and thereafter, about how much HG's heart was with the women's cause, no less than the individual women. If there were doubts in *Ann Veronica*, he removed many of them in *The New Machiavelli*. Remington himself encountered and described the whole scene on that critical night in 1909, 'the heroic tension which seemed to possess the whole company, the mood of a revolutionary outbreak. He knew then, as he had never comprehended before that the women's movement was being carried forward on an irresistible current.'

Another individual woman reader may be quoted to show how HG could strike feminine chords even when his characters were supposed to be dealing with different topics altogether. Winifred Horrabin was a young Socialist critical on occasions of HG's comments on Karl Marx and feminist questions. But she marked this passage in *The New Machiavelli*:

I prayed that night that my life might not be in vain, that in particular I might not live in vain. I prayed for strength and faith, that life might not overwhelm me, might not beat me back to futility and a meaningless acquiescence in existing things. I knew myself for the weakling I was, I knew that nevertheless it was set for me to make such order as I could out of these disorders, and my task cowed me, gave me at the thought of it, a sense of yielding feebleness . . . Break me, O God, I prayed at last, disgrace me, torment me, destroy me as you will, but save me from self-complacency and little interests and little successes and the life that passes like the shadow of a dream.

A close friend of Winifred's read him and reacted in the same spirit, another young woman scarcely twenty, a new arrival from another part of that rebellious England, Storm Jameson: 'When I was a young adolescent he [HG] had a prodigious influence on me and on all my friends. He formed a whole generation, throwing himself at us in a rage of energy, overwhelming us with his ideas, some absurd, all explosively liberating. Unlike

Bernard Shaw, who did no more than instruct and amuse us, he changed our lives.'*

His own individual affairs played their part, and why not? Richard Remington himself seemed to be shaken to the core of his political being by that 'amazingly effective' Parliament Square demonstration; he was a much better man thereafter. 'It wasn't a simple argument based on a simple assumption; it was the first crude expression of a great mass and mingling of convergent feelings, of a widespread confused persuasion among educated women that their relations with men were oppressive, ugly, dishonouring, and had to be altered.' Or maybe this last was a different Richard Remington and maybe that was the weakness of the book itself. The Remington who succumbed to the advances of Isabel Rivers was not so easily recognizable as the Remington who had prepared so immaculately every step forward in his political advancement.

At this stage in his literary career, it almost appeared that HG was more interested in the women than in the men. No small part of his offence was that, as he himself said years later, 'I would not drop the subject of the passionate daughter'. The most passionate daughter he had ever encountered was Amber Reeves; nothing else ever to equal her. He could still reproduce the intensity of their feelings when he wrote on the subject in his autobiography twenty-five years later, and the words still scorched so fiercely that they could not be published until thirty years later again. But he was also constantly finding how Ann Veronica had something of Amber's spirit or at the very least would never have been possible without her. Amanda Morris in *The Research Magnificent* made her appearance four years later; she was, according to HG himself, the nearest likeness. He was less eager to acknowledge the resemblance with Isabel Rivers in *The New Machiavelli*, and yet the actual incidents, the sequence of events match or develop so clearly that the comparison must still be made. What is indisputable is that the crisis in both the novels which faces the heroes and the heroines was precisely the

---

* Storm Jameson, *Journey from the North* (1969), vol. 2, p. 25.

1. Sarah Wells: the mother who helped to make him a Socialist. Mixed with the discipline went an overpowering love.

2. Up Park: where his mother served as housekeeper, and where HG was introduced to Jonathan Swift and Thomas Paine.

3. The three-year-old HG and his elder brother, Frank.

4. Bromley's Market Square, 1870. At the Town Hall, in the centre, and at the local museum and library, they still honour HG's cockney genius.

5. Joseph Wells, more famous for his cricket than his chess, was a bosom companion of his adoring son until his dying day. Here he is aged eighty.

6. How Joseph advertised his cricket in the *Bromley Record*, 1 June 1867.

7. His great Socialist pamphlet came later, but memories of his Bromley childhood helped to shape it.

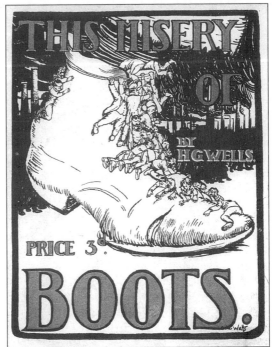

8. HG shows off as a freshman at the Normal School in South Kensington.

9. Isabel Mary Wells, the cousin whom HG married in June 1891, and then parted from two years later. She was still the heroine of *Love and Mr Lewisham*, seven years later again.

10. HG in 1895, the year which changed his fortune.

11. Jane: Amy Catherine Robbins in 1892, when HG fell for her.

12. How HG pursued her through '93 and beyond.

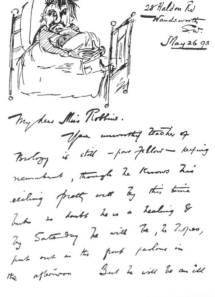

13. HG and Jane on a bicycle especially made for two in his design. He was the writer-laureate of the cyclists.

14. HG's own 'picshua' shows himself and Jane in their daily routine and full swing at work on one of his 1890 productions. For the next forty years or so, they kept up the habit.

15. He was surprised to be invited to give a lecture at the Royal Institution, Albemarle Street, on the Discovery of the Future, and happily portrayed how his audience was riveted. January 1902.

16. Three great editors of the period gave him a helping hand: W. T. Stead, of the *Pall Mall Gazette*.

17. W. E. Henley, of the *National Observer*.

18. Frank Harris, of the *Saturday Review*.

19. Building a house of his own at Sandgate, with Jane on one of the ladders.

20. HG with his mother, Sarah, just before her death in 1905. He was writing then about his younger mother, no less beloved, in *The Comet*.

21. Here, at Sandgate, with Jane presiding, their two sons were born, Gip in 1901 and Frank in 1903.

22. His *Sea Lady* was published in 1902, but he sent this particular copy, celebrating his own 'Respectability and Corpulence' to Jane in 1908.

23. Amber, later Amber Blanco White, and her daughter, Anna-Jane.

24. Max Beerbohm caricatures HG conjuring up the New Woman, 1907.

25. HG met Maxim Gorky on his first visit to America, a memorable and honorable meeting for both.

26. He met President Theodore Roosevelt (left) who showed himself an appreciative reader of *The Time Machine*.

27. 'Presently, the English Channel was bridged' – a scene from *The War in the Air*, published in 1908.

28. *The Sketch*, 29 May 1912: a Socialist but not afraid to criticize Socialism.

29. A study of six Socialists from a drawing by HG: Burns, Hardie, Shaw, Webb, Hyndman, Me.

30. Bernard Shaw and his wife Charlotte, who became a good friend of HG's despite all the quarrels.

31. Beatrice Webb. Beauty and brains together sometimes went to work to restrain the restless HG.

32. Sidney Webb, a little later but still at the same game of restraining the pace of Socialist advance.

33. E. Nesbit and her daughter Rosamund. HG was accused of having pursued them both.

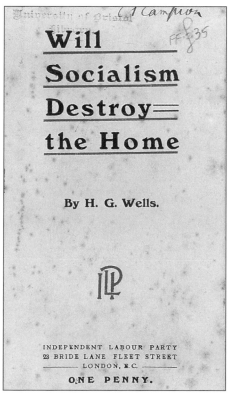

Will Socialism Destroy the Home

By H. G. Wells.

34. Most topically, HG and the Independent Labour Party produced this pamphlet, designed to set Keir Hardie's fears at rest.

35. Easton Glebe family group and guests, 1912: HG, Frank, Jane, Ella Hepworth Dixon, Cousin Ruth Neale and Gip, reclining.

36. Jane seemed in control wherever she went.

37. Little war games in the garden, Easton Glebe, 1913.

38. Rebecca West, 1912, of the *Clarion* and *The Freewoman* and herself already a match for the best Socialists of the age in an age of great Socialists.

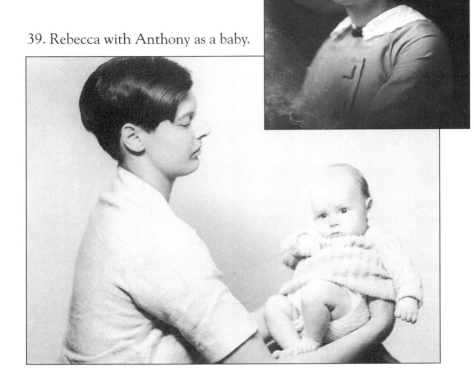

39. Rebecca with Anthony as a baby.

40. 'No letter from Panther': not for the first or last time HG laments an interruption in their correspondence, and invites a fresh, charming reconciliation.

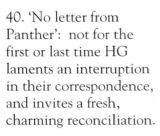

41. Bertrand Russell: friend and ally of HG's in earlier times. They were bitter yet worthy opponents in 1914, when Russell became one of the bravest and boldest opponents of the war.

42. Robert Blatchford: furiously criticized, like HG, for his pro-war stand, but he had some claim to be the best independent journalist of the age. He remained a strong ally of HG and Rebecca.

43. Charles Masterman: the most intelligent younger member of the Liberal Cabinet, a constant, welcome, appreciative visitor at Easton Glebe.

one that faced HG and Amber. Thanks to the prim relations which existed between men and women, thanks to the conduct of their enemies and friends, thanks to the pitch of scandal which the affair had reached, they must either break off the affair or suffer disgrace and destruction.

No dispute is possible about the courage with which they confronted this dilemma. Ann Veronica faced it, and won, and the acceptance of her victory was added to the charge-sheet against her lascivious creator. Isabel Rivers, with Remington at her side, made a different choice, and destroyed his political career in the process. Amber and HG after a long agony and excitement, submitted to the conventions, and years later HG was still lamenting their conformity or their cowardice. Of course, cowardice is a quite inapposite word: considering how long the passion lasted, considering how constantly HG returned to state their case by different means, it was much more the kind of courage which was needed to challenge and scatter the all-pervasive Victorian sexual oppression.

Just at the moment when he reached the climax in *The New Machiavelli* – it was published serially in the *English Review* from May to November 1910 – he received a letter from Shaw containing a Shavian–Blakean comment which showed at least that they had not come to blows; both were Blakean enthusiasts, whatever their other disputes:

'What is the price of Experiment?/Do men buy it for a song/Or wisdom for a dance in the street/No: it is bought with the price/of all that a man hath – his house, his wife, his children.' This would be a good motto for the New Machiavelli, which by the way is a frightfully unfinished masterpiece, for the truth appears to be that the parties will live happily ever after. GBS

But HG's climax, or the moral to be drawn from it, was not so clear or transparent. It might be truer to say that his hero at last had wrecked all his political prospects to sustain his love. At least William Blake, champion of free love, might have approved even while the Fabians, or most of them, were still

111

horrified. They seemed content to accept a society where the struggle for women's rights was relegated to a quite subordinate place.

Sometimes HG was accused of a weakness or a wavering in his allegiance to the feminist cause; and sometimes, alas, as we shall see, the accusation was true. But one good feature of *The New Machiavelli* was the way he used the word and the idea with a growing ease. Moreover, whatever the deficiencies or failures in appreciation – the caricature of Mrs Miniver in *Ann Veronica* was a case in point – all his real heroines were raging advocates of a liberation to match anything elsewhere on the political horizon. Ann Veronica was branded for her intolerable presumption and so was Isabel Rivers and so were all the rest.

If the conversion of H. G. Wells to a better understanding of the women's cause plays any part in our political and literary history, the credit must go to Amber Reeves. He loved her:

> Amanda in armour, the Amanda of my dreams. Sense, and particularly the sense of beauty, lies deeper than reason in us. There can be no mate for me now unless she comes with Amanda's voice and Amanda's face and Amanda's quick movements and her clever hands . . . There were things between us two as lovers . . . wordless things; and surprises, expectations, gratitudes, sudden moments of contemplation, the sight of a soft eyelid closed in sleep, shadowy tones in the sound of a voice heard unexpectedly; sweet, dear magical things I can find no words for . . .*

---

* *The Research Magnificent* (1915), p. 316. Others have sought to identify Amanda solely with Rebecca West, but this was before the publication of HG's own *H. G. Wells in Love* contained particular references to the likeness between Amber and Amanda. Amber and Rebecca joined forces in the *Research*.

FIVE

Rebecca

No other human being has ever had that effect
on me, so that I seem to feel the life and stir in
that other body more than I feel my own.

The Passionate Friends, p. 324

A pity, maybe, that his next book, *Marriage*, was not given a
more challenging title. It was mistaken in some quarters for that
rare phenomenon, a Wellsian obeisance before conventional
morals. He did, as we have seen, feel compelled at times to
embark on such wretched manoeuvres; but always, or almost
always, the moment of repentance for so deadly a sin would
come speedily and with overwhelming assurance. But *Marriage*
included no such clear-eyed recantation. His new heroine did
finish up conventionally married, but she had started out as one
of his passionate daughters who take the plot into their own
hands. Indeed, some observers or critics have portrayed Marjorie
Pope as the middle-aged Ann Veronica. Such a suggestion may
stir fierce protests among Ann Veronica's legion of admirers,
male and female. The hero and the heroine of *Marriage*, like
those in *Ann Veronica*, agreed that they must serve their
common cause with 'the keenest thought, the utmost patience,

inordinate veracity'. That was the old Wellsian message, and nothing could ever make him ashamed of it.

However, some books become famous through the responses they provoke rather than through their own merit. *Marriage* produced two sharply contrasted responses which powerfully influenced HG for the rest of his life. The first came within a few days of publication from his friend and critic, Henry James. Almost ever since they had first met, they had been real friends, and James had often expressed his genuine admiration for HG's talent as a writer. However, HG had increasingly offended against James's tastes and rules.

James concealed some of his criticism beneath his good manners; HG had no such accommodating disposition. Disputes could have come earlier. In James's estimate, HG had shown how wilfully he could stray from the true path of artistic achievement in *Tono-Bungay*. But it was *Marriage* which threw open the full argument between them. 'With tact and circum-locution James broke it to me', first in conversation and then in an elaborate critical letter which still gloried in the admission that HG's work was 'more convulsed with life and more brimming with blood than any it is given me nowadays to meet'. * Since Henry James was such an imposing figure in the Edwardian literary world, the comparatively young HG might have been expected to accept both the compliment and the rebuke. Not at all: in that same discussion about *Marriage*, HG insisted on his own conviction: 'I was feeling my way towards something outside any established formula for the novel altogether. † And then suddenly James's 'curious, intricate suavity of intimation' was interrupted by a clap of thunder.

HG was already a regular reader of the *Freewoman*. He was on excellent terms with the young, adventurous, good-looking editor of the paper, Nora Marsden, whose outstanding beauty matched her flaming temperament, as was often the case with the feminist leaders. His only complaint about her was that,

---

* *Experiment in Autobiography*, vol. 2, p. 492.
† *Experiment in Autobiography*, vol. 2, p. 497.

when they bumped into each other casually, she would demand an article from him and he would find it churlish to refuse. She had already printed a piece from him on the endowment of motherhood about which most of the *Freewoman* readers were hostile but which certainly did HG no real harm in those circles. They were hostile to the way he had presented the case, not to the case itself. Moreover, the *Freewoman*, alongside its serious, highbrow literary section, also developed fresh fields of discussion on lesbianism, auto-eroticism, or kindred topics which were not considered as proper subjects for such open inquiry. HG might not have objected on any of these counts. He prided himself on his special kinship with the young, male or female. Nora Marsden on the *Freewoman* had broken away from the general suffragist movement because she felt that the leadership of the Pankhursts was too authoritarian, and HG himself might have had some sympathy for that view. Nothing could have prepared him for the 2,000-word blast on 19 September 1912. It is the opening paragraph of the review which became so famous, and we shall shortly quote it, but it is the whole attack – and especially the sustained attack on HG's heroine in *Marriage* – which gave him the first warning that something new in his life had happened. After this, at least, he could create no new Marjorie Popes. But we must pause to consider also how HG himself read the sensational new outburst from the aptly named *Freewoman*. The whole must be quoted to show the power of the invective; it was not only a new woman in his life, but a new force in his world:

Mr. Wells's mannerisms are more infuriating than ever in *Marriage*. One knows at once that Marjorie is speaking in a crisis of wedded chastity when she says at regular intervals, 'Oh, my dear! . . . Oh, my dear!' or at moments of ecstasy, 'Oh, my *dear*! My *dear*!' For Mr. Wells's heroines who are living under legal difficulties say, 'My man!' or 'Master!' Of course, he is the old maid among novelists; even the sex obsession that lay clotted on *Ann Veronica* and *The New Machiavelli* like cold white sauce was merely old maids' mania, the reaction towards the flesh of a mind too long absorbed in airships and colloids. The Cranford-like charm of his slow, spinsterish gossip made *Kipps* the delightful book it was, but it palls when, page after page and chapter after chapter, one is told how to furnish a house . . .

Even the compliments were wrapped up in a new brand of insult, but he would have to get used to that.

And then there is Mr. Wells's habit of spluttering at his enemies. He splutters less in *Marriage* than in *The New Machiavelli*, but in the hospital atmosphere of the latter, where a soul-sick man drugged himself with the ether of sex, it seemed less offensive than in this purer, brighter air. Altiora Bailey reappears as Aunt Plessington and makes a speech that would be perfect but for its omission of the phrase, 'the morass of destitution'. There is a devilishly realistic picture of the English humorist whose parodies have drawn tears from the sentient part of the nation for the last twenty years. It is great fun, but at times it is ill-mannered. It offends one beyond measure in the last impressive pages of the book. Trafford has withdrawn from busy, sterile London, where he sold his scientific genius to buy pretty things for his wife, and now knows himself to be a commercial prostitute, and has sought the clean snows of Labrador. There, he thinks, he can clear his mind of the lies of civilisation and begin to seek God. Sickness strips him of all fear and deceit, so that he communes with God. Wonderingly he finds out what life is . . . Something trying to exist, which isn't substance, doesn't belong to space or time, something stifled and enclosed, struggling to get through. Just confused birth-cries, eyes that can hardly see, deaf ears, poor little thrusting hands. A thing altogether blind at first, a twitching and thrusting of proto-plasm under the waters, and then the plants creeping up the beaches, the insects and reptiles on the margins of the rivers, beasts with a flicker of light in their eyes answering the sun. And at last, out of the long interplay of desire and fear, an ape, an ape that stared and wondered, and scratched queer pictures on a bone . . .

In the midst of this ecstatic perception of life he stops to define Mr. Pethick Lawrence . . . A Gawdsaker? . . . Oh, haven't you heard that before? He's the person who gets excited by any deliberate discussion and gets up wringing his hands and screaming, 'For Gawd's sake, let's do something now!' I think they used it first for Pethick Lawrence, the man who did so much to run the old militant suffragettes and burke the proper discussion of woman's future.

It is good, but not worth while interrupting a triumphant meditation over the disordered earth. It is really a matter of good manners.

The *Freewoman* thus rallied to the defence of Pethick Lawrence with good reason and taste. He had served the women's cause with something much more substantial than the Gawdsaking laments attributed to him by HG. But back to the story itself and the legitimate, sustained protests of the *Freewoman* readers.

This Trafford had fallen a victim to a parasitic woman; he had laid his very soul on the altar of Our Lady of Loot. An aeroplane accident dropped him on to the lawn of a Kentish vicarage, in which was staying Marjorie Pope, a beautiful girl of twenty. At that age, when the fine body should have been protected by a vitality that bared its teeth at weakness and ugliness in fierce fastidiousness, she was seriously thinking of marrying Will Magnet, the humorist, 'a fairish man of forty, pale, with a large protuberant, observant grey eye – I speak particularly of the left – and a face of quiet animation warily alert for the wit's opportunity'. But she was willing to do it, her life being governed by gluttony and laziness . . .

After Oxbridge, unless she was prepared to face a very serious row indeed and go to teach in a school – and she didn't feel any call whatever to teach in a school; she had an invincible objection to work of any kind – she would probably have to return to Hartstone Square and share Daffy's room again and assist in the old, wearisome task of propitiating her father . . . Marriage was escape from all that; it meant not only respectful parents, but a house of her very own, furniture of her choice – that was the real attraction of Marjorie – great freedom of movement, an authority, an importance.

For the sake of sideboards and prestige she was willing to give herself to a fool and transmit folly to her children . . . And the really fine and encouraging thing about the book is that Mr. Wells sees that Marjorie is a thorough scoundrel. The horror of it is that, confused by her clear eyes and copper hair, he accepts her scoundrelism as the normal condition of women.

Indeed, was the scoundrelism of women his selected theme? It was nothing of the sort. All astonished readers, with HG himself, must have felt that they were being chastised with a new kind of satirical whip.

Something, probably Trafford's clean physical vigour, overcame her natural carelessness of destiny, that cold sensuality that made her think of her body as a thing to barter for sideboards. So she eloped with him, and henceforth mastered his life and beggared it. She wanted 'things' – old Dutch clocks and wonderful dinner-dresses and Chippendale chairs. And she claimed them from him because she was his wife and the mother of his child.

There is something sinister about a figure such as the great Christ who hangs on the cross athwart the Catholic cathedral at Westminster. The blood about his brow, the distortion of his mouth, the tension of his body, the changeless attitude of pain, convey at last the sense of an eternal hunger. The lights of a thousand candles, all the incense of the pious, the daily worship of millions, have whetted him to the remorseless acceptance of the lives of men and the reason of nations. Not till the roof of the world falls in will that hunger cease from feeding on the hearts of men; and then, amid the dust of the universe, one can imagine a God impatiently making a new world of worshippers. Perhaps it is because of this harsh lien on the world's love and sympathy that blasphemy is the one crime that all men commit before they die.

And women have taken for themselves the right to claim worship, by virtue of the suffering through which they pass to bring men into the world – although a casual glance at the worshippers might show them that they had done it carelessly and without exclusiveness – and of the beauty of their lives. There is no end of their hunger. They send men they do not know into the snowy wastes to trap silver foxes, and set the men they do know working at barren, profitable commercial muddles to buy the pelts. For in particular they demand material, inessential things. And they get them; but also they get hatred and curses that are the inevitable offerings to divinity.

Trafford had a genius for scientific reasearch. 'I want research,' he moaned when delirium overtook him in Labrador, 'and that still silent room of mine again, that room, as quiet as a cell, and the toil that led to light. Oh! the coming of that light, the uprush of discovery, the solemn joy as a generalisation rises like a sun upon the facts – floods them with a common meaning. That is what I want. That is what I have always wanted . . .' Marjorie began her attack on his soul by disliking his work and putting a background of domestic dispeace to the splendid foreground of his laboratory.

He went home about half-past five and found a white-faced, red-eyed Marjorie, still dressed, wrapped in a travelling-rug, and crumpled and asleep in his study armchair beside the grey ashes of an extinct fire . . . 'Oh, where have you been?' she asked almost querulously. 'Where have you been?' 'But my dear!' he said, as one might speak to a child, 'why aren't you in bed? It's just dawn.' 'Oh,' she said, 'I waited and waited. It seemed you must come. I read a book. And then I fell asleep.' And then, with a sob of feeble self-pity, 'And here I am!' She rubbed the back of her hand into one eye and shivered. 'I'm cold,' she said, 'and I want some tea.'

The repulsive desire for tea is a masterly touch. It reminds one of the disgust one felt as a healthy schoolgirl when one saw the school-mistresses drinking tea at lunch at half-past eleven. It brings home to one poignantly how disgusting the artificial physical weakness of women, born of loafing about the house with only a flabby mind for company, must be to an ordinary, vigorous man.

A little later he discovered that to furnish her house daintily with Bokhara hangings and brass-footed workboxes she has spent every penny of his income of six hundred and frittered away a thousand of his capital. She avoids discussion by having a baby in a sentimental and rather pretentious way. Although she knows that his work is being cut out of his life as one might cut a living man's heart out of his breast, and that its place is being taken by popular lectures to the scientifically-minded of Pinner and such parts, she continues to ruin him by buying post-impressionist pictures and hoarding up bills. Finally, she breaks his spirits by having another baby.

So he drops research and takes up the manufacture of synthetic rubber. For nine years he runs this business and plays tedious games with rubber shares, while Marjorie lets herself go with the price of his perdition in a great, beautiful house filled with the creations of genius and silly, chattering people. 'Look at this room,' cries Trafford in despair, 'this litter of little satisfaction! Look at your pretty books there, a hundred minds you have pecked at, bright things of the spirit that attracted you as jewels attract a jackdaw. Look at the glass and silver, and that silk from China!' He suddenly rebels. He takes Marjorie away to the heights of Labrador where, between combats with lynxes and wolverines, sickness and famine, they brood on Life. Marjorie, somewhat impertinently, uses her own worthlessness as the basis of a generalisation as to the worthlessness of all woman.

The impertinence, by now, was all HG's own. The *Freewoman* was now speaking for all women, all would-be free ones, and HG was taught his lesson in a new language.

What are we women – half savages, half pets, unemployed things of greed and desire – and suddenly we want all the rights and respects of souls! . . . I've begun to see what it is to be a woman . . . We're the responsible sex. And we've forgotten. We think we've done a wonder if we've borne men into the world and smiled a little, but indeed we've got to bear them all our lives. A woman has to be steadier than a man and more self-sacrificing than a man, because when she plunges she does more harm than a man . . . And what does she achieve if she does plunge? Nothing – nothing worth counting. Dresses and carpets and hangings and pretty arrangements, excitement and satisfaction and competitions and more excitements. We can't do things. We don't bring things off! And you, you Monster! You dream you want to stick your hand out of all that is and make something that isn't begin to be! That's the man!

Trafford confirms her suspicions. You're a finer individual than me. You're more beautiful by far than I, a woman for my man. You've a keener appetite for things, a firmer grip on the substance of life. I love to see you do things, love to see you move, love to watch your hands; you've cleverer hands than mine by far . . . and yet–I'm a deeper and bigger thing than you. I reach up to something you don't reach up to . . . You're in life – and I'm a little out of it. I'm like one of those fish that begin to be amphibian. I go out into something where you don't follow – where you hardly begin to follow . . . And they go home in a very good temper.

And Mr. Wells agrees with them. That is the terrible thing, for there is no author who has a more religious faith, nor one who speaks his gospel with such a tongue of flame.

His first sin lies in pretending that Marjorie, that fair, fleshy being who at forty would look rather like a cow – and the resemblance would have a spiritual significance – is the normal woman; and the second lies in his remedy, which Marjorie discovers in a period of spiritual turmoil brought on by debt. 'A woman gives herself to a man out of love, and remains clinging parasitically to him out of necessity. Was there no way of evading that necessity?' she meditates sentimentally. 'Suppose the community kept all its women, suppose all property in homes and furnishings and children vested in them . . . Then every woman would be a princess to the man she loved.' The cheek of it!

The mind reels at the thought of the community being taxed to allow Marjorie, who could steal her lover's money and barter the brightness of his soul for brass-footed workboxes, to perpetuate her cow-like kind. I can see myself as the one rebel in this humourless State going forth night after night to break the windows of the barracks of Yushiwara where Marjorie was kept in fast ease, and going to prison month after month until . . .

But 'all women!' 'Suppose the community kept all its women . . .' Heavens, I shall be inside too! I object to living under the same roof as Marjorie.

I wonder about the women who never come across any man who is worth loving (and next time Mr. Wells travels in the tube he might look round and consider how hopelessly unlovable most of his male fellow passengers are), who are not responsive to the lure of Dutch clocks and forget, as most people do, the colour of the dining room wall-paper, who, being intelligent, can design a becoming dress in five minutes and need think no more about it. I wonder how they will spend their time. Bridge-parties, I suppose, and possible State-facilitated euthanasia . . .

Let Mr. Wells and any other man who loathes the daughter of the horse-leech reflect a minute: 'What would happen to Marjorie if she had to fend for herself?' That is a very important reason why women should be made to work. Under present conditions Marjorie is a handsomely subsidised young woman. For she is to many the typical wife and mother, since she has not her more sensitive sister's objection to the monotony and squalor of domestic drudgery that men have thrust on the wife and mother. But supposing she had to work. How long could she stand it? The weaker sort of Marjorie would be sucked down to prostitution and death, the stronger sort of Marjorie would develop qualities of decency and courage and ferocity. It is worth trying. Not only because men ought to be protected from the monstrous demands of Our Lady of Loot, but because women ought to have a chance of being sifted clean through the sieve of work. *

The article was signed Rebecca West. Her real name was Cicely Isabel Fairfield. She had adopted the pseudonym which she was to make famous partly because she was inspired by the character of that name which she saw in the Ibsen play *Rosmersholm*, but partly also to conceal from her own family that she was writing for the outrageous *New Freewoman*. Her mother and her sister were supporters of the women's cause in most of its guises, but they, too, would have been horrified to see her writing for that journal. HG's household and, more especially, HG himself were less reticent. Within a few days she received an invitation to Easton Glebe, and a new world opened for them all.

---

* *The Freewoman*, 19 September 1912, reprinted in *The Young Rebecca*, ed. Jane Marcus, (1982), p. 64.

Anyhow, no more Marjorie Popes! With a single stroke, Rebecca had achieved that work of demolition. Neither the proud author nor the juvenile critic might have summarized the matter thus, but it was so, as we shall see. A friendly contemporary critic writing about *Marriage*, as it happens, said that 'he was always a little impatient with his heroines. He regarded his heroes with greater indulgence'. *

Almost imperceptibly at first, but none the less significantly, HG started to transform the character of his heroines. They could acquire at least a new political sophistication; they knew they must face Rebecca's scrutiny, and what fate would await them if they failed to pass the test. Not only on so-named feminist questions, but across the whole range of Edwardian politics and literature, she was the most scorching, iconoclastic surveyor of the scene. No-one could believe that this phenomenon which challenged their universe was a young woman not yet twenty. She, too, had learned the trade from the best classical tutors: Swift had helped to teach her how propaganda and art could serve the same master or mistress. But her feelings cannot be constrained or curbed by any recital of precedents. She was a feminist, a suffragette and a Socialist, dedicated with equal fervour to the service of both causes. Like so many of the young people of her time, she believed that the women's cause and the workers' cause would make together spectacular advances in the immediate years ahead. Fainthearts who would split them asunder must be pushed aside. And that was HG's temperament and understanding, too. He had shared the spirit of the younger generation right from the beginning of the century. And he would not be left behind now, with the Marjorie Popes holding him back. Not likely; not after the release brought in her own original language by Rebecca. Despite the divergence in their ages, it soon became a marriage of true minds. It was not exactly love at first sight – at least, not on his part – but true love soon mingled with all the other excitements. If she or he had turned their backs on the new

* Somerset Maugham, *The Vagrant Mood* (1952), p. 216.

world which opened before them, neither would have developed to the full their individual genius, and our century would have been so much the poorer.

The world and the women: he seemed always to be torn between the two or, rather, to glory in the predicament. He would turn back and forth, from the worldwide scene to the affairs of his own heart, and he wanted a philosophy which would accommodate both. After *Marriage*, which with all its defects did seek such a larger synthesis, he wrote over the next three years four more novels, designed on the most ambitious scale, which tackled afresh these combined themes and showed no weakening in his taste for adventure. None of the four – *The Passionate Friends* (1912), or *The World Set Free* (1914), or *The Wife of Sir Isaac Harriman* (1914), or *The Research Magnificent* (1915) – has been accepted by the critics, even friendly ones, as a real success. As the dates indicate, they cover some of the most momentous years of the century; and he was striving, as he had discussed in the famous essay 'The Contemporary Novel', to use the forum without any restraints or inhibitions. Again, as with *Tono-Bungay*, he must have been deeply disappointed by the reception. But he was always willing to follow his own star, especially when he had made new companions among fellow astronomers. He had many natural allies among the new women readers of Nora Marsden's *Freewoman* or Robert Blatchford's *Clarion*. They would follow him on his bicycle trips or on the excursions across the planet which figured in these volumes, too. Sometimes these odysseys were imaginary; sometimes they were the real thing. He felt the tug to see for himself, not merely in the old Europe, but in the new America, the new Russia, the new India, the new Africa, the whole wide world. And Rebecca could share these enticements and enthusiasms, although for her the London which she had invaded with her own individual daring was the centre of the universe.

First of all, Rebecca's closest political association was with Robert Blatchford of *The Clarion*. He was that rare bird, a born editor, one of the best ever, who could not only write divinely or

earthily himself but who inspired the best writing in others. His
Clarion had always been a faithful friend of the women. When
Liberal leaders seemed likely to betray the cause or, even worse,
when Labour leaders seemed tempted to follow their cowardly
example, he had no reason in his *Clarion* to pull his punches and
soften his invectives. Rebecca was a woman after his own style.
On 28 February 1913, Blatchford produced a modern sequel to
Swift's *Modest Proposal*, called 'A Short Way with the
Suffragettes':

> Cut off the women's heads my countrymen; cut off their heads while
> there is yet time. Don't flog them nor brand them or they will be
> wanting to do the same to us. Cut off their heads, and get rid of their
> rebellious brains and silence their exasperatingly logical tongues.
> Cut off all their haughty heads; it will buck up the Dean of St. Paul's
> no end.

Never before in HG's now not inconsiderable experience had
there been such an old head on such young shoulders with both
parts of the anatomy expressing an equal beauty with the same
toss of the hair and flashing eyes. Considering how scandalously
recent had been the developments in the liberation of women,
never before in history perhaps had there been such a phenomenon; such sustained, epigrammatic force in her style, such
confident critical judgement, such burning invective, such floods
of wit, the rarest of all gifts. It is true these various
qualities had made their appearance in the journalism of the day:
it was a golden age adorned by such masters as Robert
Blatchford, H. W. Nevinson, H. N. Brailsford, and Shaw and
Wells themselves. But Rebecca was the first to unsheathe such a
sword for the feminist cause. And HG himself was the first, apart
from her percipient editor, to recognize the quality of her early
writings. He suggested to her (in a letter, October 1913) that she
should collect all her early journalism together in a book, a
piece of advice which, alas, was not followed until seventy years
later. * What this compilation would have involved from HG's

* *The Young Rebecca.* See above, Preface.

own particular standpoint at the time was the reprinting of the formidable indictment of himself and, more especially, the exposure of his own understanding on which he prided himself, his relations with the new woman. Sometimes it was said that criticism exposed him as being touchy and thin-skinned, but his relationship with Rebecca reveals a quite different side to his nature. He would take from Rebecca what he would never tolerate from, say, Edith Nesbit or Beatrice Webb, and how justified was the discrimination.

Rebecca did represent the new woman in the new world, a development startlingly different even from the character he and others thought they had discerned in the 1890s. Certainly he had misread lessons which he should have learned from the great suffrage campaign. But, with Rebecca's aid and provocation, he showed how women could and would play an ever larger part in the world's affairs. He believed that men and women must be equal partners in the great crusade. Whenever Rebecca or some part of her appears on the scene in his novels, the reader senses the excitement. She made that first sensational appearance, as we shall see soon, in *The Passionate Friends*. She was there next, one part of Amanda, in *The Research Magnificent*. But between the two creations much else intervenes. *

---

* Most of us, the outside world, had our introduction to the Rebecca–HG idyll, the Panther–Jaguar affair, through Gordon N. Ray's *H. G. Wells and Rebecca West* (1974). It remains a delightful and indispensable book, since some of the essential letters were printed here for the first time, and since Ray had the advantage of a full-scale discussion with Rebecca on the subject. Apart from anything else, it proves, if proof was still necessary, how much she loved and respected and honoured HG right till the end, and this by itself should have been enough to forbid the flood of libels about his sex-life and much else which we have had to endure since.

My own chief debt in this period is to John Hammond's *H. G. Wells and Rebecca West* (1991), a masterpiece of a book which has not received its deserts in recognition. Hammond explores and excavates Wells's own writings, especially the novels, in a way no-one else has done. Mainly, I follow in his footsteps, although I think I may have made a few original minor diversions. Anyhow, Hammond's view of Wells's place in modern literature – thanks partly to Rebecca's intervention – stands unchallenged. And everyone should read his

The years 1913 and 1914 were crowded and tumultuous, even by the exacting standards which HG had developed for himself. Rebecca pursued him and he pursued her, or maybe the momentum from each side was just about equal. Since he was more than double her age, the responsibility was plainly and overwhelmingly his, especially after the Amber Reeves denouement. Thereafter he had formed a lively, informal liaison with Elizabeth von Arnim, * but that could be ended without too much commotion or too many tears on either side. What Jane thought of Rebecca in those first years is not clear; she seemed to be

book to see how unchallengeable is this verdict. I have also here followed – closely, I hope – those who have written about Rebecca West: her own writings, those especially covering this period in *The Young Rebecca*, Victoria Glendinning's excellent *Rebecca West: A Life* (1987), and then the forthcoming full-scale biography of Rebecca by Carl Rollyson, who has kindly allowed me to read his typescript and proofs, and offered much further assistance. I am sure his biography will be worthy of the subject, a great subject indeed.

A cautionary word may be added here from V. S. Pritchett's review in the *New Statesman*, 22 November 1974, of Gordon N. Ray's book when it first appeared. 'Letters', he emphasized, 'are far from being reliable evidence for the biographer; they flash out imaginary selves, imaginary rights and wrongs. Under stress they are often no more than the day-dream mutterings one practises as one walks alone down the street.' And in this case the unreliability of letters by themselves was underlined by the fact that all of Wells's were available while he had destroyed hers. When Rebecca herself read the Ray book in its first form, she protested that it presented the two of them as 'a couple of irreparably quarrelsome people who brawled their sexual relationship'. The later volume was better than that, but all the awkwardness this indicated had not been removed. Some of their relationship was more truly represented in several of his later novels, as John Hammond claims in his 'labour of love', as he calls his book on the subject – and as I claim, too.

* If anyone doubts the claims about HG's comic genius, he or, more especially, she may be advised to remedy the matter by reading HG's account of his affair with Elizabeth which appears under the title of 'The Episode of Little E' in *H. G. Wells in Love*. Of course, nothing like this could have been contemplated for publication at the time. He might have presented the whole affair as a comic short story or, better still, sought to translate the tale into an *opéra bouffe*, Rossini at his most irreverent. Elizabeth remained a firm friend of his ever afterwards. A little later she made her appearance in a less amenable mood as Mrs Harrowbean in *Mr Britling Sees It Through*. There her manner seemed to be more winsome than appealing; but, even so, she herself raised no objection. If she had ever had the chance of hearing the Rossini arias in *H. G. Wells in Love*, she would have been captivated afresh.

reconciled but she could hardly have known what was happening. For the two of them, for HG and Rebecca, all these were minor questions compared with the thrilling ramifications of the great affair. And sometimes, in those early days, the thrills almost turned to tragedy. When HG appeared to start the affair with her and then to break it off, Rebecca thought the burden too heavy to bear and she threatened suicide. The threat looked real. HG had the excuse, although he never seemed to invoke it, that at one decisive moment she was the one who had set the pace. What they had started together needed no excuse or subsequent palliation: by her creed no less than his, what they had done was right, and the rest of the world would have to learn.

Marriage had seen HG's hero and heroine transported to Labrador, the most artificial of his escape-routes. Then Marjorie had performed feats of rejuvenation which intensified Rebecca's resentment. All the more discerning was her reception of *The Passionate Friends* in *The New Freewoman* of 1 October 1913; she could pick and choose her own way through his prose style with an eye, a political judgement, which seldom failed. Sometimes he would allow his eloquence to blur his vision, and she saw it:

> This film of pretences that falls so surprisingly on the quality of Mr. Wells's prose, like gilding on bright steel, which was not at all in *Tono-Bungay* or *The New Machiavelli*, is a deliberate vice. It is the pusillanimous effort of a fierce brain to seek conformity with the common tameness, the lapse of a disorderly prophet who does not see that to be orderly is to betray his peculiar gospel.

If the charge were true, a vice indeed, and one which Wells would find deeply wounding. And then she adds an even sharper accusation when the book's hero 'marries a phantom doormat called Rachel who lives to Mr. Wells's eternal shame in one sentence; "It sounds impudent, I know, for a girl to say so but we've so many interests in common" '.

How could any volume survive such critical surveillance! And yet in the same few thousand words she underlined unforgettable felicities. She thought that a description of his father – it must have been HG's as well as the fictional hero's – is 'among the very greatest artistic representations of parenthood. It is certainly the only literary expression of the pride of fatherhood which is wholly free from the suspicion of being mere male clucking over a female achievement.' To see how HG always saw his own father was an inspired insight; it was, as we have seen, an inseparable part of him. But, then, she also saw that the whole new book was 'infinitely nobler' than his previous one.

His Lady Mary Justin, his new heroine, was a distinctive creation. Without Rebecca, and her iconoclastic fling of the hair, she could never have happened. It is surely no coincidence that at the moment when she makes the chief impact she was exactly Rebecca's age. If anyone thought that his Mary was too sharp, too intellectually confident, too assured to perform such a role, there was the Rebecca of *The Freewoman* or *The Clarion* to clinch the case. HG made several further efforts, as we shall see, to portray Rebecca in his novels, and some of these might be thought to be more apposite and brilliant. But Lady Mary should not be displaced from her rightful position in the gallery. Rebecca herself in her *Freewoman* review wrote that 'the letters from Mary on the position of women are a rather florid elaboration of a point that Mr. Wells has raised more than once before'. True perhaps: he had said such things before; he wrote with such rapidity and ease that he was bound to do so. But never before had he put the case for the world to be turned upside down, the English case for Socialism, the spirit of the new world, in the mouth of a woman who would not be denied. The chapter 'Mary Writes' could be read then, and can still be read today, as a Molly Bloomish takeover of the whole case, a transformation of the supposedly sedate *The Passionate Friends* into a revolutionary document.

One spectacle which could always stir him was the English rulers so devoutly dedicated to their task:

How amazing, it seemed, that those people didn't understand and wouldn't understand any class but their own, any race but their own, any usage than their use . . . Somehow that picture of a narrow canvas tent in the midst of immensities has become my symbol for the whole life of the governing English, the English of India and Switzerland and the Riviera and the West End and the public service . . .

And he would contrast these ancient, accepted absurdities with what was happening in the new world, and why the new country there, the United States, had become 'the living hope of mankind'. And yet the real England might still appear:

> the English reality which is a thing at once bright, and illuminating and fitful, a thing humourous and wise and adventurous – Shakespeare, Dickens, Newton, Darwin, Nelson, Bacon, Shelley – English names every one – like the piercing light of lanterns swinging and swaying among the branches of dark trees at night. *

It was in *The Passionate Friends*, we may note, that he first used the phrase 'the open conspiracy' which was to become for him a potent thought, a perpetual incitement against suffocating orthodoxies.

HG's storyteller, reporting Mary's letter in *The Passionate Friends*, insists that there are some parts of what she wrote which he cannot repeat to his son – presumably the most intimate sexual parts. Thirty years later this inhibition would have been lifted by the revolutionary changes in the discussion of sexual questions which HG did as much as anyone to introduce. His Molly Bloom spoke, if not with the riveting, original candour of Joyce's lover, at least in terms rare in Edwardian fiction. Even as the reader may read Mary's letter today, he or she may see HG striving, as he had never done before, to make the feminist declaration the dominant part of the book, as Mary herself was, incomparably, the most striking figure.

The reader should sit back for a few moments to listen, without too many interruptions, to the new voice. This was HG

---

* *The Passionate Friends* (1913), p. 235.

taking his instruction from Rebecca, and learning much more about the temper of the true woman's cause than he had ever heard before. It is a woman still in her prime explaining how she had been hurt by the elementary denial of women's rights. Mary was reminding and rebuking her Stephen; they could have gone off together in their youth, if the conventional morals of the age had not dictated wretched, ignoble lives for both of them.

Too much of my life and being, Stephen, has been buried, and I am in rebellion. This is a breach of the tomb if you like, an irregular private premature resurrection from an interment in error. Out of my alleged grave I poke my head and say 'Hello' to you. Stephen old friend! dear friend! how are you getting on! I rise, you see, blowing my own Trump. Let the other graves do as they please . . .

Stephen, I've been wanting to do this for – for all the time. If there was thought-reading you would have had a thousand letters. But formerly I was content to submit, and latterly I've changed more. I think that as what they call passion has faded, the immense friendliness has become more evident, and made the bar less and less justifiable. You and I have had so much between us beyond what somebody the other day – it was in a report in *The Times*, I think – was calling Materia Matrimoniala. And of course I hear about you from all sorts of people, and in all sorts of ways – whatever you have done about me I've had a woman's sense of honour about you.

Oh, my dear! I am writing chatter. You perceive I've reached the chattering stage. It is the fated end of the clever woman in a good social position nowadays, her mind beats against her conditions for the last time and breaks up into this carping talk, this spume of observation and comment, this anecdotal natural history of the restraining husband, as waves burst out their hearts in a foam upon a reef. But it isn't chatter I want to write to you.

Stephen, I'm intolerably wretched. No creature has ever been gladder to have been born than I was for the first five and twenty years of my life. I was full of hope and I was full, I suppose, of vanity and rash confidence. I thought I was walking on solid earth with my head reaching up to the clouds, and that sea and sky and all mankind were mine for the smiling. And I am nothing and worse than nothing; I am the ineffectual mother of two children, a daughter whom I adore – but of her I may not tell you – and a son, – a son who is too like his father for any fury of worship, a stolid little creature . . . That is all I have done in the world, a mere blink of maternity, and my blue Persian who is scarcely two years old, has already had nine kittens. My husband and I have never forgiven each other the indefinable wrong of not pleasing each other.

Stephen, my dear, my brother, I am intolerably unhappy. I do not know what do so with myself, or what there is to hope for in life. I am like a prisoner in a magic cage and I do not know the word that will release me. How is it with you? Are you unhappy beyond measure or are you not; and if you are not, what are you doing with life? Have you found any secret that makes living tolerable and understandable?

Do please remember how long ago you and I sat in the old Park at Burnmore and how I kept pestering you and asking you what is all this for? And you looked at the question as an obstinate mule looks at a narrow bridge he could cross but doesn't want to. Well, Stephen, you've had nearly – how many years is it now? – to get an answer ready. What is it all for? What do you make of it? Never mind my particular case, or the case of Women with a capital W; tell me your solution. You are active, you keep doing things, you find life worth living. Is publishing a way of peace for your heart? I am prepared to believe even that. But justify yourself. Tell me what you have got there to keep your soul alive.

I won't praise your letter or your beliefs. They are fine and large – and generous – like you. Just a little artificial (but you will admit that), as though you had felt them give here and there and had made up your mind they shouldn't. At times it's oddly like looking at the Alps, the real Alps, and finding that every now and then the mountains have been eked out with a plant and canvas Earl's Court background . . . Yes, I like what you say about Faith. I believe you are right. I wish I could – perhaps some day I shall – light up and *feel* you are right. But – but that large, *respectable* project, the increase of wisdom and freedom and self-knowledge in the world, and calming of wars, the ending of economic injustice, and so on and so on . . .

When I read it first it was like looking at a man in profile and finding him solid and satisfactory, and then afterwards when I thought it all over and looked for the particular things that really matter to me and tried to translate it into myself – nothing is of the slightest importance in the world that one cannot translate into oneself – then I began to realise just how amazingly deficient you are. It was like walking round that person in profile and finding his left side wasn't there – with everything perfect on the right, down to the buttons. A kind of intellectual Lorelei – sideways. You've planned out your understandings and tolerance and enquiries and clearings-up as if the world were all just men – or citizens – and nothing doing but racial and national and class prejudices and the exacting and shirking of labour, and you seem to ignore altogether that man is a sexual animal first – first, Stephen, first – that he has that in common with all the animals, that it made him indeed because he has it more than they have – and after that, a long way after that, he is the labour-economizing, war- and feud-making creature you make him out to be. A long way after that . . .

Man is the most sexual of all the beasts, Stephen. Half of him, womankind, rather more than half, isn't simply human at all, it's specialised, specialised for the young not only naturally and physically as animals are, but mentally and artificially. Womankind isn't human, it's reduced human. It's 'the sex' as the Victorians used to say, and from the point of view of the Lex Julia and the point of view of Mr. Malthus, and the point of view of biologists and saints and artists and everyone who deals in feeling and emotion – and from the point of view of all us poor specialists, smothered up in our clothes and restrictions – the future of the sex is the centre of the whole problem of the human future, about which you are concerned. All this great world-state of your man's imagination is going to be wrecked by us if you ignore us, we women are going to be the Goths and Huns of another Decline and Fall. We are going to sit in the conspicuous places of the world and loot all your patient accumulations. We are going to abolish your off-spring and turn princes among you into undignified slaves. Because, you see, specialized as we are, we are not quite specialized, we are specialized under duress, and at the first glimpse of a chance we abandon our cradles and drop our pots and pans and go for the vast and elegant side possibilities – of our specialization. Out we come, looking for the fun the men are having. Dress us, feed us, play with us! We'll pay you in excitement – tremendous excitement. The State indeed! All your little triumphs of science and economy, all your little accumulations of wealth that you think will presently make the struggle for life an old story and the millennium possible – we spend. And all your dreams of brotherhood! we will set you by the ears. We hold ourselves up as my little Christian nephews – Phillip's boys – do some coveted object, and say Quis? And the whole brotherhood shouts, 'Ego!' to the challenge . . . Back you go into Individualism at the word and all your Brotherhood crumbles to dust again.

How are you going to remedy it, how are you going to protect that Great State of your dreams from this anti-citizenship of sex? You give no hint.

You are planning nothing, Stephen, nothing to meet this. You are fighting with an army all looting and undisciplined, frantic with the private jealousies that centre about us, feuds, cuts, expulsions, revenges, and you are giving out orders for an army of saints. You treat us as a negligible quantity, and we are about as negligible as a fire in the woodwork of a house that is being built . . .

I read what I have written, Stephen, and I perceive I have the makings of a fine scold in me. Perhaps under happier conditions . . . I should certainly have scolded you, constantly, continually . . . Never did a man so need scolding . . . And like any self-respecting woman I see that I use half my words in the wrong meanings in order to emphasize my point. Of course when I write woman in all that has gone before I don't mean woman. It is a woman's privilege to talk or write incomprehensibly and insist upon being understood. So that I expect you already to understand that what I mean isn't that men are creative and unselfish and brotherly and so forth and that women are spoiling and going to spoil the game – although and notwithstanding that is exactly what I have written – but that humans are creative and unselfish et cetera and so forth, and that it is their sexual, egotistical, passionate side (which is ever so much bigger relatively in a woman than in a man, and that is why I wrote as I did) which is going to upset your noble and beautiful apple-cart. But it is not only that by nature we are more largely and gravely and importantly sexual than men, but that men have shifted the responsibility for attraction and passion upon us and made us pay in servitude and restriction and blame for the common defect of the species. So that you see really I was right all along in writing of this as though it was women when it wasn't, and I hope now it is unnecessary for me to make my meaning clearer than it is now and always has been in this matter. And so, resuming our discourse, Stephen, which only my sense of your invincible literalness would ever have interrupted, what are you going to do with us?

I gather from a hint rather than accept as a statement that you propose to give us votes. Stephen! do you really think that we are going to bring anything to bear upon public affairs worth having? I know something of the contemporary feminine intelligence. Justin makes no serious objection to a large and various circle of women friends, and over my little sitting-room fire in the winter and in my corners of our various gardens in the summer and in the walks over the heather at Martens and in Scotland there are great talks and confessions of love, of mental freedom, of ambitions and belief and unbelief – more particularly of unbelief, a great list of the things that a number of sweet, submissive, value-above-rubies wives have told me they did not believe in. It would amaze their husbands beyond measure.

It's no good telling us to go back to the Ancient Virtues. The Ancient Virtues haven't *kept*. The Ancient Virtues in an advanced state of decay is what was the matter with Rome and what is the matter with us. You can't tell a woman to go back to the spinning wheel and the kitchen and the cradle, when you have power-looms, French cooks, hotels, restaurants and modern nurseries. We've overflowed. We've got to go on to a lot of New Virtues. And in all the prospects before me – I can't descry one clear simple thing to do . . .

But I'm running on. I want to know, Stephen, why you've got nothing to say about all this. It must have been staring you in the face ever since I spent my very considerable superfluous energies in wrecking your career.

It was like a gust of madness – and I care, I found, no more for your career than I cared for any other little thing, for honour, for Rachel, for Justin, that stood between us . . .

My dear, wasn't all that time, all that heat and hunger of desire, all that secret futility of passion, the very essence of the situation between men and women now? We are all trying most desperately to be human beings, to walk erect, to work together – what was your phrase? – 'in a multitudinous unity', to share what you call a common collective thought that shall rule mankind, and this tremendous force which seizes us and says to us: 'Make that other being yours, bodily yours, mentally yours, wholly yours – at any price, no matter the price', bars all our unifications. It splits the whole world into couples watching each other, until all our laws, all our customs seem the servants of that. It is the passion of the body swamping the brain; it's an ape that has seized a gun, a beautiful modern gun. Here I am, Justin's captive, and he mine, he mine because at the first escapade of his I get my liberty. Here we are two, I and you, barred for ever from the sight of one another, and I am writing – I at any rate in spite of the ill-concealed resentment of my partner. We're just two peeping through our bars, of a universal multitude. Everywhere this prison of sex. Have you ever thought just all that it means when every woman in the world goes dressed in a costume to indicate her sex, her cardinal fact, so that she dare not even mount a bicycle in knickerbockers, she has her hair grown long to its longest because yours is short, and everything conceivable is done to emphasize and remind us (and you) of the fundamental trouble between us? As if there was need of reminding! Stephen, is there no way out of this? Is there no way at all? Because if there is not, then I would rather go back to the hareem than live as I do now imprisoned in glass – with all of life in sight of me and none in reach. If it isn't nonsense, tell me what it is. For me at any rate it's nonsense, and for every intelligent woman about me – for I talk to some of them, we indulge in seditious whisperings and wit – and there isn't one who seems to have been able to get to anything solider than I have done. Each of us has had her little fling at maternity – about as much as a washerwoman does in her odd times every two or three years – and that is our uttermost reality. All the rest – trimmings! We go about the world, Stephen, dressing and meeting each other with immense ceremony, we have our seasonal movements in relation to the ritual of politics and sport, we travel south for the Budget and north for the grouse, we play games for their own sake, we dabble with social reform and politics, for which few of us care a rap except as an occupation, we 'discover' artists or musicians or lecturers (as though we cared), we try to believe in lovers or, still harder, we try to believe in old or new religions, and most of us – I don't – do our best to give the gratification and exercise the fascinations that are expected of us . . .

Something has to be done for women, Stephen. We are the heart of life, birth and begetting, the home where the future grows, and your schemes ignore us and slide about over the superficialities of things. We are spoiling the whole process of progress, we are turning all the achievements of mankind to nothingness. Men invent, create, do miracles with the world, and we translate it all into shopping, into a glitter of dresses and households, into an immense parade of pride and excitement. We excite men, we stir them to get us and keep us. Men turn from their ideas of brotherhood to elaborate our separate cages . . .

Something has to be done for women, Stephen, something – urgently – and nothing is done until that is done, some release from their intolerable subjection to sex, so that for us everything else in life, respect, freedom, social standing, is entirely secondary to that. But what has to be done? We women do not know. Our efforts to know are among the most desolating of spectacles. I read the papers of those suffrage women; the effect is more like agitated geese upon a common than anything human has a right to be . . . That's why I turn to you. Years ago I felt, and now I know, there is about you a simplicity of mind, a foolishness of faith, that is stronger and greater than the cleverness of any woman alive. You are one of those strange men who take high and sweeping views – as larks soar. It isn't that you yourself are high and sweeping . . . No, but still I turn to you. In the old days I used to turn to you and shake your mind and make you think about things you seemed too sluggish to think about without my clamour. Once do you remember at Martens I shook you by the ears . . . And when I made you think, you thought, as I could never do. Think now – about women.

Stephen, there are moments when it seems to me that this futility of women, this futility of men's effort *through* women, is a fated futility in the very nature of things. We may be saddled with it as we are with all the animal infirmities we have, with appendixes and such like things inside of us, and the passions and rages of apes and a tail – I believe we have a tail curled away somewhere, haven't we? Perhaps mankind is so constituted that badly as they get along now they couldn't get along at all if they let women go free and have their own way with life. Perhaps you can't have two sexes loose together. You must shut one up. I've a horrible suspicion that all these antisuffrage men like Lord Cromer and Sir Ray Lankester must know a lot about life that I do not know. And that other man Sir Something-or-other Wright, who said plainly that men cannot work side by side with women because they get excited . . . And yet, you know, women have had glimpses of a freedom that was not mischievous. I could have been happy as a Lady Abbess – I must have space and dignity, Stephen – and those women had things in their hands as no women have things in their hands to-day. They came to the House of Lords. But they lost all that. Was there some sort of natural selection?

Stephen, you were made to answer my mind, and if you cannot do it nobody can. What is your outlook for women? Are we to go back to seclusion, or will it be possible to minimize sex? If you are going to minimize sex how are you going to do it? Suppression? There is plenty of suppression now. Increase or diminish the pains and penalties? My nephew, Philips's boy, Philip Christian, was explaining to me the other day that if you boil water in an open bowl it just boils away, and that if you boil it in a corked bottle it bangs everything to pieces, and you have, he says, 'to look out'. But I feel that's a bad image. Boiling water isn't frantically jealous, and men and women are. But still suppose, suppose you trained people not to make such an awful fuss about things. Now you train them to make as much fuss as possible.

Oh, bother it, Stephen! Where's your mind in these matters? Why haven't you tackled these things? Why do you leave it to me to dig these questions into you – like opening a reluctant oyster? Aren't they patent? You up and answer them, Stephen – or this correspondence will become abusive . . .

What you call 'social order', Stephen, all the arrangements seem to me to be built on subjection to sex even more than they are built (as you say) on labour subjection. And this is an age of release, you say it is an age of release for the workers and they know it. And so do the women. Just as much. 'Wild hopes', indeed! The workers' hopes are nothing to women's! It is not only the workers who are saying, 'Let us go free; manage things differently so that we may have our lives relieved from this intolerable burden of constant toil', but the women also are saying 'Let us go free'. They are demanding release just as much from their intolerable endless specialization as females. The tramp on the roads who won't work, the swindler and the exploiter who contrive not to work, the strikers who throw down their tools, no longer for twopences and sixpences as you say, but because their way of living is no longer tolerable to them, and we women, who don't bear children or work or help; we are all in one movement together. We are part of the General Strike. I have been a striker all my life. We are doing nothing – by the hundred thousand. Your old social machine is working without us and in spite of us; it carried us along with it and we are sand in the bearings. I'm not a wheel, Stephen, I'm grit. What you say about the reactionaries and suppressionists who would stifle the complaints of labour and crush out its struggles to be free, is exactly true about the reactionaries and suppressionists who would stifle the discussion of the woman's position and crush out her hopes of emancipation.*

Mollie Bloom may have had a more intimate case to put and better guidance from her lover, but HG was learning all the time, and Mary's outburst to Stephen deserves a place in feminist literature.

Rebecca could never forget – and, if she did, he would be there to remind her – that he was engaged on a commission to save the world, if only he could persuade enough people to

* *The Passionate Friends*, pp. 281–306.

listen. And one part of the business was to accumulate expert knowledge about what was happening across the planet, and how he might disseminate his ideas. That meant travelling to the places where he thought he could learn and teach best. Sometimes he made the actual journeys and sometimes he imagined them. He had acquired the means to learn and teach at first hand. He went to Russia and renewed his acquaintance with Maxim Gorky. His interest in Russia was growing apace, fostered partly by the introduction to some Russians by his friend Arnold Bennett in the same column in the *New Age* where he had extolled the virtues of *Tono-Bungay* and *The New Machiavelli*. At a diplomatic function in Petersburg he exchanged glances with Moura von Benckendorff, a ravishing 19-year-old niece of a former Russian ambassador in London. She remembered his bright, gleaming blue eyes even if he was not quite so precise about hers. He made a bizarre trip through the Balkans, and described their bristling national problems with scorn and perception. He went for a fresh holiday in the Swiss Alps and produced, almost overnight, in a matter of a few weeks, something fresh or, at least, something slightly different again from the various genres he himself had tried out before.

Quite often the books of his own which he liked the best were least popular with the general public – his output was so vast that these contrasting discernments were inevitable, but this was also a sign that he would let loose his imaginative powers in regions unexplored by most of his contemporaries, even those who were seeking to apply original scientific judgements to the world around them. One such volume where these discrepancies between his own verdict and that of almost everybody else emerged most sharply was *The World Set Free*, published in the early months of 1914. He himself called it 'a distinctly prophetic book'. At least nobody could deny that. He had seized upon some recent highly tentative revelations about the splitting of the atom and transformed them into a full-scale description of what an atom-bomb war might entail: first and foremost, a shattering exposure of what would be the scale of the disaster, with the addition of such niceties as the warning that, fearful as the explosions might be, the subsequent ineradicable effects of the radiation might be even more fearful and some debate about whether the menace would become especially dangerous when terrorists could carry their world-destructive potions in suit-cases. So remote were these possibilities from the actual terrors which crowded one upon another in 1914 and 1915 that few would take him seriously. Moreover, he seemed to add to his own intellectual discomfiture by suggesting that, faced with these realities, these terrors, the world would, at the last minute of the eleventh hour, come to its senses. He prophesied a war starting with a German invasion of France by way of Belgium, but then prophesied also that 'a wave of sanity' would sweep the world – 'a disposition to believe in these spontaneous waves of sanity may be one of my besetting weaknesses'. *

His sojourn in Hampstead, it seems, contributed to his last-minute recovery of faith in his own or the world's destiny. He delivered a whole range of useful hints about the way the world might control the new power, argued across those beaten tracks with politicians who might seem more interested in their dogs than in the new menace, was shocked himself to discover that a new breed of beggars were being allowed to infest the streets of central London, reasserted his newly developed doctrine about women, a world set free for love-making – 'There is no end between men and women that is not a common end'. But, most potent of all, his exposure of the English contempt for science: 'Do tricks for us, little limited tricks. Give us cheap lighting. And cure us of certain disagreeable things, cure us of cancer, cure us of consumption, cure our colds, and relieve us after repletion . . .' But in the name of everything which Victorian England or Edwardian England holds holy: 'Don't find out anything about us, don't inflict vision upon us, spare our little ways of life from the fearful shaft of understanding.' Above all, *The World Set Free* strove to set the atomic age in its full historical setting, as no-one else had ever done before.†

* *Experiment in Autobiography*, vol. 2, p. 666.
† Brian Aldiss, in his introduction to the 1988 edition of *The World Set Free*, stresses how much HG himself would have agreed that he owed much to his

True, the final word of salvation, spoken by his Russian character Michael Karenin, swept forward on his wave of sanity, was naturally engulfed by the sudden tempests of the 1914 war itself, but another section of Karenin's message was especially designed to warn those who might seek to twist his words to suit some other purpose altogether. 'I do not see why life should be judged by its last trailing thread of vitality . . . Don't believe what I may say at the last.' Thus Michael Karenin sought to provide himself with a prophylactic protection against the distortion of his last utterances which pious observers so often contrive for the glory of their church and maker. The choice of a Russian spokesman to deliver this warning has a particular interest. HG's own internationalism had a strong Russian strand woven into it. Some others were beginning to mark these messages brought to the West especially in the writings of Prince Kropotkin. Michael Karenin had more than a touch of him, too.

Lady Harman, the heroine of *The Wife of Sir Isaac Harman*, was a distinctive creation, a committed feminist, too, but with no touch at all of Lady Mary's acquired sophistication and non-chalance. Supposedly, she was modelled on Amber Reeves's mother who had in her time stunned London society with her youthful beauty and radical politics. HG had spoken of the 'matrimonial flattening' which Amber's mother had suffered from Pember Reeves, but even HG with all his sustained animosity could not have compared Amber's father with the ogre Sir Isaac, the most repulsive villain he ever portrayed. What Sir Isaac represented, even in its grossly caricatured form, was the husbandly conviction that wives were merely part of the property which clever men could righteously accumulate and must obey their lords accordingly. The women's movement was partly a revolt against this primitive conception, a revolt with which HG himself had quick sympathy, especially since he was

predecessor in the field, Winwood Reade's *The Martyrdom of Man* (1872). HG himself wrote in 1924 how he 'had thought *The World* a good book, but nobody else has ever done so'. How thrilled he would have been today to read the Aldiss introduction and the Winwood Reade tribute.

ready to show how not only outrageous figures like Sir Isaac held this view about property relationships but how it could, insidiously, infect supposedly decent people, too. Even Lady Harman's bumbling guardian and suitor, Mr Brumley, could not, at hours of crisis, forget about the money. Poor Lady Harman at times had nowhere to turn except to her own high ideals. At one moment in her ineffectual tours round London society, she bumps into the seemingly successful but still sceptical novelist Wilkins (who is, of course, HG himself). He would like to advise; he is obviously impressed by Lady Harman's combined beauty and innocence and zeal for good causes. Wilkins is no cynic, but he finds that his own capacity to give advice to anyone, especially beautiful women, is impaired by his own *disgraceful*, yes, *disgraceful* conduct towards them. The italics were his, and the confession was tucked away in the latter pages of the Harman book.

Most of HG's love affairs were long-lasting, and the plain reason was that he wanted it that way and so did the women. These bare assertions bear little relation to his customary Don Juan reputation: the portrait of a man always lasciviously on the prowl and usually succeeding in his conquests. If HG had been one of these specimens, it is safe to suppose that he would never have secured Rebecca. She wooed him as much as he wooed her, not merely in the early days, but later. The moment when she became pregnant was critical in every sense, and since HG was the one who had the experience, and since the case of Amber was fresh in both their minds, his was the chief responsibility. No-one could doubt that: he never did but, rightly or wrongly, he welcomed the development, and believed at once that the love between them would sweep aside all obstacles. Both of them understood – he, maybe, better than she – that they could not risk a repetition of the Amber scandal. Sensible precautions would have to be taken to avoid publicity. Both Rebecca's family and Jane would have to be warned, and their connivance secured. They found a convenient place at Hunstanton on the Norfolk coast, far away enough from London but convenient for HG to visit from Easton Glebe. Everything did seem to go according to plan, when Anthony West was born on the morning of 5 August 1914. Rebecca was safe; her mother was forgiving; Jane was content; HG himself was radiant; and even the child, Anthony, showed as yet no sign of what was to develop later, a disgruntlement against the universe in general and his mother in particular. *

How they fell in love and how they stayed in love and how they triumphed over all the fearful combined events of 1914 is best described in his own *The Research Magnificent*, not published until 1915. By that time all concerned had many other interests and pursuits to divert their attention, and both the quality and the revelations contained in that volume might be overlooked by the reading public and the individuals concerned. But HG himself thought the book was good, and so did Rebecca, and their combined judgement on a matter on which they had such a close common interest deserves a special respect. As we have seen previously, HG could describe a composite character in his portraits, and he might have had a special interest in this case to protect Rebecca. Some part of his heroine still recalled features from Amber Reeves, as he himself later remarked. So the Amanda Morris who takes immediate command of *The Research Magnificent* from the moment of her first appearance cannot be accepted as Rebecca in every particular, every shake of the head, but clearly the two cannot be kept separate for long. 'Something in the clear, long line of her limbs, in her voice, in her general physical quality' convinced

* If the hasty reader imagines that this judgement is unfair to Anthony, let me add that he will have every opportunity to put his case. His own book, *H. G. Wells: Aspects of Life* (1984), is an indispensable as well as a highly readable document. However, what he read in Gordon N. Ray's book provoked him, or so he claimed, to his most savage comment, as he explained in his new introduction to his novel, *Heritage* (1983). Ray's book claimed that HG had intentionally omitted the usual precautions in the hope that the pregnancy might bind her to him, and that Rebecca had obviously been a party to the dissemination of this tale. Compared with all that she had done to him, he thought his own novel to be a positively genial and good-humoured work. Except in this remark, geniality and good humour were positively not the qualities which Anthony inherited from his parents.

the susceptible hero of the book that 'she was the freest, finest, bravest spirit that he had ever encountered', and he wrote in his notebook that night: 'I felt there was a sword in her spirit; I felt she was as clean as the wind.'

Quite frequently in his later novels he would seek to describe again her appearance on the scene; she never failed to take command but, even when allowances are made for the disguises he had to practise, her role in *The Research Magnificent* remains the most subtle and entrancing. It was not only, on both sides, a true, ecstatic, enduring love; it was also an exploration of their dissimilarities which might lead to discontents or ruptures, all these being compressed into what was called 'The Spirited Honeymoon', staged most curiously in a journey through the Balkans where neither HG nor Rebecca had set foot. They had some really tremendous arguments, not so much necessarily about the way men and women should treat one another, but about how mankind and womankind could be rescued from the unspeakable cruelties which they saw all around them. One discussion which arose – not yet a dispute but of particular interest because of the real arguments he was having with some others, notably Henry James – concerned the relationship between art and HG's other interests such as science and history and the politics which had plunged Europe into war. The young hero of *The Research Magnificent* was impatient: 'Art that does not argue nor demonstrate nor discover is merely the craftsman's impudence.' At first, he was subdued by the young Amanda, who seemed to appreciate these matters better than himself; but then, by unnoticed gradations in the debate, he would reassert his own view. But still the phenomenon would display itself afresh and captivate him.

The suppression of his discovery that his honeymoon was not in the least the great journey of world exploration he had intended, but merely an impulsive pleasure hunt, was by no means the only obscured and repudiated conflict that disturbed the mind and broke out upon the behaviour of Benham. Beneath that issue he was keeping down a far more intimate conflict. It was in those lower, still less recognised depths that the volcanic fire arose and the earthquakes gathered strength. The Amanda he had loved, the Amanda of the gallant stride and fluttering skirt, was with him still; she marched rejoicing over the passes, and a dearer Amanda, a soft whispering creature with dusky hair, who took possession of him when she chose, a soft creature who was nevertheless a fierce creature, was also interwoven with his life. But – But there was now also a multitude of other Amandas who had this in common – that they roused him to opposition, that they crossed his moods and jarred upon his spirit. And particularly there was the Conquering Amanda, not so much proud of her beauty as eager to rest it, so that she was not mindful of the stir she made in hotel lounges, nor of the magic that may shine memorably through the most commonplace incidental conversation. This Amanda was only too manifestly pleased to think that she made peasant lovers discontented and hotel porters unmercenary; she let her light shine before men. We lovers, who had deemed our own subjugation a profound privilege, love not this further expansiveness of our lady's empire. But Benham knew that no aristocrat can be jealous; jealousy he held to be the vice of the hovel and farmstead and suburban villa, and at an enormous expenditure of will he ignored Amanda's waving flags and roving glances. So, too, he denied that Amanda who was sharp and shrewd about money matters, that flash of an Amanda who was greedy for presents and possessions, that restless Amanda who fretted at any cessation of excitement, and that darkly thoughtful Amanda whom chance observations and questions showed to be still considering an account she had to settle with Lady Marayne. He resisted these impressions, he shut them out of his mind, but still they worked into his thoughts, and presently he could find himself asking, even as he and she went in step striding side by side through the red-scarred pinewoods in the most perfect outward harmony, whether after all he was so happily mated as he declared himself to be a score of times a day, whether he wasn't catching glimpses of reality through a veil of delusion that grew thinner and might leave him dis-illusioned in the face of a relationship.

Sometimes a man may be struck by a thought as though he had been struck in the face, and when the name of Mrs. Skelmersdale came into his head, he glanced at his wife by his side as if it were something that she might well have heard. Was this indeed the same thing as that? Wonderful, fresh as the day of Creation, clean as flame, yet the same! Was Amanda indeed the sister of Mrs. Skelmersdale – wrought of clean fire, but her sister? . . .

But also besides the inimical aspects which could set such doubts afoot there were in her infinite variety yet other Amandas neither very dear nor very annoying, but for the most part delightful, who entertained him as strangers might, Amandas with an odd twist which made them amusing to watch, jolly Amandas who were simply irrelevant. There was for example Amanda the Dog Mistress, with an astonishing tact and understanding of dogs, who could explain dogs and the cock of their ears and the droop of their tails and their vanity and their fidelity, and why they looked up and why they suddenly went off round the corner, and their pride in the sound of their voices and their dastardly thoughts and sniffing satisfactions, so that for the first time dogs had souls for Benham to see; and there was an Amanda with a striking passion for the sleekness and soft noses of horses. And there was an Amanda extremely garrulous who was a biographical dictionary and critical handbook to all the girls in the school she had attended at Chichester – they seemed a very girlish lot of girls – and an Amanda who was very knowing – knowing was the only word for it – about pictures and architecture. And these and all the other Amandas agreed together to develop and share this one quality in common – that altogether they pointed to no end, they converged on nothing. She was, it grew more and more apparent, a miscellany bound in a body. She was an animated discursiveness. That passion to get all things together into one aristocratic aim, that restraint of purpose, that imperative to focus, which was the structural essential of Benham's spirit, was altogether foreign to her composition.

There were so many Amandas, they were as innumerable as the venuses – Cytherea, Cypria, Paphia, Popularia, Euploea, Area, Verticordia, Etaira, Basilea, Myrtea, Libertina, Freya, Astarte, Philommedis, Telessigamma, Anadyomene, and a thousand others to whom men have bowed and built temples, a thousand and the same, and yet it seemed to Benham there was still one wanting.

The Amanda he had loved most wonderfully was that Amanda in armour who had walked with him through the wilderness of the world along the road to Chichester – and that Amanda came back to him no more. *

And most of this was written within three years of their first meeting, just after the arrival of Anthony, years before there was any sign of any real estrangement between them. But let Rebecca herself, with the aid of their common tutor, Jonathan Swift, have the last word at this most delicate moment. She wrote in the *Daily News* of 14 August 1915 a review of a book called *The World of H. G. Wells* which had appeared in America. She set about the offending American author as she had once tackled HG himself.

He mentions *The Passionate Friends* as though it were not the worst book written since *Robert Elsmere*, and he talks of *The Modern Utopia*, with its vision of the world governed by a guild of stuffed bishops called Sumurai, as though it were a settled and sober judgement instead of the last frenzied attempt of Mr. Wells to set his steed at the Fabian fence. He mentions *Mr. Polly* as though it were not one of the great books of the world, and a good fellow to *Don Quixote*, and has not been struck by the epic quality of *Tono-Bungay*. It is evident from his guarded references to Mr. Wells's work that, for lack of a personal palate he accepts the current vulgarism that books which aim at the expression of ideas are not art. It is an entirely mystic belief that a piece of work can be deprived of beauty by its intention. One might as well allege that a girl walking along the street is more or less pretty according to whether she is going to a music hall or a sacred concert. Swift, who wrote pamphlets like an angry angel whose tongue had got the better of its wings; Shelley, who sang not as the linnet does, but because he was a crank; Anatole France, who still produces the socialist monthly for which he wrote *Crainquebille* – all these bear witness that beauty is the fruit of any intensity, even if it be moral.

* *The Research Magnificent* (1915), pp. 221–4.

As Mr. Wells himself has put it, 'Beauty isn't a special inserted sort of thing. It is just life, pure life, life nascent, running clear and strong.' And Mr. Van Wyck Brooks is as wrong about wisdom as he is about beauty. *

If Rebecca's invectives of 1912 can still sear the page, how infinitely soothing must have been the balm when she applied it thus. It was still only 1915.

* *The Young Rebecca*, p. 303.

SIX

War to End War I

I feel we are not being properly done by.
Hugh Britling to his father, 1916

No writer of his time, prophet or propagandist, foretold more clearly how individual nation states, left to their own feverish devices, would plunge mankind into catastrophe. The paradox was that, when the catastrophe came, he himself seemed to be swept along by the same fevers. Moreover, his change of attitude, if change it was, soon became for him extremely advantageous and lucrative. The H. G. Wells who could suffer such startling setbacks in his fortunes, induced by the shifts or recklessness in his personal conduct, suddenly discovered that all these anxieties and pitfalls were behind him. He could not be destroyed any more by the world's afflictions, as he had so often feared he might be. He could command an audience whenever and wherever he wanted. He could write what he pleased, and the test of his allegiance to the truth might be all the more severe amid his suddenly acquired wealth and high prospects. It was Mr Polly, confronting every obstacle, and finding himself in charge of an even larger enterprise than the Potwell Inn.

The book which did the trick was *Mr Britling Sees It Through*, which purported to tell the story of England's fate from just before the outbreak of the war until the winter of 1916 when the losses and defeats everywhere were so fearful that no-one could prophesy the outcome. *Mr Britling* seemed to capture every nuance in every change of mood, and since the consequences for HG himself were so beneficial it might be regarded as a brilliant, well-judged piece of opportunism. It was nothing of the kind, but the full circumstances must be explored.

What HG could always legitimately claim was a sense of proportion about what was happening to the world at large and what was happening to himself. Successful or unsuccessful, outlawed from decent society and circumspectly readmitted, the suddenly acclaimed author of *Anticipations* or *The Time Machine* or the suddenly exposed creator of Ann Veronica or Isabel Rivers, he could properly comfort himself with the knowledge that he was always seeking to discover the truth about the society in which he was living and to tell it, not to present himself in some new pose of authority. And here was one cause of his quarrel with Henry James which mounted to a strange climax in the early months of the war. It had nothing whatever to do with the war, but something to do with Rebecca, which made it all the stranger.

Despite the deep-seated historical rights and wrongs of the matter, HG made up his mind about the war with breathless speed. He had often foretold how the international anarchy would lead to war, but in the most recent period – despite the description of a German invasion through Belgium in *The World Set Free* – he had inclined to the view that Germany would draw back from the precipice. It was the suddenness and the perfidy of the attack on Belgium which seemed to clinch the case. This is what multitudes felt at the time, and this was the feeling which HG expressed, more vividly than anybody else.

Neither the Cabinet in London nor the country at large were prepared for what was to come, but once the decision was made one agency of government leaped into action with immediate success. Charles Masterman, the most lively mind among all the junior ministers in the Asquith government, was put in charge of the propaganda war, although it was never given so vulgar a name. His operations were conducted as secretly as possible from Wellington House. A mighty throng of writers and journalists responded to his appeal, HG at their head. He and Masterman were close friends already; he and his wife had often been enthusiastically received at Easton Glebe. So there was nothing forced or false in their common response now. Within a few weeks, HG had written a whole series of articles about the war which were later, but not much later, incorporated in a book, *The War to End War*. It was HG's phrase, and he lived to be half-proud and half-ashamed of it. Liberal England, to use the term in its broadest sense, could not make up its mind as swiftly and as surely as HG; indeed, sections of it were offended by what they saw as his vulgar pugnacity. Two members of the Liberal cabinet had resigned rather than accept the decision; several others had deep doubts almost up to the last moment. Most of the leaders of the Labour Party shared these doubts and never abandoned them. Keir Hardie was broken-hearted to see his own Socialist dream of international action against war betrayed or broken in one country after another. Nothing like an easily defined, clearly defined platform for those who still opposed the war was available, but several brave Socialist spirits were determined to raise their voices. Bertrand Russell wanted to answer HG directly, although he soon found that it was not easy to get his awkward views printed.* But after a while the *Labour Leader*, Keir Hardie's old paper, did give him space. 'All wars are thought to be righteous', he wrote, 'but no war hitherto has put an end to war. If this war is to end differently, it must produce a different spirit, and, above all, it must make us forget, in the claims of humanity, our fiery conviction of the enemy's wickedness.' That last claim in particular was a brave thing to say in August and September 1914, and the response which he

* Caroline Moorehead, *Bertrand Russell* (1990), pp. 164–5.

152

received illustrated afresh how the war spirit was stampeding all before it. One friendly note which Russell did receive came from Bernard Shaw whose 'Common Sense about the War', published in the *New Statesman* in November, was denounced even more fiercely. 'Our job', wrote Shaw to Russell, 'is to make people serious about the war. It is the monstrous triviality of the damned thing, and the vulgar frivolity of what we imagine to be patriotism that gets at my temper.' Russell confessed to himself that he was 'tortured by patriotism'. HG was tortured, too, and he strove – all his life almost – to offer a new and improved definition.

Meantime, in those liberal circles, HG shared the obloquy with his and Rebecca's old friend Robert Blatchford, editor of *The Clarion*. Even before August 1914, he had dared to identify militarist Germany as the enemy, the enemy which democratic Socialists must be ready to oppose and defeat. He had even been prepared to publish these outrageous opinions in the Northcliffe press, which in liberal eyes, almost all liberal eyes, was the deepest offence. Northcliffe was the warmonger, helping to incite war against Germany to sell his newspapers. When Blatchford wrote on these matters in the *Daily Mail*, although he would say there nothing which he would not print in his own *Clarion*, he was blackguarded by many of his own friends. Neither HG nor Rebecca would join that cry; they knew him better. But what Blatchford had said before August HG was saying afterwards, and he was saying some of it in that hated Northcliffe press. For many of his old friends, or even some of the new ones, it was such an act of treachery that it seemed he would never be forgiven.

One life he led in the sudden glare of London fame and publicity – if ever that head was to swell to bursting-point, this was surely the most feverish moment – but he devised for himself, as we shall see, a quite different remedy. A second life, intimately interwoven with the first, was conducted at Easton Glebe – the Matchings Easy of *Mr Britling* – where he could write and sustain old friendships, and make new ones, and unloose without any inhibitions whatever his high spirits. Some of those who became his enemies were foolish enough to talk or write as if there was too much exhibitionism about it. His real friends knew better, and one after another they have described the scene with overflowing affection. Charles Masterman was one, Frank Swinnerton was another; J. B. Priestley (a little later) was a third. All of them testified not only to HG's gift as a host but also to his pre-eminent quality: his absolute dedication as a writer to telling the truth. What he himself saw as the truth was constantly changing, but his determination to tell it was the essence of his genius – and never more so than at the moment when he and his world were hit by the cataclysm of 1914.

He was leading a third life with the beleaguered Rebecca and the unexpected Anthony. But he shared with her, too, an intellectual life of absorbing fascination. Although they might each have had premonitions of how their minds might develop differently, the common interest was still overwhelming, and happily HG produced a book which tells the real story. The book itself was called *Boon*, and it was published in strange circumstances. Only the brief, noncommittal, ambiguous introduction was said to be written by H. G. Wells. The author was named Reginald Bliss. The full title was *Boon, the Mind of the Race, the Wild Asses of the Devil, and the Last Trump*. And the subtitle read: *Being a First Selection from the Literary Remains of George Boon, Appropriate to the Times*.

Boon was chiefly noted at the time and has attracted interest since, in so far as there has been any interest, through its attack on Henry James. But that was certainly not HG's primary intention. Several leading figures in the literary world had attacked him on what he might construe as pretentious grounds. Just occasionally, Henry James had seemed to join the cry, although he had always striven to sustain the courtesies between them. But after *Boon* all the chivalry was presumed to be on James's side and all the crudity on HG's. HG was not interested in manners; he wanted to probe his own mind and the mind of other people at a particular moment of crisis for mankind. He found at hand some old pieces on the literary themes involved which he had written but not sought to publish round about the time when he was engaged in the *Ann Veronica* controversies, but then he added the chapters directly inspired by the impact of the war. He himself called *Boon* 'the frankest and most intimate' book he had written – 'although esoteric'. Even with this qualification, the rest of the testimonial stands, especially since the whole was contrived under Rebecca's astringent eye.

The satire against Henry James still sticks. 'It is Leviathan retrieving pebbles. It is a magnificent but painful hippopotamus resolved at any cost of its dignity upon picking up a pea which has got into the corner of its den. Most things, it insists, are beyond it, but it can, at any rate, modestly, and with an artistic singleness of mind, pick up at that pea . . .' This and more in the same vein; considering the kind of vituperation of which he himself had been the victim, he must have considered this positively lighthearted. And Rebecca could develop a similar tone on the same subject. She was soon embarking on her own first book of criticism, which had Henry James as its subject. She did not seek to dismiss him altogether; she wrote that 'the great glow of the book, the emotional conflagration, is always right'. Jamesian devotees might have warmed their hearts at that verdict, but most of them were still too much offended by the wit. She described a Jamesian sentence as 'a delicate creature swathed in relative clauses as an invalid in shawls'. Some of her critics accused her of stealing her sharpest barbs from Wells; he could have told them better at any time in their relationship. Always the Rebecca wit was all her own. Literary criticism, covering the reputations of many of HG's contemporaries, formed a notable part of *Boon*. Mostly HG would be exalting the lowly or striking the overmighty, as Henry James was in the general estimate. He rushed to the defence of Ford Madox Ford when several Tory critics were defaming him; he called Stephen Crane 'the best writer of English for the last half century'; he mocked Bernard Shaw and his Life Force; and interrupted the brothers Chesterton arguing about immortality and 'whether it extends to semitic and oriental persons'. He even stumbled across a novelist 'strange to me, but one who must certainly be pronounced "a first rater", James Joyce'. He was provoked, too, to execute a full-scale reappraisal of past reputations, knocking the Great Men off their pedestals – the German intellectuals in particular. No doubt some of these assessments and assassinations were provoked by the fresh intolerance of the war itself, but who would deny their element of justice?

> The greatness of Goethe. Incredible dulness of *Elective Affinities*, of *Werther*, of *Wilhelm Meister's Apprenticeship* . . . Resolve of the Germans to have a great Fleet, a great Empire, a great Man. Difficulty in finding a suitable German for Questioning. Expansion of the Goethe legend – German efficiency brought to bear on the task. Lectures. Professor Goethe compared to Shakespeare, compared to Homer, compared to Christ, compared to God. Discovered to be incomparable . . .

And from this exposure of German Great Men, with some English idols similarly treated to prove that he himself was not succumbing to a new racism, a new nationalism, to 'a predominant intellectual degeneration', as he called it, in the writings of Houston Stewart Chamberlain, even some of Nietzsche's 'boiling utterances', some of Schopenhauer. Indeed, the whole outburst against that 'invalid Englishman, Houston Stewart Chamberlain' must be emphasized since it gave hints of so much of his own later work, even if he could not tackle it there and then.

> Poor Jenghiz Khan who had founded the Mogul Empire in India just about that time, and was to lay the foundations of the Yuen dynasty, and prepare the way for the great days of the Mings, never knew how mere his relations were with these marvellous men from the north. The Tartars, it is true, were sacking Moscow somewhere about twelve hundred . . . But let us get on to more of the recital of Teutonic glories.

Sometimes the changing author of *Boon* is outraged and justly so, but often he will relapse into quite different moods. 'Presentations of the men and the women whose characters might be flawed, whose visions might be incomplete, but whose courage was all the more to be recognised if it was less flamboyant.' His Swift of *The Battle of the Books*, who would soon dismiss any Great Man-making; his Laurence Sterne, with 'his unpopular vice, greatness blighted by want of dignity,' or his old favourite, Shelley; he could never be overlooked. Or closer still, if conceivable, the young phenomenon at his side: 'Insurrection of the feminine mind against worship. Miss Rebecca West as the last birth of time. A virile-minded generation of young women indicated, Mrs. Humphry Ward blushes publicly for the *Freewoman* in *The Times*. Hitherto greatness has the applause of youth and feminine worship.' And on the very next page the same invincible Rebecca had a whole page and picture to herself. 'Miss Rebecca West pensive, after writing her well-known opinion of that great good woman-soul, Miss Ellen Key.'

But *Boon*, with all these dazzling preliminaries and diversions, also described the crash: the coming of the kind of war which no-one had properly described, the mockery of heroic language, the swift exposure of all the war-to-end-war talk, 'a new sense of deep tremendous things'. * Complacencies, fatuities have to be destroyed; we have to learn and relearn what Boon once called 'the bitter need for honesty'. That was not the whole of the message, but it was part of it, and the question was whether he could apply it to himself: the slightly plump but still bright-eyed H. G. Wells who had suddenly stepped into a position of fame and power such as none of his dreaming heroes and heroines could ever have conceived.

His answer to the challenge was *Mr Britling*, and it may still be a matter of absorbing interest to see how the deed was done.

---

* The first commentator to recognize the pre-eminence of *Boon* as a war book, one of the first and one of the most important, was Samuel Hynes in his *A War Imagined: The First World War and English Culture* (1990). And this, of course, is only one of the minor insights contained in Hynes's magnificent book, better even than his *Edwardian Turn of Mind*. Readers of that volume may recall his frequent criticisms of H. G. Wells's works, his writing and his conduct – which makes the fresh appreciation of HG's achievements in this new book all the more significant.

Soon after publishing *Boon* he must have thought that something more was required, something less 'esoteric', to use his own word, something more ambitious and comprehensible. *Mr Britling* was certainly a new projection of the old HG, the kind of creation which Henry James had warned him to abjure. But, in these particular circumstances, it would have been absurd for him to present a hero without some assortment of Wellsian virtues and vices. If he had been made to appear saintly or sanctimonious in any sense whatever, he would never have escaped the ridicule. He must be allowed all the frailties of character which Laurence Sterne would prescribe, but he must never flinch in probing the depths of Swiftian horror. Still, he must not lose his humour, as some critics had alleged he had done in some of his recent productions. He knew better than anyone else that that was a gift which could not be switched on and off; Mr Polly always insisted on choosing his own moment. Some serious dilemmas appeared, especially if he wished to use Easton Glebe as the English country home disrupted by Armageddon. And what about the women? How could they be honestly presented? Looking back on these tender choices, with a very special kind of hindsight, Anthony West selected from *Mr Britling* a special epigraph for his second chapter: 'Mr Britling had got into it very much as he had got into the ditch on the morning before his smash. He hadn't thought the affair out and he had not looked carefully enough. And it kept on developing in just the ways that he would rather that it didn't.' That might have been intended as a reference to his own procreation, but in *Mr Britling* itself it clearly refers to HG's attempt to extricate himself from the affair with Elizabeth von Arnim.

Neither Rebecca nor Anthony makes a direct appearance in *Mr Britling*. Two sisters, Cissy and Letty, seem to take their names but not much else from Rebecca's family; and Jane, too, is heavily disguised. The Mrs Britling who presides over Matchings Easy seems sharply removed from the emotions of the other characters which developed to govern the story. Was this the necessary concession to the absent Rebecca? She could be ferociously jealous of the real Jane, naturally enough; for a while, she was content to live on the glowing compliments of *Boon*.

So Mr Britling in the book makes an open confession of his misdemeanours in this field, and gains a further touch of credibility in the process. He has a whole range of other Wellsian idiosyncrasies which all decent readers, male and female, can still relish. He makes no pretensions for his morals, or even his particular brand of foresight. If anything, he underrates the foresight which the real H. G. Wells had shown throughout the previous decade, and overstresses the absurdity of some of his antics in the early days. But all these perceptions, explicit or implicit, help to confirm the justice of his judgement about the war itself; how it had to be fought, despite all the monstrous mismanagement which had brought it about or the even more monstrous mismanagement of the war itself. None of these elements is falsely or feebly presented. Above everything else, it is the cry of youth which is heard: the cry of young men, torn from their families and their wives and lovers, to engage in a senseless, endless massacre. How did we ever get into it? How could we get out? How could we stop another drift to Armageddon? These were the kinds of question which mounted in their intensity as the whole picture grew darker through the terrible year 1916:

> What was the good of making believe that up there they were planning some great counter-stroke that would end in victory? It was as plain as daylight that they had neither the power of imagination nor the collective intelligence even to conceive of a counter-stroke. Any dull mass may resist, but only imagination can strike. Imagination! To the end we should not strike. We might strike through the air. We might strike across the sea. We might strike hard at Gallipoli instead of dribbling inadequate armies thither as our fathers would sit at their tables replete and sleepily, and shake their cunning old heads. The press would chatter and make odd ambiguous sounds like a shipload of monkeys in a storm. The political harridans would get the wrong men appointed,

would attack every possible leader with scandal and abuse and falsehood. The spirit and honour and drama had gone out of this war. Our only hope now was exhaustion. Our only strategy was to barter blood for blood – trusting that our tank would prove the deeper . . . While into this tank stepped Hugh, young and smiling . . . The war became a nightmare vision . . .*

These were the questions which the 17-year-old Hugh sent back to Mr Britling until his mouth was stopped, too.

When *Mr Britling* was published in September 1916, the first sentence in the *Times Literary Supplement* review read: 'For the first time we have a novel which touches the life of the last two years without impertinence.' And that was true, and the achievement was already immense. No other novelist had achieved anything comparable; no poet as yet had done so, either, although many did later. No other direct reporter from the scene had surpassed the letters of HG's fictitious son. No other writer had shown the same taste, as the *TLS* reviewer discerned; to write about these matters, without that quality, would have destroyed the whole effect. And yet, added to this essential quality, was a whole range of other ones: the under-standing of the international character of the war; how the Americans saw it; how German sons were killed no less than British sons; how the only kind of peace which could win in the end was one in which the victors would have to concede no less than the vanquished.

Nothing in *Mr Britling* sounded false, neither the expressions of patriotism at the beginning nor the appeal to religion at the end. The England he loved was real, but how could that love be stated? 'The meaning of England . . . The deep and long-unspoken desire for kindliness and fairness. Now is the time for speaking. It must be put as straight now as her gunfire, as honestly as the steering of her ships.' And the closeness of God at the end, that was real, too, in the mind of the bereaved Mr

---

Mr Britling Sees It Through (1916), p. 318.

Britling, who had seen and shared the feelings in the many broken English homes. And then the reply to his questioning, still rebellious children.

> No life is safe, no happiness is safe, there is no chance of bettering life until we have made an end of all that causes war.
> We have to put an end to the folly and vanity of kings, and to any people ruling any people but themselves. There is no convenience, there is no justice in any people ruling any people but themselves; the ruling of men by others, who have not their creeds and their languages and their ignorance and prejudices, that is the fundamental folly that has killed Teddy and Hugh – and these millions. To end that folly is as much our duty and business as telling the truth or earning a living . . .
> 'But how can you alter it?'
> He held out a finger at her. 'Men may alter anything if they have motive enough and faith enough.'

He had written, like all the great writers about war before him – Tolstoy, Stendhal, Byron, Swift himself – to strip war of its glory and pretensions. He gave the proper treatment to the epic theme. Unwittingly, none the less directly, he answered all his critics. Bernard Shaw sent him the most friendly letter of greeting he had ever written to him: apart from anything else, HG had produced 'a priceless historical document'. He offered Siegfried Sassoon a passage to copy into his diary: 'the war that has lost its soul'. He provided for the Jamesians a work of art more powerful than any propaganda pamphlet. So Mr *Britling* can be read today by all who still retain HG's eyes and HG's heart. It is not so surprising that Thomas Hardy could still write four years later: '*Mr Britling* is the best war book we have had. It gives just what we thought and felt at the time.' Yet even that is not enough. Thomas Hardy believed in fate; HG was also still determined to shape the future.

SEVEN

War to End War II

Youth grew wise very fast in those tremendous
years.

Joan and Peter, p. 32

One of the accusations made against him as a result of his
wartime popularity, by old friends or new enemies, was that he
had betrayed the cause of youth. * Nothing anyone could have
said could have been more hurtful; his chief purpose had been to

---

* A book which reached this severe judgement was Douglas Goldring's
Reputations (1920). Goldring's essay is fair and discerning; he is an old-fashioned
Socialist who hated some of the ideas which Wells developed in the war, but still
understood his qualities: 'His great virtues are his sensitiveness to ideas: his eager
scanning of the future, his belief in a love for humanity, his imagination and his
ability at his best moments to combine emotional warmth with a scientific
clarity.' All the worse after such perceptions comes the jolt: 'One of the worst
things about this novel [*Joan and Peter*] was the way it showed how completely Mr
Wells had lost touch with youth'. A deadly blow indeed. I was sent the Goldring
volume by my old friend Peter Eaton, and I would love to know whose side he
would have been on.

encourage the acceptance of exactly the opposite deduction. Ever since his belated awakening to new vitalities in his mid-thirties, he had wanted to make up for lost time. He thought of himself as being perpetually young; and, if it was delusion, most of his mistresses happily shared it. Anthony West would remark that this was one of the reasons why his father had renewed his wooing of his mother: she was another part of his young aspiration which nothing could make him surrender. Moreover, if there were such misunderstandings about his allegiance, *Mr Britling* should have swept them all away. All his heroes in the novel were young and individual: his young, animal-loving German, a young American who could speak the language Americans wanted to hear: 'I don't see how anyone can be very much in love with your Empire, with its dead-alive Court, its artful publications, its lords and ladies, and snobs, its way with the Irish and its way with India, and everybody shifting responsibility, and telling lies about the common people.' Yes, that was indeed part of the convincing message to take back. *Mr Britling's* Mr Direck was just about the best two-way ambassador we had travelling back and forth across the Atlantic since Benjamin Franklin.

But, above all, the most important character in the book was the young Hugh, who was the purest Wellsian invention. He came near to choosing the pacifist path; he might have had the sheer luck to escape; he was the very best that England could produce; he had a reticent charm to match his wayward will and his eventual courage. The sheer wantonness of the killing of Hugh, and a million Englishmen, and Frenchmen, and Germans, and Americans: no-one who had truly read *Mr Britling* could see this charge of betrayal as a proper one against the author. All his young heroes and heroines had been given the chance to speak and they all did it with lasting effect, and Mr Britling himself was young in spirit and action, too, ranged as HG always had been against the greybeards. And yet HG himself was not quite satisfied.

He could misjudge his own work, especially when he was seeking, according to his own recipe, to raise the contemporary novel to its highest level of achievement. But never did this feature in his literary-cum-political character, his readiness for self-criticism, offer a sharper contrast than in the period which followed *Mr Britling*. In the immediate years thereafter, he set out to produce a worthy sequel – or, rather, something even more ambitious. He saw for himself that *Mr Britling* had serious deficiencies. The unexpected success was partly a lucky accident, or maybe some hidden artistic hand had intervened at critical moments. HG would not himself stop to analyse these aspects of his craft; he had done so when he produced *Boon* or, more deliberately still, with the 'Contemporary Novel' essay in 1911. But in 1916 he could be excused for being much more interested in the practice than in the theory. A new and better *Mr Britling* was what he turned his hand to at once. He permitted some other diversions, some of them distinctly outside his customary work. He was immediately engaged and increasingly for the next two years in work directly concerned with the war. He visited the war fronts in the winter of 1916 and was ready to accept direct work in a government department. But any and all of these activities were diversions from the paramount task he set himself: to use the instrument of the novel to tell the truth about the Great War.

The book into which he poured all these aspirations was *Joan and Peter*. He thought at the time that it was much better than *Mr Britling*, and never saw any reason to alter that appraisal. His own judgement and the sudden, brutal condemnation from his contemporaries had a most potent effect on his whole future. The weaknesses and the strengths of *Joan and Peter* help to expose the real, often-concealed HG of that particular period who is sometimes paraded as either a craven convert to the flag-wagging, patriotic camp or a reversion to something nearer his pre-war liberalism. Neither of these conclusions is justified, but what of the charge which might be common to both interpretations – even more deadly, if it were true – that somehow he had betrayed the rising generation, for whom he claimed to speak? He was still doing so more openly and at the same time more intimately than anyone of his generation – better, at least, than any of Rebecca's list of uncles, for a start – but better than a whole range of others who had not applied their minds to the challenge of the war as he had done by common consent in *Mr Britling*.

Joan and Peter, compared with *Mr Britling*, has some weaknesses, structural perhaps, but HG's own estimate must not be dismissed altogether. A drawback from the reader's immediate point of view is that the apparent leading character, Oswald Sydenham, is no Mr Britling. He has no endearing, obvious weaknesses: he is much more the old Remington than a new Mr Polly. Another true quality is his unwavering and constantly reiterated devotion to Winwood Reade's *The Martyrdom of Man*.* Since Oswald Sydenham is credited with really knowing something about the modern Africa of those times, his devotion to Winwood Reade is all the more commendable. HG honoured Reade for a range of reasons, but he would especially emphasize how he had developed his defence of heresy and how, in the process, he had developed his understanding of other cultures, other intellectual traditions and accomplishments, than those comprised in the Judaeo-Christian tradition. 'It was a book of sombre optimism productive of dark hopefulness – *provided we stick to it*,' wrote the author of *Joan and Peter*, introducing one of his most promising pupils. Who thereafter could accuse either of them of an imbecile optimism or a black despair? So Oswald Sydenham did certainly have a much wider vision of how his world had been shaped and how it might be shaped in the future than most of the prophets and all the priests on his side of the political fence. He longed to teach the rising generation the significance of these and kindred truths. But mostly, absolutely, he was blocked; and, since the blockages happened at the doors of the schools and universities where the sons and a few of the daughters of the most powerful nation on earth were supposed to

* This is the first reference in Wells's own writing to Windwood Reade's classic. His later reference to it in his introduction to *The Outline of History* (1920) became much better known. No doubt is possible about the valuation which he placed upon it, and the commendations became more frequent until, almost literally, his dying day.

be educated, the point had some significance for the world at large and for the world at war. Sometimes Oswald Sydenham put his case with a slightly ponderous touch; and perhaps his creator intended that, too. HG was never as much at home with his English aristocrats as he was with his belligerent cockneys, of the first or second generation. However, Oswald strengthens his perceptions during the war itself, which is another virtue of the novel.

But what of Joan and Peter? It had always been intended, as the title implies, that they should be the dominant characters. They, too, came from a class in the community several rungs above the top of the Bromley ladder, but one which he aspired to delineate with authentic intimacy. His Joan and Peter were reared amid all the comforts and educational contrivances of Edwardian England, and then they are hit by the utterly unforeseen, implacable events of August 1914. Never was the terrible suddenness of that catastrophe better recaptured than in *Joan and Peter*. And the art with which HG created them has seldom been recognized. Peter's political brain had not been fully developed before the crash came, but it was obviously a sharp and brilliant one. Among others he had taken a cursory look at the young Fabians – not the old fogies, the Webbs and the Brands, but the young ones, the Coles and the Mellors, who had tried to engineer a coup against the leadership not so different from the one HG and his friends had attempted seven or eight years before. Peter would call himself a Socialist, but – like Blatchford's *Clarion* readers – he had already been asking the question: How long must we wait? So bitter and corrupt was the whole system in the eyes of Peter and his friends that some of them openly argued for 'a general smash-up' as the only way forward since all other paths were blocked.

Oswald tried to restrain some of these ardours in his ward, but not to break his fiery temperament, his passion to do something much more effective than seemed possible so long as they were content to stay in the old political rut. When the war came Peter found his role in the Royal Flying Corps. His real education was compressed into these tumultuous months of achievement, the

166

exultant flights and the terrible casualties. He could learn and teach, better than ever before, a new kind of *esprit de corps*, which the English airmen, but not only the English, learned in their new kind of fighting. HG captured that mood better than anyone had done before, and Peter lived to acquire a fuller personality to reach out for his new world.* Peter was real enough. He had not quite the same intellectual interests as Hugh Britling – he didn't yet read Heinrich Heine, but he soon might remedy that deficiency.

But it is the case of Joan which must be most carefully weighed. HG confessed later that he had fallen in love with her, and he deeply regretted that no-one else would follow his example; A. A. Milne was the only exception to this rule. However, no such laments are needed for those who read the book. Joan is different from any previous heroine he had drawn. She is one of those passionate daughters who were not supposed to exist but whom he had still dared to introduce into his previous novels, but her passions were directed – with a greater propriety, I suppose it must be conceded – towards one man, one hero. She gets her Peter in the end, in circumstances of tremendous tension and excitement, but her character, too, has developed in the war itself. Of course, she has a strong streak of Rebecca's independence in her, but there are other elements, too.

Joan's education, Rebecca's education, and the speed with which they developed the education of their lovers or their parents are essential parts of the book. Oswald discovers his Joan, still in her teens, reading Oscar Wilde, and the *Freewoman* or even more shamelessly *The New Freewoman* which took over when the other one died: 'it existed, it seemed, chiefly to mention everything that a young lady should never dream of mentioning.' But Havelock Ellis was even worse. None of the writers she and Peter seemed to alight upon had the kind of breeding Oswald had been taught to admire: 'Except for

* Anyone reading these pages in *Joan and Peter* today must be reminded of the descriptions of the even more famous exploits of the airmen who flew from English bases in 1940.

Cunningham Graham there was not a gentleman among them.'
But somehow these did get hold of the intelligent young because
'they did at least write freely where the university teacher feared
to tread'. And then they started to teach him, about some of the
writers who were daring to write, especially about religious
matters, in a way no-one had done before.

> Adolescence was once either an obedience or a rebellion; at the
> opening of the twentieth century it had become an interrogation
> and an experiment. One heard very much of the right of the parent
> to bring up children in his own religion, his own ideas, but no one
> ever bothered to explain how that right was to be preserved. In
> Ireland one found Dublin educational establishments surrounded
> by ten-foot walls topped with broken glass, protecting a Catholic
> atmosphere for a few precious and privileged specimens of the Erse
> nation. Mr. James Joyce in his 'Portrait of the Artist as a Young
> Man,' has bottled a specimen of that Catholic atmosphere for the
> astonishment of posterity. The rest of the youth of the changing
> world lay open to every wind of suggestion that blew. The parent or
> guardian found himself a mere competitor for the attention and
> convictions of his charges. *

It was Rebecca, indeed, who urged HG to turn aside even
from his fascination with his newly created Joan to review the
recently published *Portrait*. Critical reviewing of this nature was
not his strength, but when he did do it he took some trouble. At
first, he had replied that he was too busy to do it, but on
Rebecca's direct urging he relented. His highly appreciative
review appeared in *The Nation* on 24 February 1917. He was full
of well-considered praise for 'the most memorable novel' and its
quintessential and unfailing reality. He said that Laurence
Sterne himself could not have done better the Christmas-dinner
scene and that 'the whole book's claim to be literature is as good
as the claim of the last book of *Gulliver's Travels*'. No higher
praise from HG was possible, but then he added a less agreeable
Swiftian footnote: Joyce, he suggested, might, like Swift

* *Joan and Peter* (1918), p. 208.

himself, seem to suffer from 'cloacal obsession', which was why he felt forced to use all the indecent words. Joyce himself demurred about that, and then added the famous taunt: 'Why, it's Wells's countrymen who build water closets wherever they go' – a charge he renewed in *Ulysses*. But the review itself was the great event for Joyce; he had never received kindlier and more perceptive encouragement from such a well-known figure in the literary world. And some time later, indeed, on the indelicate 'cloacal question', Joyce would confirm 'How right Wells was!'*

It was a two-way education all right between Joan and Peter.

---

* Richard Ellmann's *James Joyce*, (1959) p. 414, which also records:
Wells complained that the hero, while intolerant of sounds, was singularly indulgent of smells. Joyce wrote a limerick of which only three lines have survived.

> There once was an author named Wells
> Who wrote about science, not smells
> The result is a series of cells

Patrick Parrinder states that HG 'here shows himself the only early reviewer apart from Ezra Pound, who was able to do justice to the magnitude and originality of Joyce's novel' (Patrick Parrinder and Robert M. Philmus, eds, *H. G. Wells's Literary Criticism*, 1980). The whole review has point and substance: let us quote one more paragraph:

> The interest of the book depends entirely upon its quintessential and unfailing reality. One believes in Stephen Dedalus as one believes in few characters in fiction. And the peculiar lie of the interest for the intelligent reader is the convincing revelation it makes of the limitations of a great mass of Irishmen. Mr. Joyce tells us unsparingly of the adolescence of this youngster under conditions that have passed almost altogether out of English life. There is an immense shyness, a profound secrecy, about matters of sex, with its inevitable accompaniment of nightmare revelations and furtive scribbling in unpleasant places, and there is a living belief in a real hell. The description of Stephen listening without a doubt to two fiery sermons on that tremendous theme, his agonies of fear – not disgust at dirtiness such as unorthodox children feel, but just fear – his terror-inspired confession of his sins of impurity to a strange priest in a distant part of the city, is like nothing in any boy's experience who has been trained under modern conditions. Compare its stuffy horror with Conrad's account of how in analogous circumstances Lord Jim wept.

He said he was blind until she opened his eyes, and at every turn they were learning afresh. He was outraged that he had been told so little about the Empire for which they were supposed to be fighting. 'You see, we don't see or learn anything about India.' Nothing now could be suppressed, and soon both could hear the most authentic voice of all.

> The young soldier's mind found a voice in such poetry as that of young Siegried Sassoon, who came home from the war with medals and honours only to denounce the war in verse of the extremest bitterness. His song is no longer of picturesque nobilities and death in a glorious cause; it is a cry of anger at the old men who have led the world to destruction; of anger against the dull, ignorant men who can neither make nor end war; the men who have lost the freshness and simplicity but none of the greed and egotism of youth. Germany is no longer the villain of the piece. Youth turns upon age, upon laws and institutions, upon the whole elaborate rottenness of the European system, saying: 'What is this to which you have brought us? What have you done with our lives?'*

Since the story of the whole century was to be compressed into these pages, he wanted to portray groups as well as individuals. He was hard on the pacifists, so hard that some of them never forgave him, and he never quite forgave himself. But he was much harder still on the old Tory English, brilliantly portrayed in his Lady Charlotte. All through the war she, or

> a voice indistinguishable from hers, had bawled unchastened in *The Morning Post* . . . The old lady had played a valiant part in the early stages of the war. She had interested herself in the persecution of all Germans not related to royalty, who chanced to be in the country; and had even employed private detectives in one or two cases that had come under her notice. She had been forced most unjustly to defend a libel case brought by a butcher named Sterne whom she had denounced as of German origin and a probable

Joan and Peter, p. 325.

poisoner of the communists, for the very laudable belief that his name was spelled Stern . . . She subscribed liberally to the British Empire Union, an organisation so patriotic that it extended its hostility to Russians, Americans, Irishmen, neutrals, President Wilson, the League of Nations and similar infringements of the importance and dignity of Lady Charlotte and her kind . . . She included several rich Jewesses of Swiss, Dutch, German and Austrian origin to relieve the movement of their names, and, what was still better, of the frequently quite offensively large subscriptions with which they overshadowed those who had the right to lead on these occasions . . . She was deeply shocked by the stories she had heard of extravagance among our overpaid munition workers . . . She was in London during the early Gothic raids, but she conceived such a disgust at the cowardice of the lower classes, on this occasion, that she left town the next day and would not return thither. The increasing scarcity of petrol and the onset of food rationing, which threatened to spread all over England, drove her to Ulster . . . She warmed up tremendously over the insidious attempts of the Prime Minister and a section of the press to get all the armies in France and Italy under one supreme generalissimo and end the dislocated muddling that had so long prolonged the war. It was a change that might have involved the replacement of regular generals by competent ones, and it imperilled everything that was most dear to the old lady's heart. It was 'an insult to the King's uniform', she wrote. 'A revolution, I knew that this sort of thing would begin if we let those Americans come in. We ought not to have let them come in. What good are they to us? What can they know of war? A crowd of ignorant republican renegades! British generals to be criticised and their prospects injured by French Roman Catholics and Atheists and chewing, expectorating Yankees and every sort of low foreigner. What is the world coming to? Sir Douglas Haig has been exactly where he is for two years. Surely he knows the ground better than any one else can possibly do.'

Once the theme of Lady Charlotte got loose in Oswald's poor old brain, it began a special worry of its own. He found his mind struggling with assertions and arguments. As this involved trying to remember exactly what she had said in this letter of hers, and as it was in his pocket, he presently chose the lesser of two evils and took it out to read over: 'I suppose you have read in the papers what is happening in Clare. The people are ploughing up grassland. It is as bad as that man Prothero. They raid gentlemen's houses to seize arms; they resist the police. That man Devil-era – so I must call him – speaks openly of a republic. Devil-era and Devil-in; is it a coincidence merely? All this comes of our ill-timed leniency after the Dublin rebellion. When will England learn the lesson Cromwell taught her? He was a wicked man, he made one great mistake for which he is no doubt answering to his Maker throughout all eternity, but he certainly did know how to manage these Irish. If he could come back now he would be on our side. He would have had his lesson. Your Bolshevik friends go on murdering and cutting throats, I see, like true Republicans. Happily the White Guards seem getting the upper hand in Finland. In the end I suppose we shall be driven to a peace with the Huns as the least of two evils. If we do, it will only be your Bolsheviks and pacifists and strikers and Bolos who will be to blame.*

These lesser voices were all part of the wartime reality, and HG recorded them with a conscientious skill which rarely lapsed. If he was unfair, he would relent later and say so quite openly. But much more important still was the eloquent climax in the debate in which a rejuvenated Oswald rises to the occasion. He tells them more movingly than ever before what *his* patriotism means.

'Yours is a great inheritance, Joan and Peter,' he said to the darkness. 'You are young; that is a great thing in itself. The world cries out now for the young to enter into possession. And also – do you ever think of it – you are English, Joan and Peter . . .

'Let me say something to you before we have done, something out of my heart. Have I ever canted patriotism to you? No! Am I an aggressive Imperialist? Am I not a Home Ruler? For Ireland. For India. The best years of my life have been spent in saving black men

* *Joan and Peter*, pp. 398–90.

172

from white – and mostly those white men were of our persuasion, men of the buccaneer strain, on the loot. But now that we three are here together with no one else to hear us, I will confess. I tell you there is no race and no tradition in the whole world that I would change for my English race and tradition. I do not mean the brief tradition of this little Buckingham Palace and Westminster system here that began yesterday and will end tomorrow, I mean the great tradition of the English that is spread all over the earth, the tradition of Shakespeare and Milton, of Newton and Bacon, of Runnymede and Agincourt, the tradition of the men who speak fairly and see fairly, without harshness, and without fear, who face whatever odds there are against them and take no account of Kings. It is in Washington and New York and Christchurch and Sydney, just as much as it is in Pelham Ford . . . Well, upon us more than any other single people rests now for a time the burthen of human destiny. Upon us and France. France is the spear-head but we are the shaft. If we fail, mankind may fail. We English have made the greatest empire that the world has ever seen; across the Atlantic we have also made the greatest republic. And these are but phases in our task. The better part of our work still lies before us. The weight is on us now. It was Milton who wrote long ago that when God wanted some task of peculiar difficulty to be done he turned to his Englishmen. And he turns to us today. Old Milton saw England shine clear and great for a time and then pass into the darkness . . . He didn't lose his faith . . . Church and crown are no part of the real England which we inherit.'*

He advised them, too, now.

'You and your generation have to renew and justify England in a new world. You have to link us again in a common purpose with our kind everywhere. You have to rescue our enemies, the destinies of the world, from these stale quarrels; you have to take the world out of the hands of these weary and worn men, these old and oldish men, these men who can learn no more. You have to reach back

*Joan and Peter, p. 396.

and touch the England of Shakespeare, Milton, Raleigh and Blake and that means you have to go forward. You have to take up the English tradition as it was before church and court and a base imperialism perverted it. You have to become political. Now. You have to become responsible. Now. You have to create. Now. You, with your fresh vision, with the lessons you have learned still burning bright in your minds, you have to remake the world. Listen when the old men tell you facts, for very often they know. Listen when they reason, they will teach you many twists and turns. But when they dogmatise, when they still want to rule unquestioned, and, above all, when they say "impossible", even when they say "wait – be dilatory and discreet", push them aside. Their minds squat crippled beside dead traditions . . . That England of the Victorian old men, and its empire and its honours and its court and precedences, it is all a dead body now, it has died as the war has gone on, and it has to be buried out of our way lest it corrupt you and all the world again . . ."*

Having written such a book, having exerted his powers to the uttermost, having thought that at least the triumph of *Mr Britling* could be repeated, he must have been deeply pained by what followed. He was quite accustomed to giving offence to his different audiences. Here he offended them all afresh at the same time, even though he had taken special precautions to be on his best behaviour on the sexual questions. However, he may have taken comfort, as sensitive authors will, from some insignificant sentences which seemed to be squeezed into the lengthy but no means laudatory review which appeared in *The Times Literary Supplement* on 19 September 1918. The last sentence in the review cried out to be requoted and frequently was: it gave a strong hint that most of HG's work might receive 'the unconcealed boredom of posterity', but previously the same reviewer had discerned:

One part of what he has achieved has some relation to a work of art.

* *Joan and Peter*, pp. 497–8.

44. Max Beerbohm was partly mocking HG's Patent Mechanical New Republic, and his spirit of Pure Reason, but this was April 1914, when some of his prophecies seemed to be coming true.

45. Keir Hardie addresses a peace meeting from a plinth in Trafalgar Square, 1914.

46. HG quickly publishes a collection of his early wartime articles with a title that would become famous.

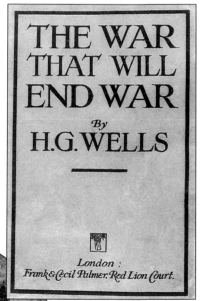

THE WAR THAT WILL END WAR

By

H.G. WELLS

London :
Frank & Cecil Palmer. Red Lion Court.

47. Following the publication of *Mr Britling*, HG visits the Western Front.

48. He met two men who would reshape his world and theirs: Max Aitken, later Lord Beaverbrook.

49. Lord Northcliffe, as portrayed by Max Beerbohm. HG had seen him like that eighteen years before in his *Anticipations*.

50. Max Beerbohm (1920) exposes Urgent Conclave of Doctrinaire
Socialists wishing to reinstate themselves as Visionaries. HG argues with
his old friend and enemy, Sidney Webb.

51. Petrograd, September 1920: HG with his host, Maxim Gorky, and
interpreter, Moura Budberg.

52. Robert Bruce Lockhart, Britain's envoy and Moura's lover, and, a little later, Beaverbrook's employee.

53. HG and Churchill engaged in a furious controversy about his Russian trip, and Max Beerbohm was at the ringside.

The Churchill-Wells Controversy.

Churchill: "You were only 14 days in Russia!"

Wells: "Your mother's an American!"

December '19

54. Arnold Bennett, like HG, was sometimes accused of attempting too much. They were lifelong friends and allies in most good causes.

55. Frank Swinnerton, just about the truest friend HG or anybody else ever had, and he honoured Jane no less.

56. J.B. Priestley, another younger Wellsian ally, who saw him as the most honest writer of the age.

57. How novelists write: the *Strand* in 1924 produced a page from HG's *The Dream*, one of the best of his later books.

58. Max Beerbohm (1925) pictured the old Wells confronting the young one and suggesting that neither had much to confess.

59. Jane among her mountains: they had some wonderful holidays, but she loved Switzerland best.

60. At Lou Pidou, the home he made for Odette Keun, receiving Anthony West and his partner.

(LEFT TO RIGHT)
A "FRANK" WOMAN NOVELIST, SHAKESPEARE, SHAW, WELLS, BENNETT, ALDOUS HUXLEY,
D. H. LAWRENCE, JAMES JOYCE. EACH IS ACCOMPANIED BY HIS LITERARY INSPIRATION;
(AT BACK) DICKENS AND JANE AUSTEN

JIX, THE SELF-APPOINTED CHUCKER-OUT.

61. Jix, Sir William Joynson-Hicks, the Tory Home Secretary of the 1920s, expels all the best writers of this century, and a few others, including of course HG.

62. Bernard Shaw, Hilaire Belloc and G. K. Chesterton at the time of the Belloc-Wells row. Belloc tried to destroy HG's *Outline of History* and the sales soared still further.

63. HG addressed the Reichstag, Berlin, in 1929, and Moura was in the audience.

64. HG leaves for the United States, 1934.

65. Meets President Franklin Roosevelt at the White House.

66. A family party in Estonia; HG one from the left, Moura one from the right.

67. Visits Soviet Union, 1934; welcomed at the airport.

68. How the controversy looked back in London. HG more than held his own.

69. Meets Ivan Maisky, new Soviet Ambassador in London.

70. HG in Dubrovnik, 1934, at a famous meeting of the PEN Club, puts the Fascists, Italian and German varieties, in their place.

71. A publicity stunt for his film, *Things to Come*.

72. Greeted by Priestley and his wife, at his seventieth birthday celebration.

73. Meets Churchill and Maugham at Maugham's villa at Cap Ferrat.

74. With Moura at the Gargoyle Club, Soho, 1939.

75. The great photographer, Karsh, called this *The Ageing Wells*, but he still could capture HG's reflective intelligence.

76. His 1940 publication and a most creditable one, putting all the appeasers of Fascism in their place.

77. He could still argue with George Orwell.

78. HG, 29 January 1944, still arguing for a better world.

IT'S H. G. WELLS COMING UP

79. Vicky, a true Wellsian and the author's dearest friend, still put a glint in HG's eye as he despatched him on that last voyage.

If you could isolate the seed from which the whole fabric has sprung, you would find it, we believe, to consist of a fiery passion for the rights of youth . . . But if Joan and Peter are merely masquerading rather clumsily at being the heroes of the ages, Mr. Wells's passion for youth is no make-believe. The sacrifice, if we choose to regard it so, of his career as a novelist has been a sacrifice to the rights of youth, to the needs of the moment, to the lives of the rising generation.

Who could be the critic so much concerned for HG's artistry? A repentant Henry James risen from his recent grave? The anonymous reviewer was in fact the Virginia Woolf who shared some of those youthful feelings and dilemmas. This was not exactly a peace offering from the Bloomsbury which he had offended so deeply; and, if it was, many others who had taken shelter there would have protested against so gracious an offer of reconciliation. But she had detected the genius which drove him: his all-else-devouring mission to serve the cause of youth.

Even with this final, awkwardly executed half-sentence of commendation, Virginia Woolf had damned *Joan and Peter* in a manner which she and her circle must have thought would be conclusive. She had thought that almost everything else was wrong with it, and in a sense in the subsequent years it is her judgement which has prevailed. *Joan and Peter* has not kept any kind of place in the Wellsian cannon. HG himself would not accept that decree, but seemingly he could find few valued allies to support him. And yet there was another widespread opinion of long-lasting significance which sustained his spirits. The author of *Mr Britling* had understood the mood of 1916 better than any other writer at the time; he expressed the tragedy and the despair without a trace of defeatism, and then produced a companion volume with its taste of victory without a trace of vainglory – indeed, with a foreboding how even such a triumph could be poisoned if political leaders failed to use the occasion. He seemed to recruit a new army of common readers who would take the defence of human decency into their hands and dictate a different outcome. An unknown reader wrote from Surrey: 'I don't know how you can write a book like *Joan and Peter* and escape pestering letters. This is one of them . . . I have closed it with a bang and an indrawn breath . . . You have turned our minds up towards the sun and made things grow. You have made us infinitely indebted to you.' But there was much more in this same wonderful vein from this particular reader and a host more: men and women, mostly young but not all so, who had been similarly stirred by *Mr Britling* and understood how *Joan and Peter* was the inseparable climax. *

The H. G. Wells of wartime might seem to be a quite different man from the earlier incarnation, and some of his old admirers might be amazed or horrified by his sudden, sweeping popularity. But a few of those who knew him even better appreciated that he, too, was an artist of the first order who somehow raised his gift to an even higher pitch with his wartime output. One of these was Ivor Brown, a fellow journalist who watched his hero at close quarters. He swiftly repudiated any accusation that HG had betrayed his trust; the very opposite. 'How much of wisdom and of feeling there is, in fact, in this profound and moving document . . . Into the passage of Hugh's death comes a masterful and beautiful compassion . . . Wells spoke for all; for the father of Herr Heinrich, the pleasant, docile, German tutor of the young Britling, as for Mr Britling himself. When loneliness spoke like a bloom.' But it was his whole experience in the war, Ivor Brown insisted, which equipped him to face the postwar challenge.†

---

* Except to HG himself perhaps, the full scale of this flood of support for what he was writing at this period was not revealed until Robert Crossley delivered his lecture at the 'H. G. Wells under Revision' seminar in 1986: 'He was their voice, their intellectual leader, their champion, their substitute parent, their comrade-in-arms, their vocational counsellor, their psychotherapist, their neighbour across countries and continents . . .' Reprinted in Parrinder and Rolfe (eds), *H. G. Wells under Revision*.

† Ivor Brown's book appeared in 1922 in the Writers of the Day series published by Nisbet. At the time of Wells's death, Brown wrote: 'We can never think of him as finished: he is not a past, but a presence – and radiantly so.' His own little volume serves that purpose – radiantly, too. If you find a copy on the secondhand stalls, buy it, whatever the marked price.

Sometimes he did stray from his own straight and narrow path, his truly sacred mission to serve the rising generation: or maybe we can indicate better what happened in 1917 and 1918 by defining where he went on a couple of detours, one into the hands of the Government and the other for a brush with an even older and higher authority.

Soon after the publication of *Mr Britling*, he found himself lionized even by those who would scarcely have recognized his existence before. It would be absurd to say that he was never influenced by these official flatteries but, as with the Adlai Stevenson recommendation, he never inhaled. He consented for a while to serve Northcliffe's wartime propaganda organization, but he soon became disgusted by the evidence of how the good work done there was so much outweighed by the evil. Most of his associates had no idea of making a real peace for the world in the momentous epoch ahead; they were much more interested in the political dividends to be drawn for themselves or their political parties from the process. HG's own most immediate interest in this business was the acquaintance he found with Beaverbrook, Northcliffe's understudy in his ministry. No-one could say that Beaverbrook ever lacked interest in dividends of any kind, but the two men had other common interests, too, which each was amazed to discover.

He wrote three other pieces in this period: *God the Invisible King, The Soul of a Bishop* and *The Undying Fire*, which seemed to explore further a new kind of relationship with a real God, not a Wellsian one which Mr Britling had revealed. *The Undying Fire* was the Book of Job brought up to date, but since Job has always been the bible for doubters, and since this new version was offered in one overwhelmingly effective Wellsian sweep, no-one could object – not even the author. The mood which produced the others was much less venial, and only a few years later he underlined how much he regretted these lapses which could lead others astray. And considering the themes which he presented so boldly in the black days of the winter of 1917 or the early months of 1918 which were not much brighter – a moment of deadly danger in English history to compare with 1805 or 1588 or 1940 – no-one could accuse him of opportunism or weakness or any other kindred crime. *Joan and Peter* was a brave and comprehensive statement of his combined love of England and faith in a world citizenship. It was as eloquent as William Hazlitt and as far-seeing as Thomas Paine. He had chosen the novel as the best way to speak the whole truth, and the failure of *Joan and Peter* was a wound which never healed. But since so few seemed to hear he must find some other way.

'The League of Free Nations, to enforce Peace throughout the earth.' So spoke Oswald Sydenham at the end of *Joan and Peter*. It was not, of course, the first mention of the subject. Various committees in London had been meeting to discuss the general subject in London throughout 1916 and 1917, and the whole idea was spurred by the declaration which President Wilson made on the subject in 1917. HG was an eager member of these London committees, although he hated committee work and acquired a general reputation, dating from the old Fabian quarrels, for breaking up any committee of which he was a member. Several of those on the Research Committee for the League of Nations were old colleagues or old rivals from previous committees: Gilbert Murray, Ernest Barker, Leonard Woolf. Several of them reminded him of how rich was the tradition of the writing of history – not that the author of *Joan and Peter* needed much reminding. 'All history', he had said,

is the record of an effort in man to form communities, an effort against resistance – against instinctive resistance. There seems to be no natural and proper limit to a human community. (That's my great point, that. That is what I have to tell them.) That is the final teaching of History, Joan and Peter; the very quintessence of History; the limitlessness of the community . . . All history is one dramatic story, of man blundering his way from the lonely ape to the world commonwealth. All history is each man's adventure. But what teacher makes history much more than a dwarfish twaddle about boundaries and kings and wars? Dwarfish twaddle! History! It went nowhere. It did nothing.

A real history: it had to be done. He would do it himself, with the aid of several of the splendid allies who were ready to help. And the idea might be even more important than the work for this embryo League of Nations – although he did not neglect that, either.

Even while these preparations were being made, before the ink was dry on the last pages of his own beloved *Joan and Peter*, he had to conclude his business with the Government for which he had been a servant. It was sometimes held against him that his actual experience of real politics was indeed so flimsy. It was, indeed, short and sweet; it all turned out entirely to his honour, and he himself put the story on the record with a touch of his own special humour:

> The government had created two new ministries for the sake of keeping the inquisitive nose of Lord Northcliffe and his younger competitor, Lord Beaverbrook, out of the ancient mysteries of the Foreign Office. This could be done most unobtrusively by busying them elsewhere. The Ministry of Information was devised to prevent Lord Beaverbrook from becoming too well-informed and the Ministry of Propaganda served a similar purpose in occupying and disordering the always rather fertile mind of Lord Northcliffe. *

HG always seemed to be able to get on reasonably well with both of them. All three had a common streak of irreverence; all three had made their own way in the world against the will and style of what was later called the British Establishment. But HG soon discovered that he was much more seriously concerned than they could ever be about the immediate plans for making a good peace and especially the project for establishing the League of Nations. But the Foreign Office was still effectively in charge. Wells and his fellow committee members were just being used as decoys. HG himself soon left the job with no hard feelings towards Northcliffe or Beaverbrook, but with a fresh and deeply entrenched contempt for the Foreign Office. No guidance came

* *Experiment in Autobiography*, vol. 2, p. 697.

from them about how they could make a good peace: 'Men of my way of thinking were left helpless, and altogether baffled outside the fiasco of Versailles. What had seemed to be the portal of a World Control standing wide open to us, was shut and slammed in our faces.'* All the more eagerly could he turn to his own devices.

The Outline of History was published, first of all, in fortnightly parts, in the late autumn of 1919, and then, finally, all together in September 1920. He had been hard at work at it for the previous twelve months; but, even so, the pace and the achievement seems incredible. The original edition was a double-spaced coloured book of 620 pages. Two special features, both designed by HG himself, were immediately evident: first, an elaborate display of charts and illustrations, especially designed and arranged by J. F. Horrabin; and, second, extensive footnotes in almost every section, contributed by the experts whom HG had recruited to challenge his own judgements in the text itself. Gibbon's footnotes, as HG knew so well, had contributed most powerfully to the success of his book, but *The Outline* carried that addition a step further. Several of these footnotes were written by experts on their particular periods, and HG positively encouraged them to contest his own opinions if they wished. Thus the whole book became a colossal argument. However, even these various aids and incitements to understanding would not have availed if the text had been presented without the array of Wellsian gifts which he had developed in other fields: lucidity, honesty, eloquence and, along with these essential qualities, his own individual, iconoclastic vision.

It was the idea and the writing together which made 'a great book', as E. M. Forster described it.† Millions of readers all over

---

* *Experiment in Autobiography*, vol. 2, p. 707.

† E. M. Forster was rarely lavish in his praise, but in his review of *The Outline*, whatever his criticisms, he returned always to his claim about the book's greatness. My own copy of *The Outline* belonged to my father, who never read any book he really liked without covering it with marks and exclamations. Being a strong Christian and a militant Methodist, he was certainly not a Wellsian in any full sense. But all the more perhaps did he appreciate *The Outline*'s verdict on

the world, introduced on the commendation of others, must have agreed with him. The original *Outline* in English sold 2 million copies. Translations were made into several other languages. *A Short History of the World*, based on this original and published in 1922, sold no less extensively. HG himself was overjoyed, as any sensible author would be. 'My self-conceit', he wrote, 'has always had great recuperative power; it revived bravely now.'

If Versailles represented a great defeat for the human intelligence, *The Outline of History* was a comparable essential victory.

Roman Catholicism in general and on the English Cromwellian revolution in particular. But then I turned over page after page, covering other periods which he had greeted with comparable approval or excitement; a clinching proof, if any is needed, of my father's magnanimity – and HG's.

I add here, too, a comment taken from a comprehensive review of a new edition of *The Outline* published in *The Times Literary Supplement*, 30 June 1972. The writer offers a series of criticisms, just as Forster had done, but also finds himself forced back to Forster's verdict about the greatness of the book. He writes at the end of 'the radiance of his artistic genius and humanity which he shared with a very few contemporaries in his own country – perhaps only Bertrand Russell and Winston Churchill'.

EIGHT

The Open Conspirator

Hunting the truth is an art.

The Open Conspirator, p. 17

A number of good reasons encouraged HG to consider a visit to the new Russia, but the most compelling was the invitation from his friend Maxim Gorky. The political paths of the two men had conveniently crossed ever since HG had defended Gorky on his visit to New York in 1906. They had had their next agreeable meetings in St Petersburg when they met there in 1914; HG incorporated an account of his mood in his *Joan and Peter*. They were kindred, experimental spirits; as writers, they both seemed to have fought their way up from nowhere. But, then, most potent of all, Gorky had quite spontaneously welcomed *Mr Britling* and started to translate it into Russian, calling it 'the best, boldest, most veracious and human book written in Europe in this accursed war'. That was literary comradeship of a high order indeed; Gorky had a heart, and this tribute came straight from it. And, when revolution broke out in Russia in 1917, Gorky on the spot and HG in London responded to events with a common sympathy. Gorky did not seek to excuse or justify everything he saw happening around him: 'I do not close my eyes to the negative results of war and revolution – but I see on the other side how there awakens in the Russian masses the creative power, how the people, gradually, become an active force.' Gorky also did his best to assure HG that Lenin was not the ogre portrayed in capitalist newspapers of the West. 'He is', said Gorky, 'free from any intoxication with his own power. By nature he is a Puritan, lives in the Kremlin just as simply and quietly as he did in Paris when an emigrant. He is a great man, and an honest man, as much as a politician can be honest.' Every clause in that sentence could appeal to HG. Anyhow, he could go and see for himself. He and his boy Gip spent a fortnight in the new Russia in September 1920.

His own story of what he saw and felt, even on such a brief visit, was told in a series of seven newspaper articles, later incorporated in a book of 20,000 words called *Russia in the Shadows*. Whatever else might be said, it was brilliant journalism: direct reporting, original insights, sharp character-studies, daring forecasts of the future. Several others, professional and amateur writers, were attempting the formidable task of telling the outside world – chiefly Britain and America – what this entirely new kind of revolutionary epoch entailed and what it could mean for the future. Some wrote as starry-eyed supporters of the new Communist regime, and they had some excuse since the vilification on the other side passed all bounds of decency or credibility. Some others wished to be sympathetic, but were determined to be honest, and their honesty could get them into trouble with the Communist hierarchies either in Moscow or in London. Bertrand Russell was one honest, liberal observer who soon found himself assailed on this account. HG thought he might be better able to steer clear of these pitfalls on every side, thanks to the fact that his visit was organized by Maxim Gorky. He stayed with him instead of with the journalists at the hotel, and could hear for himself Gorky's views; or sometimes these criticisms, elaborations, guidances were related to him by the woman he described on the first page of his first article:

> The guide and interpreter assigned to assist us was a lady I had met in Russia in 1914, the niece of a former Ambassador in London. She was educated at Newnham, she has been imprisoned five times by the Bolshevist Government. She is not allowed to leave Petersburg because of an attempt to cross the frontier to her children in Estonia, and she was, therefore, the last person likely to lend herself to any attempt to hoodwink me. I mention this because on every hand at home and in Russia I had been told that the most elaborate camouflage of realities would go on, and that I should be kept in blinkers throughout my visit.

He had another reason, too, for mentioning this matter so demurely, but no-one who read his report would properly question his journalistic integrity. It shines through every paragraph.

Thanks to his reintroduction to Russian affairs through the Gorky-Benckendorff household, HG was given or gave himself a unique introduction to Russian affairs which influenced him for the rest of his life. Theoretically, he questioned all forms of flag-wagging patriotism, and no-one did more than he to expose the perils for the world at large if allegiance to 'King and country' was allowed to become the single basis of virtue. However, British patriots had customarily been willing to make special allowance for the patriotism of other countries which happened for the moment to be in alliance with us, and even English patriots on the Radical Left, like HG (he could never bring himself to use the word 'British' in this connection), often shared this curious but venial lapse from an absolutist standard. HG, as we have frequently seen in quotations from him, had a passionate devotion to the England of Cromwell and Milton, Paine and Shelley. But he saw, too, how our French allies or our American allies could draw sustenance from similar, overlapping, patriotic revolutionary traditions, and many of these strands had been quite properly woven into his *Outline of History*. And maybe this was also an added reason why the HG of that period understood the Russia of his time better than many of his own compatriots: why he could be so outraged by their expressions of unthinking hostility, especially when this development in turn was translated into highly dangerous excursions deriving from circumstances which had nothing to do with the real situation in Russia. Oddly, but not inappositely, he had written just two years before, in his *Joan and Peter*, a whole chapter about the pre-revolution St Petersburg and its culture. He had thus an early introduction into the great themes of Russian history: how the people of Russia, through their own genius, had resisted foreign tyrants and defeated the most powerful of them, Napoleon Bonaparte. Moura could tell him about that, almost from their first meeting. He and his friends, old and new, at Gorky's house had plenty to talk about, and they were all good talkers. Gorky's household, indeed, both here and elsewhere later, bore some resemblance to the kind of parties which the Wellses staged at Easton Glebe where no intellectual holds were barred, and everyone, writers and politicians, were required to argue for their supper. He was always impressed by Gorky's flights of rhetoric, which could include denunciations of some follies and crimes being perpetrated around them; he wrote in his report – a little inadvisedly maybe – that Gorky 'is no more of a Communist than I am'. Moura could talk, too; she had a beautiful, rough voice and a rough command of English, to match her other charms, which her friends might falsely claim she had learned at Amber Reeves's Newnham. What exactly her relationship with Gorky might be, no outsiders knew for sure. She was the daughter of a Russian senator and she had married Benckendorff in 1911. He was shot by the Bolsheviks, and later she married Baron Budberg.

The perpetual topic in the Gorky household was the state of the new Russia and how it might be pushed over the precipice into even more hopeless devastation or how, just conceivably, the world outside might come to the rescue. This was the most significant choice to which HG turned in his *Russia in the Shadows*. As the title indicates, there was nothing starry-eyed in his report. Rather, he was shaken by the scale of the disaster, which he had not appreciated before he got there. But, of course, he was also impressed by the conclusion which Gorky and his friends hammered home to him. If the regime which had taken charge in St Petersburg and Moscow was now to be overthrown by sabotage or direct attack from the Western nations, the calamity would be immeasurable. Moreover, the men in charge were not fools or knaves, as he would be able to test for himself. He had a meeting with Lenin, which he famously described in his chapter 'The Dreamer in the Kremlin'. He was impressed, as were most people who met him, by Trotsky's achievements as an organizer and talker. He thought the Bolshevik government had within it 'a few individuals of real creative imagination, who may with the opportunity, if their hands are strengthened, achieve great reconstructions'. And holding such views, and seeing how much might depend on British and American responses to the situation, he thought he must do everything in his power to tip the balance in the right direction.

This choice, this balance in the possibilities for the future, was not so different from that reached a little earlier by another actor-performer on the crowded Russian stage. At least this description fits Robert Bruce Lockhart better than the title of 'diplomat' which brought him back to the British embassy in 1918. He had had his first diplomatic post for a short spell there just before the war, but he came back now in the circumstances of revolutionary turmoil which seemed to suit his talent better. Even in faraway London he had had the acumen to see that some different kind of British representation in Moscow on the spot was needed. He was not greatly impressed by the way the Foreign Office was dealing with the matter – but nor was Lloyd George, the Prime Minister. Bruce Lockhart made contact with Maxim Litvinov, who had just arrived in London as the new Bolshevik ambassador, and Litvinov gave him a kindly letter of introduction to one of the arch-villains, Leon Trotsky. He returned to Moscow in February 1918. But all these intelligent arrangements and precautions were not quite enough to keep him out of mischief or trouble or adventure. At some moments he seemed to be responding too sympathetically to the desires of the bloodthirsty new Bolshevik regime, and his sponsors in the

Foreign Office became alarmed and critical. At other times he seemed to be acting too successfully or intimately on behalf of his British masters, and at these moments the Russians with whom he had acted too successfully or intimately were involved, too. This was the reason or excuse why Moura von Benckendorff had spent periods in the Moscow jail. She had fallen in love with Bruce Lockhart, and he had fallen in love with her. They could hardly have known it at the time, but, for both of them, this was the greatest affair of their highly emotional lives. What they could know, and what became strongly reinforced in their mutual acceptance, was the proposition which became the dominant one in the Gorky household during HG's visit: how to stop the combined crime and folly of a fresh attempt by the Great Powers in London, Paris and Washington to renew the war and strangle the new republic in its cradle.

This was, for sure, the same Moura appointed as HG's official interpreter on his visit in September 1920. How much she told him there and then of her relations with Bruce Lockhart is not clear; how deep were her feelings for him may not have been so clear, either. She was an adventurous woman who had to protect herself in a highly dangerous world. She was certainly qualified to enter all the arguments from every quarter. As a matter of hard fact, she had never been educated at Newnham, never been to England. Indeed, some of these misconceptions, if invented by others, had not been positively denied by her. HG's description of her – written twenty years later – seems to make every other description utterly trivial:

> She was wearing an old khaki British army waterproof and a shabby black dress; her only hat was some twisted-up piece of black stocking, I think – and yet she had magnificence. She stuck her hands in the pockets of her waterproof, and seemed not simply to brave the world, but disposed to order it about. She was twenty seven then . . . And she presented herself to my eyes as gallant, unbroken and adorable. I fell in love with her, and one night on my entreaty she flitted noiselessly through the crowded apartments in Gorky's flat to my embraces. I believe she loved me and I believed

every word she said to me. No other woman has ever had that much effectiveness to me. *

When he returned to England, he reported the matter – not quite in these terms, we may surmise – to Rebecca. She was considerably aggrieved and she made her grievance clear to him: it was not the first opening of an estrangement between them, but it was obviously serious.

It cannot be claimed that it was part of his normal technique to 'tell all', as the phrase is, about encounters with different lovers, and this experience with Rebecca must have warned him of the perils of any such procedure. But the memory of the magnificent Moura was, he thought, something new; he could tell her, if nobody else. And Moura, as we shall see, had her way of dealing with these complicated courses which true love may follow in such susceptible times of world crisis. The worldwide feminist movement had not made deep penetrations in Tsarist Russia or even among the Bolsheviks, but Moura Benckendorff had fashioned her own ideas on the subject, and would not be denied. It was part of her magnificence.

Other commotions awaited HG on his return to London. Winston Churchill, still a member of the Government, replied directly to his articles in the *Sunday Express*, insisting that the dislocation and starvation in Russia were the direct result of Bolshevik policy, and not the Allied intervention and blockade. He taunted HG with the 'superficiality' of his judgements on these Russian matters, and that was doubtless the provocation which drove HG to a furious reply:

> He believes quite naively that he belongs to a peculiarly gifted and privileged class of beings to whom the lives and affairs of common men are given over, the raw material for brilliant careers . . . He has smeared his vision with human blood, and we are implicated in the things he abets. He does not stand alone. This vision of his,

* *H. G. Wells in Love*, pp. 163–4.

grotesque and distorted though it may be, is no more and no less contemptible than some misshapen idol esteemed by the tribe, to which we may presently see our children sacrificed.

And then:

> I cannot call myself anti-Churchill. I have known Mr. Churchill for a dozen years perhaps, and there is much to like in him. He has an imaginative liveliness rare in politicians, and his personality is unusually amusing. But I will confess that it distresses me that he should hold any public office at the present time. These are years of great severity and Mr. Churchill is temperamentally a waster; there are dangerous corners ahead, and for two years Mr. Churchill has – if I may use the most expressive word – monkeyed with our Eastern policy. I want to see him out of any position of public responsibility whatever . . . The Government would look more serious and statesmanlike without him. His departure at any rate would not be a personal tragedy; Mr. Churchill has many resources. He would, for instance, be a brilliant painter.

Churchill's 'Eastern policy' was seen by many others, including some of his cabinet colleagues, as a disaster, and he was soon to be able to return to his painting. HG would not have counted this among his most significant prophecies. But the part he had played in securing the change in British policy towards the Soviet Republic helped to restore his own bruised relations with people on the Left in British politics and added strength to his voice in speaking afresh about the most desperately urgent task of all: how to regain the losses so wantonly thrown away in the Versailles treaty-making, how to start to build a real League of Nations, how to stop sowing the seeds of a new world war. HG was ahead of almost everybody with his forebodings, but neither would he surrender his hopes.

He was a world figure now, or, as some of his journalistic friends or admirers might say, a world force. He was proud to call himself a journalist, and nothing pleased him more than when some writing of his, despised or neglected elsewhere, was acclaimed by the particular journalists whom he honoured. A most perceptive greeting had come from his old friend, Robert Blatchford, soon after the publication of *The Outline*, and an even more welcome tribute to his eternal youthfulness from a rising star on the other side of the Atlantic, Walter Lippman. But, best of all, was the discernment of the position HG had gained in the eyes of one whose liberal reputation was much more secure than his own but who could still see how HG had the touch of genius, and how he seemed to have developed it all on his own. Henry Nevinson had served some of the same causes as HG: he had served the women's cause much better, having broken his connection with sections of the Liberal press to protest against the Asquithian betrayal. But on other matters Nevinson was more and more attracted by HG's large vision; he eagerly enlisted behind HG's banner to stop the war against Russia, and a few months later he found himself sitting next to HG among the journalists in Washington. Soon after he penned this remarkable paragraph in his own memoirs:

> In one of these years [1903] I met H. G. Wells for the first time, for he came into the office one night with 'his fair haired little wife,' and I just noted that he was 'a very attractive man, with shy and humorous grey eyes.' I had little knowledge then of his inexhaustible and devastating powers – devastating and fertilising, like the powers of a steam plough, grinding and cleaving along its way through stones and roots and flowers, remorselessly turning up the fallow, destroying the slow and sometimes beautiful growth of ages, and industriously fertilising the ground for future utility, that in time may possibly reveal some element of beauty, too. It was only long afterwards that I comprehended this, as when, at one of the vast assemblies during the Washington Conference of 1921, I realised that the small and inconspicuous figure standing beside me, far at the back and out of sight, was an incalculably greater force than all the orators, generals, statesmen, clergy, and innumerable cheering crowds celebrated by the reporters. *

* Henry Nevinson, *Fire of Life* (1935) p. 125.

HG could not make Washington, December 1921, as immediately exciting as Petersburg 1920, or maybe it was the absence of a Moura which partly accounts for the difference. He was forming a close friendship which sometimes flowered into something closer still with Margaret Sanger, the brave birth-control campaigner whose views on this principal topic and several others came so close to his own. They first met at Birth Control group meetings in London in 1920. Then they had a vague plan for an American tour together on the same subject. Sanger was soon singing his praises in terms he certainly would have enjoyed. 'He is not only loving but has a capacity for loving both individuals and humanity at the same time. He can be amusing, witty, sarcastic, brilliant, flirtatious and yet profound at once; he is quick, sensitive, alert to the slightest memory or intonation or feeling.' As he packed his bags for his new journey, she played a big part in the prospect. 'My plans in New York are indeed entirely by the wish to be with you as much as possible and *as much as possible* without other people about.' He would continue signing himself 'ever glowingly yours H.G.', and her attachment and allegiance to him never waned. All his visits to the United States were important for his education and, thanks to Margaret Sanger, this was the most important of them all. His reports from the Washington Conference, as substantial in volume at least as *Russia in the Shadows*, showed how genuinely he struggled to place the whole postwar planet in a proper perspective. He was torn, as he so often was, after an astringent review of the facts, between hope and despair.

And amid these proper assessments, all faithfully reported back to London, he gave his voice to a series of spokesmen from outlandish places all over the same planet who found the Washington doors slammed in their faces. Italy: 'Italy is troubled by its restless nationalists, a whooping, flagwaving crew of posturing adventurers without foresight or any genuine love of country. If nothing is done, I think I would give Germany about six months and North Italy two years before a revolutionary collapse occurs.' A Korean delegation came to see him: 'Korea is as much a nation as — Ireland. She has so recent an independence that she has treaties with the United States recognising and promising to respect her independence. Yet she is being "assimilated" by Japan, without any protest from her protector.' Where had poor HG heard that story before in accents not so dissimilar? He himself would never forget the claims of India, but there were Indians in Washington who approached him direct. 'I adopt almost inadvertently, as much as is adoptable of the manner and tone of the late Lord Cromer and say "yes, yes. But are you RIPE for self-government?" ' They told him of the effects of the recent Amritsar massacre, and how the complete suppression in India was intolerable: 'Everybody is talking of insurrection in India now; nobody talked of it three years ago. These have been the years of stupid "firmness".' And, lest the Americans might congratulate themselves too fulsomely that it was the old British imperialists who were responsible for the repression in India, he reminded them that he had been greeted by an array of banners outside the conference, informing him that 'that evidently most gentle and worthy man, Mr. Eugene Debs, was still in an American prison for saying his honest thoughts about conscription', or that a minor English poet, Charles Ashleigh, a supporter of the International Workers of the World, had been given a sentence of ten years for nothing at all. HG happened to be there just at the time when the land of the free was 'swept by a gale of indiscriminate suppression', and he took steps to ensure that his protests against these individual outrages were printed in the *New York World* which had originally ordered the articles or in Northcliffe's *Daily Mail* back in London which did not normally print such treasonable outbursts about India. For good measure – but here one must suppose his blind or neglectful readers must be pardoned – he prophesied that, if nothing was done by international action to check the rising imperial ambitions of Japan and the ever-developing new forms of air power, a new war might start 'with a direct Japanese raid on an American west coast city'. Such wild flights of fancy were supposed to detract from his intimate revelations; so he did his best to combine the two: 'I must need go about this present world of disorder and dalliance like an exile doing such feeble things as I can towards the world of my desire, now hopefully, now bitterly, as the moods may happen, until I die.'*

Sometimes he could be mortified or outraged by what other people said about him, and sometimes he would brush aside the insults and hurry on to his next task. Churchill's gibe about his superficiality did hurt, but at least he knew in that instance how false it was; he knew Russia much better than Churchill did and he had been stirred also by the insufferable condescension which he himself had seen in the country houses exercised by the same rulers of our country who had helped to contrive the world catastrophe of 1914, and who were now preparing a new one. So he let Churchill have a taste of his real fury, although he was prepared to write in a quite different tone about 'Winston' three years later. What did he feel, at much the same time, when the report was relayed to him of what Lenin had said about him, according to Trotsky, following his meeting in the Kremlin: 'What a little bourgeois! What a philistine!'† Whatever its exact terms, that gibe went round the world; and, considering what efforts HG had made to support the Russian people's cause at one of the worst moments in their history, he took it in good part. At that particular stage in his worldwide argument, it might have done more good than harm. The Bolshevik leaders truly had not known quite what to make of Wells. Bernard Shaw noted that they tried to pass him off as a *petit bourgeois* Volney, but since the Count de Volney had been one of the real pioneers in seeking a new way of writing history HG would have been more honoured than disturbed by that comparison. And he was all the more gratified by the manner in which Bernard Shaw was provoked to reply to Trotsky: 'he has allowed himself to speak of Mr. H. G. Wells with a contempt which shows that he has not read Mr. Wells's *Outline of History*, and has therefore no suspicion of what an enormous advance on *Das Kapital* that work represents.' That

* *Washington and the Hope of Peace* (1922), p. 232.
† The Trotsky article appeared in *Labour Monthly*, July 1924.

was Shaw writing in the *Daily Herald* at the time of the Zinoviev letter, but the point is no less sharp.

If there was any tendency to exaggerate his own importance, he applied the remedy, unusual for him, of standing as the Labour candidate in two parliamentary elections in 1922 and 1923. He did it with considerable reluctance, and only in contests for a university seat, and he developed in the process no fresh interest in the tedious aspects of electioneering. He still had time to prove himself, as in the old Fabian days, a hopelessly impatient, even irascible committee member. Not on account of any of these deficiencies, but much more owing to the still deeply reactionary nature of the universities in that era – even London, which supposedly was not as bad as Oxford or Cambridge – he came bottom of the poll. But what he did do, most creditably, was to show how, first and foremost, it was the Labour Party which had acted with a proper historic sense of the events of the postwar years, and which was committed to build a real League of Nations instead of the highly delusive fake which others were content to offer.

His dislike for British parliamentary politics could change to an inordinate contempt, especially when he saw the misjudgements which the system seemed to make about the capacities of individual leaders. Just after one of those unhappy elections he had undertaken to write a weekly article for a book which was later published under the title *A Year of Prophesying*. He permitted himself some follies or absurdities – that was always the price to be paid for engaging in this kind of journalism – but he also used the chance well. He passionately renewed his appeal for the creation of a real League of Nations. He called for the lowering of the voting age to 18, for men and, of course, women – 'making eighteen the boundary between tutelage and complete responsible citizenship' – and the plea was designed not only for the benefit of the young: 'the younger the age of enfranchisement, the greater our hopes of an early effect of the new education upon the affairs of mankind', and the sooner this was done the sooner some fresh air might penetrate 'into Congress and Parliament and these assemblies cease to be the gatherings of political butchers and tinkers representing the broken spirit and curtailed desires of a forty-year-old electorate'. And he called, too, for the protection of whales: 'These marvels of life, these strange and wonderful beings of whose vitality and impulses we know so little are being killed because they are insufficiently protected.'

He wrote, too, with a fresh, savage insight into the relations between Britain and India. Some others had their judgements formed by the massacre at Amritsar and the subsequent trial in London. He saw vividly 'the tremendous failure of the British Imperial system, after a century of opportunity, to produce any working tradition of interaction between the British people, the British garrison, and the Indian population. It has demonstrated the impossibility of any very long continuation of British rule in the peninsula.' His boiling outrage can still scorch: 'No race is fit to have the upper hand over any other race; the possession of the upper hand leads at best to an inconsiderate self-righteousness and at the worst to an extreme contempt, injustice and cruelty. There are very few instances in the world of an even moderately satisfactory alien rule.' And one of those with whom he renewed this particular debate was the politician whom, despite their furious arguments of a few years ago, he still honoured with the title 'Winston'. Winston had tried to claim that HG had changed his mind about Bolshevik Russia. He could easily defend himself against such distortion. Furthermore Churchill also made the charge that 'Wells's League of Nations would involve placing the British Empire under the control of Belgians, Chinese, Peruvians, Hottentots etc. In this sublime conception, the British inheritance accumulated by the thrift and effort of so many centuries would be liquidated and generously shared with all nations.' But HG put him right as gently as possible: 'The present British Empire is not an inheritance but a series of – shall we say – acquisitions. What is the use of canting in the face of facts? We didn't save up India; Australia wasn't the reward of abstinence.' But, if his angry wisdom could be stirred by the old imperialists, he was roused no less by the 'Elder spinsters of the Labour Party'. Their failure even to make an attempt to keep up with the times was even more inexcusable. At first it looked like a contest between age and youth; between 'Mr Ramsay MacDonald's gentility, his fine old-fashioned statesmanlike evasiveness' and the women who had set out to lead their party against the blushingly tactful Elder Spinsters:

> These younger women believe that women really are responsible citizens, that democracy does mean treating adults with respect instead of concealing anything that matters most to them from them; that women ought to know what marriage means for them and how motherhood may be undertaken or declined before diseases and children and suchlike intense and overwhelming things blot out their youth and health.

No-one could question how deep were his feelings on these subjects about which he had been arguing all his adult life. So it is not difficult to gauge the fury which he felt when he discovered that the newly elected Labour government in the person of its supposedly Socialist Minister of Health, Mr John Wheatley, proposed to bow to the pressures from the Roman Catholic Church and let that church decide 'what the poor Protestant woman shall know and do'. He was horrified that a Labour minister intended to sustain this state of ignorance as eagerly as the most extreme Tory. He could not believe it would last: 'When women fought for votes they fought for a symbol; the reality was the possession of themselves.' And then his anger rose to a fresh legitimate pitch.

> Most politicians have still to learn the significance of the women's vote. Because one or two pretty ladies on the Labour side have lost their heads, adorned themselves in trains and ostrich feathers, given themselves over to the photographers and interviewers, and succumbed to the delightful temptation of patronising the Queen, it does not follow that the mass of Labour women are not intensely sane and realise sexual questions are coming into politics, and they are coming to stay. Before the next election every parliamentary

candidate will have to make up his mind whether he stands for knowledge or ignorance in this matter.

That piece, entitled 'The Serfdom of Ignorance', was published on 7 June 1924. Even in 1995, the world has not quite caught up with him, and 'serfdom' still retains its force as the right word.

On some other great matters, he was easily enraged, and both the strength of his conviction and the particular targets for his attacks retained a long-term significance. He had remarked before on the particularly odious kind of organized terror which was shaping politics in Italy. Then came the seizure of power by Mussolini and his organized thugs. Gradually, much too gradually, but still better late than never, the world was awakening to the infernal vileness of a thing that had been plainly before its eyes for years. And then came the murder of Giacomo Matteotti, Mussolini's chief Socialist opponent, and HG innocently thought that a real awakening had come: 'Even the London *Times* has published a leading article that seems to hint at a faint reluctant perception that the Italian dictator is remotely connected with the bloody filthy terrorism on which his power rests.' That article was written on 12 July 1924. Whole aeons were still to pass before what HG called then 'the public conscience of Europe' did awake. A host of leading public figures, including Churchill himself, would combine to stifle it, but it was HG's original judgement which eventually prevailed.

Several of his prophecies – several of his books and increasingly so in the 1920s and 1930s – seemed to have been made in pairs, one foretelling what a doom would await the human race if we continued the practice which had led to 1914, the other offering the prospect, as he had done in the peroration which concluded *The Outline of History*, of how man, the student-teacher of the universe, would reach out to conquer the stars. He might easily contradict himself on these mightiest matters and, when he did so, the growing army of opponents, intellectual and otherwise, which he was mobilizing was sure to pounce, to destroy him, if they could. Often he was too proud to answer, too eager to proceed to the next argument, too resolved to pose the next lesson before the last one was accepted, having grown rich and prosperous much too fast for his own weak character to contend with such trials.

It would be absurd to claim that such charges never had any foundation; he himself might make some of the confessions before his accusers got to work. But what he could fairly protest about was the charge of dishonest or slipshod thinking when he was in fact facing the most awkward questions most intelligently. Similar accusations used to be made against William Hazlitt, when he seemed to write his essays in contradictory pairs, to extol Edmund Burke in one essay and Rousseau in the next, to see all sides of a subject, never for the purpose of searching out a muddled middle ground but rather to force an explosive fusion or an entirely new departure. Indeed, Hazlitt saw how (and was one of the first to remark) it was Shakespeare who achieved 'the combination of the greatest extremes'. The artist must be allowed the fullest latitude in striving for these beautiful syntheses; but, if they failed, they must be allowed to try again. If the political pamphleteer or the novelist tried to combine these greatest themes, he would get no mercy if he himself had been merciless in mounting his own original attacks. Some of these were arguments which remained unresolved at the time of Henry James's death; but, when they re-emerged, HG had his own peculiar interest in them.

Two ambitious books which he wrote in this ambivalent mood – the adjective seems much too restrictive in 1921–2 – were Men Like Gods written just after The Outline and The Dream, published two years later. Men like Gods gained an immediate notoriety through its satirical portraits of Arthur Balfour and Winston Churchill. Balfour was an old target of HG's, dating back to the days of The Comet; but Rupert Catskill (Winston Churchill) was selected for treatment, thanks to his leading role in the crusade against what he had called 'the foul baboonery of Bolshevism'. Rupert Catskill was accused of wantonly encouraging death and destruction across the Eastern world, and the term 'Catskill' was not intended to be friendly: cats were HG's favourite animals. Some people at the time (and Churchill's biographer, forty years later) thought the charge was grossly unfair. Throughout all the vicissitudes of the century, Churchill and Wells seemed to preserve a special relationship, a credit to them both. But the Churchill of the early 1920s was Churchill at his worst. He would not act ignobly – that would be too harsh –but he made no effort to exert the magnanimity which he liked to attribute to himself. Not only on the question of the war against Russia, but on the whole range of choices which helped to make a bad peace and prevent the creation of a real League of Nations, he contributed little or nothing to help secure a better policy. 'I swam with the stream,' was his own later confession – a rare occasion but all the more damning when it did happen.

But Rupert Catskill and his blundering associates were not supposed to be allocated so prominent a role – although their antics could still make HG himself smile ten years later. *Men Like Gods* contains some brilliant parodies of Churchillian eloquence along with the exposure of his lapse into his worst imperialist phase and still a touch of HG's own deeper friendship for him: quite a mixture and not an easy one to design. *Men Like Gods* also contained, apart from an early delightful glimpse of an ultra-young Professor Laski preaching pluralistic wisdom at the London School of Economics, an important intervention from a wayward, smiling heroine – no Wellsian Utopia would be complete without her – who appears at appropriate intervals to give the tale a last twist in his hero's favour and even to leave the scent of his favourite white lilies. If his *Time Machine*'s Weena had had such a pretty name as Lychis, all the literary critics would have accepted her charms, and no-one would have questioned the re-creation of Gulliver's Sorrel Nag. And still a proportion would have been kept in all these matters. Nothing could alter the huge commotion which the Great War had caused in HG's world vision and which came near to destroying altogether his valiant optimism. Indeed, for him, in one sense what happened afterwards, after 1918, was even worse: the sabotage of the real chance of peace at the supreme moment – 'Like Tristram Shandy's parish bull – which set about begetting the peace of the world at Versailles'. *

What the world felt like – this was in the war years – what London especially felt like, is re-created in *The Dream*, but by an HG who happily steps down from the corridors of Versailles and Washington and seeks afresh some of those glimpses of innocence. This Dream dares to recall some of the older Wellsian themes and escapades: the insolent cockneys eager to defy the universe; the all-absorbing ecstasies of young love; the immortal love for his father and mother, both the father who understood him and the mother who did not. If he was pot-boiling, it was at least to one of his own recipes, and the mixture on analysis would be found to include a new element: a new woman condemned to endure all the hardships, indignities and ostracisms of single parenthood, and who yet emerges from the trial more radiantly beautiful and independent than ever. No doubt HG underrated the hardships, both physical and mental, which Rebecca had been compelled to endure, but he still celebrated better than anyone else her resilience and her wit.

If *Men Like Gods* and *The Dream* were two real triumphs for which proper recognition was denied him by political spite or jealousy, he did deserve failure in some other instances, although he himself was loath to accept it. *The Secret Places of the Heart*, published in 1922, was one of these: Sir Richmond Hardy, the more than slightly pompous hero, was rebuked; he was 'not a dear, like Kipps', HG himself was told, and certainly that was true, but this joking with which HG turned aside the criticism was not enough. *The Secret Places* did have its redeeming moments: 'The shadow of Martin stood over him inexorable.' She for sure was Rebecca at her inexorable best. She

---

* Much the best account of *Men Like Gods* appeared in John Hammond's *HG Wells and the Modern Novel* (1988). He gives the subtitle: *The End of Innocence*. And so it was; HG never lost his understanding of the scale of the catastrophe and the small minds of the political leaders who seemed ready to tolerate a new one. Here, too, in *Men Like Gods* was the new Wellsian Utopia with all modern conveniences and many previous prospective horrors removed.

upbraided him above all else for the pitiably inadequate quality of his love:

> Your love has never been a steadfast thing. It comes and goes – like the wind. You are an extravagantly imperfect lover. But I have learnt to accept you, as people accept the English weather . . . Never in the whole of your life have you loved, wholly, fully, steadfastly – as people deserve to be loved; not your mother, not your father, not your wife nor your children, nor me, nor your child, nor any living thing . . . You do not even love this work of yours steadfastly, this work to which you sacrifice us all in turn. You do not love enough. That is why you have these moods and changes, that is why you have these lassitudes. So it is you are made . . .

Sir Richmond did not quite give up then, although he ought to have done. Perfect love indeed. 'But is there such a thing as perfect love? Is *yours* a perfect love, my dear Rebecca, with its insatiable jealousy, its ruthless criticism? Has the world ever seen a perfect lover yet?' Some part of the momentous quarrel between HG and Rebecca was described in *The Secret Places*, and Rebecca certainly did not come off second best:

> The image of Martin became very vivid in his mind. He thought of her, as he had seen her many times, with the tears close, fighting with her back to the wall, with all her wit and vigour gone, because she loved him more steadfastly than he did her . . . Was it Martin who failed him or he who failed Martin? Not much doubt about the answer to that question either; he should face it.

Whatever else *The Secret Places* was, it was an honest account of a Homeric quarrel, with Rebecca as a reluctantly rebellious Helen: 'For me, too, waste and ruin. I shall be a woman fought over. I shall be fought over as dogs fight over a bone. I shall sink back to the level of Helen of Troy. I shall cease to be a free citizen, a responsible free person . . . We shall just be another romantic story . . . No!'*

* *The Secret Places of the Heart* (1922), pp. 243–50.

The other book which adds a few strokes to the already stunning portraits which he had drawn to show how Rebecca appeared to him, and to anyone else who had the luck to set eyes on her, was *The World of William Clissold*, published in 1926. *Clissold* had many deficiencies, as even HG himself might be ready to admit: the book purported to cover the whole political-cum-philosophical waterfront. It was not tedious; considering his huge output, few of his novels were. He might fall out of fashion, and then fall back in again. But Rebecca could come to his rescue. She certainly came to the rescue of William Clissold, even if she had to be relinquished later.

This story I have to tell about myself and Helen is, I perceive, an experience different in kind from any other love affair in which I was ever involved. It is too recent for me to write about yet with complete detachment. In a sense Helen has been exorcised here in Provence; I can hardly trace how; but the scars are fresh and plain. The essence of every great passion is by its nature a thing untellable. We do not tell our love experiences; at best we tell things about them. Only the reader who was in love with Helen could see her as I saw her. For other people she was a strong, clever, ambitious actress with a charming smile, an adorable voice, a reputation for a hot temper, and an ungracious way with obtrusive admirers. Many people found her beautiful, but no one called her pretty. She was a mistress to be proud of, but only a brave man would attempt to steal her. For me she was wonderful and mystical; she was beautiful and lovely for me, as no human being has ever been; she had in my perception of her a distinctive personal splendour that was as entirely and inseparably her own as the line of her neck or the timbre of her voice. There was a sideways glance over her shoulder full of challenge; there were certain intonations, there was a peculiar softness of her profile when it was three-quarters turned away, that gave me an unanalysable delight. My passion was made up of such things. If that explains nothing, then there is nothing that can be explained.

We met before the end of the war, and then she was a comparatively unknown young woman, very fearless, and quite prepared to be interested and excited by a man of my standing and reputation. She fell in love with me and I with her, and I ceased to trouble myself about any other woman. We loved romantically, ostentatiously. Hitherto, she had despised her suitors. We became lovers, friends, allies and companions. For a time I was very happy again. I immersed myself in the reconstruction movement, and I spent all the time I could spare and refreshed myself greatly with her. She, too, was busy with her profession; she was doing fine work and becoming well-known, and almost from the first we had to fit our times rather carefully to get together as we did. But to begin with we did not mind that trouble.

I have been writing of the equal woman as an ideal. In Helen I met her. In the early days we were equal and proud to the swaggering pitch. But unless the proud and equal woman travels an identical road, how is one to keep her?

Neither Helen nor I need to be pitied as those others who are weaker and less coherent are to be pitied; both of us have something in us that sustains us and at last takes us out of all such distresses. At an early limit we grow exasperated, damn the jig-saw puzzle, and sweep it out of the way. The jig-saw puzzle is not a primary thing with us. We are more wilful and more strongly individualised than the common run of people. I have my philosophy of life, my faith, my religion, and she has the compelling impulse of her art.

A great actress is not the feminine equivalent of a great actor; being a great actress is not the same thing as acting; it is a thing peculiar to womankind. It is the sedulous development of a personality of superb proportions. *

That was HG writing about Rebecca fourteen years after she had come to Easton Glebe. No animosity in his feelings about her seemed to have developed – at least, nothing which counted against the original vision. She, too, wrote about him in a manner which showed how deep and indelible was the love and admiration, the two merging into one another, which he had aroused. A sentence appeared in a particular essay in a particular

* The World of William Clissold (1926), vol. 3, pp. 549, 815–16.

book where, most notably the essays later comprised in *The Young Rebecca*, she felt she could unloose her wit without restraint. She wrote an essay called 'Uncle Bennett' in which she put all those uncles in their particular places. But, first, before the interment of any of them, she described in language which no-one else could match what the appearance of HG on the scene throughout a whole epoch meant for young England in general and young Rebecca in particular: 'This impression of wild and surpassing generosity was not in the least one of youth's illusions. One had, in actual fact, the luck to be young just as the most bubbling creative mind that the sun and moon have shone upon since the days of Leonardo da Vinci, was showing its form.'*

Such a sentence should be left without any embellishment whatever. The HG she acclaimed was, first, the creator of *Mr Polly*, *Tono-Bungay*, and *The New Machiavelli* before she herself secured the banishment of the Marjorie Popes and their replacement by a range of Rebeccas, not so exquisite as Rebecca herself, but not bad imitations, culminating anyhow in Helen of *William Clissold*. Clissold at least was not much good before he met her and nothing like as good after they parted. And yet it must be noted again that, on HG's own insistence, neither in his own books nor in hers, did they capture 'the peculiar wit that made her companionship at its best the warmest, liveliest and most irreplaceable of fellowships . . . She went across life in the same sweeping fashion. She was a great invention. And none of it was ever written down, alas. Most of the fun in Rebecca is lost for ever.'†

How the impediments between these true minds developed is usually traced back to the last months of 1920 when she was writing her novel *The Judge*, and he was compiling his *Outline of History* instead of seeking to produce, as she thought he should, a new work of literature. All his facilities for doing his work were assembled at Easton Glebe, under Jane's supervision, and he seemed to have no idea that Rebecca needed economic security as much as he did himself to enable her to write. She, like many

* Rebecca West, *The Strange Necessity* (Viking, 1987), p. 119.
† *H. G. Wells in Love*, p. 112.

women writers, cried out for a Jane, too. As the months passed, he wrote: 'She came to hate *The Outline of History* almost as much as she hated Jane.' They tried a holiday of reparation in Italy in the winter of 1922 when they walked, argued, made love, but still renewed the quarrel about their writing. 'I was writing *The Secret Places of the Heart* at her', he recorded. And he missed! Or, rather, he gave her a good case against him. Martin Leeds is to be preferred to Sir Richmond Hardy any day or night. And there did develop an intellectual as well as an emotional conflict between them. She was appreciating better than he the real rising stars in the literary firmament – James Joyce and D. H. Lawrence – and if she trained her critical fire she seldom mistook the target; *she* would never miss.

She was making herself into one of the most formidable literary critics of the century, successfully revitalizing the young Rebecca for this purpose – an art which he never mastered, despite his own writings on Joyce, partly on her encouragement – while he thought for a while at least that she was misdirecting her talents. And, as the sympathies between them became strained, each found they could turn elsewhere. Rebecca had been shocked by his report about Moura from Moscow, but she herself developed, a good deal more gradually, an association with Max Aitken, Lord Beaverbrook, the young minister in the Lloyd George government who had, along with Northcliffe, invited HG to assist them at the short-lived Ministry of Information. She did not suddenly lose her love and admiration for HG – she never did – but there was a decline in her passionate attachment. Similarly, the affair with Beaverbrook did not come suddenly. Both processes and the comparative qualities and frailties of both her suitors were admirably described in the book she wrote at the time or soon afterwards but never published in all their lifetimes. *

* *Sunflower* was published by Virago in 1985, after Rebecca's own death. It contains, apart from anything else, an excellent expository epilogue by Victoria Glendinning. She quotes Rebecca writing to a friend, after her first meeting with Beaverbrook in 1920, how she still preferred Wells to all other men, but had this to say about Beaverbrook: 'I found him one of the most fascinating talkers I've ever met and full of real vitality – the genius kind that exists mystically apart from all physical conditions, just as it does with H. G.'

She would choose, when she was on the warpath, to deal with other miscreants of the male sex. As for Beaverbrook, he and his friends (and he did retain a few, some of them women) would have read *Sunflower* as any man would with a glowing excitement. HG could be jealous, and he no doubt would have been if he had read the whole story. Another ironic aspect of the situation is that HG would often upbraid Rebecca for her outbursts of jealousy, sudden or sustained. But let us adjust the balance once more. No other two writers of comparable literary stature in our liberated century have had the taste and opportunity to let loose their fusillades against each other, and the miracle is not merely that they both survive but they both still live now, triumphantly, for those who will read: the Marie of *The Passionate Friends* or the Joan of *Joan and Peter* or the Fanny of *The Dream* or the Helen of *William Clissold* – all passionate exponents of the feminist cause, by the way, despite HG's own lapses on this test – and he himself, on the other side, drawn by Rebecca, the new Leonardo who sought to expound and integrate all forms of knowledge.

This was the period especially when HG had strayed from the artistic path, and gone whoring after the false gods of journalism and popular appeal. Perhaps we may blame *William Clissold* for this malign suggestion. He had obviously made a superhuman effort to comprehend everything in one story, but even with Rebecca's dazzling appearance the book was a failure. However, as usual with him, if so rarely with the rest of the human race, he found a host of other interests. He started to set in motion two projects to be placed alongside his outstandingly successful *Outline of History*, one an outline of scientific knowledge and the other an outline of the field of human knowledge covering economics and wealth creation. The working titles for these projects changed over the next few years, and he could not conceivably consider writing as much for these volumes as he had for the original *Outline*. But, still, both the idea and the achievement were prodigious. And in the years while this work went ahead he wrote three other novels: *Christina Alberta's Father* (1925), *Meanwhile* (1927), *Mr Blettsworthy on Rampole Island* (1928).

Each of these showed him in a very different world, but no-one should accuse him of a weakening in his readiness to face new problems or, more difficult, to revise his own judgements, if developments in the world required. *Christina Alberta's Father* is suffused with a father's love and understanding for his child, the emotion which Rebecca especially detected and appreciated in *The Passionate Friends*. Yet Christina Alberta more than holds her own and emerges as a new Wellsian heroine all on her own. Of course, she has a dash of Rebecca herself in her make-up, but her inelegant nose and faint tomboyish manner exclude any exact identification. She represents – and most gallantly, too – a new woman of the 1920s who was learning and teaching a new brand of independence. Christina Alberta's slightly nonplussed suitor began to see a new world: 'Now that he began to understand her he began to understand a great number of bright-eyed, adventurous, difficult young women he had met in the last few years, and he had his first dim realization of the meaning of the deep wide stir among women of that kind that had won them votes and a score of unprecedented freedoms.'* So HG was learning that, too.

Meanwhile was not quite in the *Christina Alberta* class. It sought to present an argument about the industrial crisis which gripped Britain in 1926, but the Swiss lakeside retreat where the novel was staged was not the best vantage-place from which to see it. However, he did seize the chance to renew his attack on the developments in Mussolini's Italy. *Mr Blettsworthy on Rampole Island* deserves to rank with the writings which contain the most mature of political judgements, especially since the moment when it was written was one in which the world prospect began to look more settled. It was a fantasy generated rather by his pessimism, applying his Voltairean model and mood with devastating emphasis. His sense of pain, his fear of men's cruelty, could suddenly take command. 'Excruciating pain runs through that admirable late work,' wrote V. S. Pritchett; it was one of the main works which he cited as the

---

* *Christina Albert's Father* (1925), p. 406.

disproof that HG's genius had faded or, even less forgivably, that his sense of outrage, when confronted by infamy, had somehow diminished.* It never did.

Each of these volumes, written in the late 1920s, made a distinctive Wellsian contribution to the worldwide debate, which he was enabled to carry in person to the Sorbonne in Paris where he lectured in 1927, or the Reichstag in Berlin where he lectured in 1929. He published also in 1928 *The Open Conspiracy*, which formed in a sense the subject of both these lectures and in which the contradictions in his political thought, noted before, are compressed into the phrase itself. His idea of democracy was much more ambitious than most of its prac-titioners had ever dreamed of before; he was against all censorships, curtailments, proscriptions; and yet, no less insistently, he demanded swift, worldwide action, if the world itself was not to be destroyed. If he himself never solved the dilemma, and if in the process he appeared to injure, as he often did, either his claims as a democrat or his recognition of the realities of politics, he himself, at this particular period, the late 1920s and the early 1930s, had a particular defence. He was saying more clearly than anyone else what was needed to stop the next war; indeed, he had been saying most of it since the tragic failures of 1918 and 1920, and saying it with the aid of every art or device known to him.

Another argument, normally conducted on both sides with a genuine bonhomie, suddenly broke into something fiercer. Many observers forgot that, whatever their differences, G. K. Chesterton and Hilaire Belloc had mostly been on the same side in most debates. 'These two', wrote HG at an earlier stage, 'say Socialism is a thing they do not want for men, and I say Socialism is above all what I want for men. We shall go on saying that now to the end of our days.' Of course, that word and the interpretation of its real significance was a tremendous question. But HG continued in the pre-1914 argument: 'We all three hate

* V. S. Pritchett, 'Wells Marches On', *New Statesman*, 23 September 1966.

equally and sympathetically the spectacle of human beings blown up with windy wealth and irresponsible power as cruelly and absurdly as boys blow up frogs; we all three detest the complex causes that dwarf and cripple lives from the moment of birth, and starve and debase great masses of mankind.'* And then HG went on to elaborate, in that pre-1914 discussion, why state Socialism was not the only way of securing essential collective action. But in the mid-1920s these affable exchanges were completely dwarfed by the attack which Hilaire Belloc in particular launched against *The Outline of History.*

Of course, such a counter-attack was to be expected. *The Outline* was one of the most formidable critiques, not merely of the Roman Catholic church and its history, but of fundamentalist religion in general. In popular terms perhaps, it was the most comprehensive assault ever delivered. So HG must have expected a counter-attack; in one sense he had provided for it in his elaborate footnotes. What he could hardly have expected, and what he certainly resented, was the tone of academic condescension in which Belloc delivered his verdict. What more could be expected from such a provincial mind reared in some London suburb which could not be expected to have instructed its sons in the great tradition of European culture? If Belloc did not state his whole argument thus, this was the tone. HG did feel deeply insulted, especially since he had taken such pains to study the great historians. Moreover, there was no such object as the general culture which he was accused of disregarding. The historian who more than any other had sought and nearly succeeded in presenting a period which covered the Christian epoch as one spacious tapestry which still held together all the individual strands was Edward Gibbon. HG had been studying him ever since his first readings of the epic in the Up Park attic. And one essential strand in his thought was his scepticism: without that indispensable link, he could never have held his work together. HG had taken a good model to guide him; some might say the greatest historian who had

* *Social Forces in England and America* (1914), p. 257.

written in English and certainly more likely to offer good guidance than the unsung, unnamed chroniclers of Roman Catholicism – perhaps the very same who placed the essays of Montaigne on the Papal Index or the prosecutors of Galileo. Roman Catholic apologists had never been shiningly successful when they chose to fight on the battlefield of free speech and free printing, and Hilaire Belloc was no more successful than his predecessors. As for HG's upbringing in 'home counties and London suburbs', it was too late for him to attempt any remedy there; he could only express his envy for Mr Belloc 'who it seems was born all over Europe'. *

The World of William Clissold is dedicated to Odette Keun, was written at the French home near Grasse which he shared with her, and was published in 1926, a year in English history famous or infamous for reasons entirely different from anything to do with them. Maybe this combination of circumstances is responsible for its comparative failure. Yet, without *Clissold*, we might not have had Rebecca at very near her incomparable best – at least, in HG's presentation.

* *Mr Belloc Objects to 'The Outline of History'* (1926), p. 4.
It would be sad if it were thought that the whole Wells–Chesterton friendship ended on this note. Lovat Dickson in his biography used a real exchange between them as an epigraph:

H. G. WELLS TO G. K. CHESTERTON
(1933)
'If after all my Atheology turns out wrong and your Theology right, I feel I shall always be able to pass into Heaven (if I want to) as a friend of G.K.C's. Bless you.'

G. K. CHESTERTON TO H. G. WELLS
(In Reply)
'As to the fine point of theology you mention. If I turn out to be right, you will triumph, not by being a friend of mine, but a friend of Man, for having done a thousand things for men like me in every way, from imagination to criticism. The thought of the vast variety of that work, and how it ranges from towering visions to tiny pricks of humour, overwhelmed me suddenly...'

Originally, Odette got him on something like a rebound from Rebecca: 'In form, she gave: in effect, she grabbed.' That summary of the relationship which he later elaborated on a series of occasions placed that affair in a quite different category from all the others and injured the work in progress. Did his conscience prick him with a rare kind of double incision? The storms of industrial strife, first in the coalfields and then in the General Strike, were shaking the whole country, and he was far away. Moreoever, he had lost the companionship of Rebecca, who would certainly have shared his interest in those mighty events; and, whatever substitute Odette might be, she was developed from a different species altogether.

If he could not describe his relations with women with all the candour which he thought the subject deserved, he certainly made a huge effort in that direction. The more honest the exposition, the better: that was his creed, and he stuck to it, even when describing his humiliations at the hands of Odette. And he would not deny her her best moments such as the uproarious one when she castigated a Tory Home Secretary, Joynson-Hicks, the most strait-laced of the century, for his failure to fold Radclyffe Hall, author of *The Well of Loneliness*, to his bosom. Sometimes, as we have seen, he would refer some of man's or woman's sexual escapades at the height of crisis to what he called the Assize of Jealousy. It was not always clear who was the prosecutor and what happened to the defendants, or what was his own final verdict on all these fascinating complexities.

Early in 1927, he received an invitation to lecture at the Sorbonne in Paris, and he despatched a happy message to Jane at Easton Glebe to come over and join him. He was a world figure in Paris as he had been in Washington, and they both greatly enjoyed being fêted. He drew one of his old picshuas for Jane: 'Democracy under Revision – Marianne asks Dadda to tell her all about it!' Considering how sharp and persistent he had been in criticism of post-1918 French policy, it was all the more generous that they should have given him such a welcome and such a platform.

He expressed his thanks in glowing language: 'France, the

custodian of the world's artistic conscience, the exponent of intellectual freedom, the mighty mother of valiant and liberal thought for all mankind.' He meant every word of it, especially at the Sorbonne, 'a very magical name to every intellectual worker'.

He was still proud to call himself a journalist, although he was inspired especially in such a company and such a place to describe how the democratic spirit had found its natural vehicle in the novel – 'the great master, Cervantes with his Don Quixote, scoffing at aristocracy, scoffing at privileged responsi-bility, mocking the final futility of chivalrous mastery, putting his wisest words into the mouth of a clown and letting the flourmills of the common bread-eater overthrow his knight in armour'. Jane, at his side, could share that particular triumph, as she had many others before, despite all the breaches and estrangements between them.

She returned to Easton Glebe; he went back to Grasse; but, within a few days, quite out of a clear sky, came the news from their younger son Frank that Jane had cancer and that the doctor's report could hardly be more serious. He came back at once, and stayed the next six months at Easton Glebe, watching her die but lost in admiration, as they all were, for the courage with which she did it. A curious by-product of this news was a renewal of the old oft-broken but oft-repaired friendship with Bernard Shaw and Charlotte. Charlotte especially wrote as if any idea of political disagreement between them counted for nothing beside their friendship. Shaw seized the occasion to write a loving but none the less tactless letter about doctors and how unwise it would be for HG to take their advice too uncritically in the case of Jane. Charlotte saw the peril and pleaded with him not to send it. But Shaw persisted. Charlotte sent a covering letter: 'He is very fond of you and Jane: I do think you are our most special friends and G.B.S. is really worrying about you both dreadfully just now and would do anything in his power to help. Then – by some evil fate he is impelled to do what I fear has hurt you.'* She pleaded for a reply which, it seems, was

* *Bernard Shaw Collected Letters*, vol. 4, *1926–1950*, ed. Dan H. Laurence (1988), pp. 60–1.

never sent. Events overtook them. But Charlotte had shown a real discernment: despite all their quarrels, which were certainly not yet at an end, there was a deep sympathy between them. They had both been wedded in their youth to a dream of Socialism, and they were not prepared to see that destroyed.

When the day of Jane's death came, he wrote a most moving address spoken just before the cremation. 'Hers was a life freed from all supernatural terrors and superstitious illusions . . . It was said that there was much wisdom and comfort for us in these words of Spinoza: "The free man thinks of nothing so little as of death and his wisdom is a meditation not upon death but upon life." ' She was truly 'great minded', as he described her in that same address. Nothing that was said was untrue, and everything that was said was to her honour. And he soon compiled thereafter *The Book of Catherine Wells*, in which his introduction movingly described the events leading to her death, and which reproduced several of her own writings, short stories and poems, some of which he himself had never seen before. *

A few of these re-created moods must have shaken his whole being. Some of the poems expressed the anguish he had caused her; and, if she had never told him before, she told him now. She put the case against him more sharply than anyone else. If he had not been honest, he could have conducted a suppression, there and then. Instead, she had the last word. She, like him, loved gardens and Chopin, and she combined the two:

> The garden of the roses
> Is loveliest at night,
> When the red are like black shadows
> The white ones still more white.
> In the garden of the roses;
> A woman walks alone;
> She listens for a footstep,
> Knowing it will not come.

* *The Book of Catherine Wells* (1928), p. 256.

Whatever his shortcomings as a husband, some compensation was offered as a father. All his children, legitimate and illegitimate, came to love him. They were all favoured, like his lovers, not only with loving letters, but with the even more entrancing pictures which came with them. He was a wonderful natural teacher himself, and naturally wanted all his brood to share all these good things which his mother and family had been so shamefully denied, and which he and Jane had had to skimp and scrape for in their arduous young days. He didn't want any future generation to suffer what they had. His idea was that the human race could put behind it all the remnants of that cringing, parsimonious age. Of course, it was much easier for him, the father who had suddenly come into wealth beyond the dreams of avarice, as he described it, to lead his children on reckless spending escapades than the hard-working, home-loving mothers: easier for him than for Jane or, most certainly, Rebecca. But still these qualifications should not be allowed to shake the earlier claim: HG could excite and enlighten his own children just as he had sought to instruct a whole earlier generation. He had taught his Hugh Britling how to soak himself in Tristram Shandy or to turn aside to Heinrich Heine's *Florentine Nights*; or, maybe, he in turn had been prepared to learn from his Joan, his Rebecca, how he should accustom himself to hear and appreciate the new voices.

It would have been high treason to his own heretical faith if he had not tried to listen with a special care to those who had something important to say in what might have seemed to him a strange way of saying it. When he had appeared to lapse from his standard of tolerance, Rebecca had rebuked him; and remonstrances from that quarter, kindly or caustic, could still smart more than from anybody else. It was partly on her urging, through the good offices of Harriet Weaver, that he had been persuaded to write his outstanding review of A *Portrait of the Artist as a Young Man* in 1917, and it was this exchange which made him agree to a meeting with Joyce in the late summer of 1928. HG could still bask in the enthusiastic response he had incited at the Sorbonne; he was now the most famous literary figure in the world. James Joyce's fame was of a quite different order: his *Ulysses* was still a banned book across most of the planet. He himself seemed to learn no lesson from this scandalous ostracism; and even some of his modernist friends, like T. S. Eliot and Wyndham Lewis, seemed to be deterred by his latest project, *Work in Progress* which would later see the light of day or, rather, attract even darker denunciations, when it appeared as *Finnegans Wake*. But the meeting in Paris was a happy one for the two writers or, we should immediately add, for the world at large. After their meeting, HG wrote a letter to which he had obviously given deep thought. One or two sentences have sometimes been extracted from it to try to prove that any meeting-point about Joyce was beyond the Wellsian comprehension. The whole letter tells a quite different story.

My dear Joyce,

I've been studying you and thinking over you a lot. The outcome is that I don't think I can do anything for the propaganda of your work. I've an enormous respect for your genius dating from your earliest books and I feel now a great personal liking for you but you and I are set upon absolutely different courses. Your training has been Catholic, Irish, insurrectionary; mine, such as it was, was scientific, constructive and, I suppose, English. The frame of my mind is a world wherein a big unifying and concentrating process is possible (increase of power and range of economy and concentration of effort), a progress not inevitable but interesting and possible. That game attracted and holds me. For it, I want language and statement as simple and clear as possible. You began Catholic, that is to say you began with a system of values in stark opposition to reality. Your mental existence is obsessed by a monstrous system of contradictions. You really believe in chastity, purity and the personal God and that is why you are always breaking out into cries of cunt, shit and hell. As I don't believe in these things except as quite provincial values my mind has never been shocked to outcries by the existence of waterclosets and menstrual bandages – and undeserved misfortunes. And while you were brought up under the delusion of political suppression I was brought up under the delusion of political responsibility. It seems a fine thing for you to defy and break up: To me not in the least.

Now with regard to this literary experiment of yours. It's a considerable thing because you are a very considerable man and you have in your crowded composition a mighty genius for expression which has escaped discipline. But I don't think it gets anywhere. You have turned your back on common men, on their elementary needs and their restricted time and intelligence and you have elaborated. What is the result? Vast riddles. Your last two works have been more amusing and exciting to write than they will ever be to read. Take me as a typical common reader. Do I get much pleasure from this work? No. Do I feel I am getting something new and illuminating as I do when I read Anrep's dreadful translation of Pavlov's badly written book on Conditional Reflexes? No. So I ask: Who the hell is this Joyce who demands so many waking hours of the few thousands I have still to live for a proper appreciation of his quirks and fancies and flashes of rendering?

All this from my point of view. Perhaps you are right and I am all wrong. Your work is an extraordinary experiment and I would go out of my way to save it from destruction or restrictive interruption. It has its believers and its following. Let them rejoice in it. To me it is a dead end.

My warmest good wishes to you Joyce. I can't follow your banner any more than you can follow mine. But the world is wide and there is room for both of us to be wrong.

Yours,
H. G. Wells[*]

Joyce was greatly encouraged, even excited, by such a letter, as well he might be. He certainly would not accept several of the individual criticisms – in particular, the claim that language was fixed or exclusively national. But he could draw more encouragement from HG's still small voice, if we may use a musical term, than from Ezra Pound's 'big brass band' to which he was customarily allotted. As for the argument on HG's side, he could not help reaching the

[*] The whole letter was printed in Richard Ellman's *James Joyce*, pp. 607–9.

conclusion that Joyce, with all his greatness, was turning his back on the common man; and that, for him, if there had been such a spectre, was the sin against the Holy Ghost. And how much, if he had had the chance, he would have loved to have welcomed Joyce in that crusade with his fellow Irish campaigners-cum-artists.

Several of HG's writings and lectures at the time – in the late 1920s and early 1930s – revolved around his individual interpretation of the word 'democracy'. He understood how the revolutionary tradition had developed in his own Miltonic England, or in Voltaire's France, or in Thomas Paine's or Thomas Jefferson's America. But when he came nearer to modern times, and felt called upon to examine the achievements of modern forms of government, including parliamentary government, he thought that the performance was pitiable, indefensible. He was often quoted, and more often misquoted, as having been tempted himself, in his frustration, to follow the Fascist or some other false gods which appeared on the scene. This was a wretched misapprehension or a calculated calumny – especially so since, as we have seen, he was among the first to denounce Mussolini's rise to power in Italy when others such as Bernard Shaw on the Left or Churchill on the Right were still deceiving themselves about its real nature. Where the new Wellsian prescriptions for the salvation of mankind did not seem to improve on what he had projected before was his definition of the Samurai, the effective receivers, the new administrators required to take over the operation. And his failure was not for want of trying, which seemed to make it all the worse.

Confronted with such problems of misinterpretation or worse, the best corrective is to turn to what he himself wrote: the general declaration which he published under the title *The Open Conspiracy* in 1928, and then the two further *Outlines* which he was working on at the time. He had first mentioned the idea, as we noted, at the end of *The Passionate Friends*, published in 1912. He constantly returned to it, and even after the publication, on both sides of the Atlantic, in

1928, would seek republication in one form or another, to offer further clarification; but, whether the 1928 version or its later variations are relied upon, *The Open Conspiracy*, as presented by himself, still offers his original thought on a whole range of themes.

'We do not give our children a chance of discovering that they live in a world of universal change.' He proposed his own remedy that would accept 'the immense necessities that now challenge us'. It was 'the Great War' and all its accompaniments and consequences which had brought it home to him. He wrote of 'a great dispersed crowd of ordinary people, all wanting to know, all disgusted with the patriotic, litigious, twaddling, gossiping stuff given them as history' which persuaded him to produce first his *Outline* and then the others. He wanted something sound and comprehensive for the future – an 'ideology', as people say. Not enough people had seemed to understand that the 'knowledge of today is the ignorance of tomorrow'. Each fresh development of religion in the world had so far been proclaimed in perfect good faith as the culmination and final truth. But that conception is the enemy of truth: 'A lucid, dispassionate and immanent criticism is the primary necessity, the living spirit of a world civilisation.' And, if this scepticism was properly implanted in our hearts and minds, we should know also who and what are our enemies. 'Our antagonists are confusion of mind, want of courage, want of curiosity and want of imagination, indolence and spendthrift egotism. These are the enemies against which the open conspiracy arrays itself: these are the jailers of human freedom and achievement.'

Let them look to the next essential steps. 'Flags, uniforms, national anthems, patriotism sedulously cultivated in church and school, the brag, blare and bluster of competing sovereignties, belong to the phase which the Open Conspiracy will supersede. We have to get clear of that clutter. Especially as the European disease had crossed the Atlantic. America for example – both on its Latin and on its English speaking side – is in many ways a triumph of the old order over the new. Men like Winwood Reade thought the new world would be indeed a new world. They idealised its apparent emancipations.' HG himself and a few others since have indulged in that same idealization. Yet, this edition of *The Open Conspiracy* – or, rather, we write more generally, the HG of those times – struggled at the same time, in the same synthesis, to face the facts about what was happening in the new America, but not to stifle the hope of a new emancipation. And he could show himself equally wise and imaginative in his estimate of some other conflicts where his critics or enemies might allege that he was blinded by his old prejudice against Karl Marx. He did understand the tumults which were developing in the industrial world. 'Once the horrors of subjection produced only a fatalistic acquiescence. An objection to direction and obligation, always mutely present in the toiling multitudes since the economic life of man began, becomes articulate and active. It is the taste of freedom that makes labour desire to be free.' Yes, and it was the ruling class in England which had originally prosecuted that struggle with such relentless zeal:

The class war was invented by the classes; it is a natural tradition of the upper strata of the old order. It was so universally understood that there was no need to state it. It is implicit in nearly all the literature of the world before the nineteenth century, except the Bible, the Koran and other sequelae. The 'class war' of the Marxists is merely a poor, snobbish imitation, a *tu quoque*, a pathetic, stupid, indignant reversal of retort to the old arrogance, a pathetic upward arrogance . . .

Of course, the Marxists of almost every brand hated these strictures – the nearer the bone, the more they hurt – but the author seemed only to be incited to deliver braver and larger speculations which could hurt the dogmatists even more.

It is no small part of the practical weakness of present day Communism that it attempts to centre its intellectual life and its directive activity in Moscow, and so cuts itself off from the free and open discussions of the

219

Western world. Marxism lost the world when it went to Moscow and took over the traditions of Tsarism as Christianity lost the world when it went to Rome and took over the traditions of Caesar.

That deadly sentence might be left to stand on its own, but the deduction also is hardly less prophetic: 'Entrenched in Moscow from searching criticism, the Marxist ideology may become more and more dogmatic and unprogressive, repeating its sacred creeds and issuing its disregarded orders to the proletariat of the world . . .' Bold words indeed, but he would hasten on and expose some other myths, across an even wider world of which he was supposed to know little.

Man interbreeds with all his varieties, and yet deludes himself that there are races of outstanding purity, the 'Nordic', the 'semitic' and so forth. These are phantoms of the imagination. The reality is more intricate, less dramatic, and grips less easily upon the mind: the phantoms grip only too well and can incite to terrible suppressions.

That was the HG who was sometimes so absurdly and monstrously accused of being a racist. He looked to the time when 'the colour of a man's skin or the kink in a woman's hair cease to have the value of shibboleths' – and, maybe, even the use of the Jewish word 'shibboleth' could get him into trouble. He had read at his mother's knee, even if she did not understand, how that discrimination had been enforced. Altogether, he guided that first full expression of his open conspiracy to a tremendous climax.

Our battle is with the cruelties and frustrations, stupid, heavy, and hateful things from which we shall escape at last, less like victors conquering a world than like sleepers awaking from a nightmare in the dawn. The Open Conspiracy is the awakening of mankind from a nightmare, an infantile nightmare, of the struggle for existence and the inevitability of war . . . A time will come when men will sit with history before them, and ask incredulously: 'Was there ever such a world?'

In the spring of 1929 he had another invitation which he felt he could not refuse. Berlin was not Paris, the Reichstag was not the Sorbonne, but the German capital was continuing to play a prominent part, sometimes hopeful, sometimes threatening, in European politics. The invitation to address, not the German Parliament itself, but a literary club which held meetings there came from Antonina Vallentin whom HG had met in London and who was working in the office of Gustav Stresemann, the German Chancellor of the day. She had written a good book about him and she was preparing an even better one – 'a classic', as HG later described it – about Heinrich Heine. Their common interest in Heine was an exciting discovery. HG had long since had his interest in the man awakened; he was accepted as a bigger literary figure in the England of the 1880s and the 1890s than he seemed to become later. Antonina was making herself an expert on the subject, and her book when it appeared four years later had the passionate charm which the subject deserved. Heine dared to call himself a citizen of the world, and the claim could cause offence with his Jewish family in Hamburg or his German tutors in Berlin or even with a few of his new French comrades in Paris. But Heine wrote the best love-lyrics the Germans had ever heard, revolutionary anthems worthy of Shelley, satires fit to take their place beside Byron's *Vision of Judgement*, and still he pleaded to be recognized not as a poet but as a soldier in the campaign for the liberation of humanity. Heinrich Heine was the specimen which Henry James had insisted could not or should not exist, but there he was helping to beckon HG to Berlin. The lecture itself was not such a success. Harold Nicolson, a junior member of the British embassy at that time, reported to his wife, Vita: 'One simply could not hear a word. Not a single word. It was rather a disaster.' Whether this was caused by the Reichstag arrangements or HG's lecturing habits or a combination of the two is not clear. The lecture was published and reads well enough; it was a good German version (actually translated by Antonina) of the Sorbonne exposition of his views about democracy. But two other events of that Berlin expedition put everything else in the shade, then and thereafter. The first was the dinner for Wells at the Adlon Hotel at which Professor Albert Einstein presided. 'He looks', wrote Harold Nicolson, 'like a child who has put on a mask painted like Einstein. He is a darling.' They all had plenty to talk about. Einstein, too, was a lover of Heine as he was a true admirer of HG. And at the lecture itself the other event had occurred which had distracted HG from these delightful compliments. As the lecture audience dispersed Moura had appeared: 'Tall and steady-eyed, shabbily dressed and dignified', she at least had been able to hear: 'Its Moura,' I said. 'Aige-gee,' said she. Next day they met again, and the following evening terminated in her shabby little apartment. He wrote later but he obviously knew then: 'From the moment we met we were lovers, as though there had never been any separation between us. She has always had that unquestionable attraction for me, and unless she is the greatest actress in the world, I have something of the same un-analyzable magic for her'.* Heinrich Heine's last love was unalterably true whatever the tragic or melancholy strands in the previous ones. So it was with HG.

The history of all his open conspirators was the one he had devised for them. More people in that world of the 1920s had read it in the form he had devised than any other. Moreover he had some distinguished readers who would soon be making history as well as reading it – which, of course, had been his favourite dream. One of these was Jawaharlal Nehru, who was, between October 1930 and August 1933, serving sentences in various prisons under the British Raj. Not merely did the Wellsian hand of history give general encouragement to such pupils, but he helped to inspire the chapter which Nehru wrote on 30 March 1932 entitled 'Ashoka, the Beloved of the Gods'. 'From the Volga to Japan, his name is still honoured. China, Tibet, and even India, though it has left his doctrine to preserve the tradition of his greatness. More living men cherish his memory today than have ever heard the names of Constantine or Charlemagne.' High praise indeed, added Nehru, but deserved – 'for an Indian it is an especial pleasure to think of this period of India's history'. Again, high praise: but it is HG with

---

* H. G. *Wells in Love*, p. 140. These words were written four or five years after the event.

his grand conception of world history who has done the most to reawaken, and not merely to preserve, the appreciation of Ashoka. *

The worldwide success of *The Outline* had come as an amazement to HG himself; until it happened, he had thought it impossible. His own main deduction was to produce two more 'Outlines': *The Science of Life*, written with Julian Huxley and his son, GP, published in 1930, and *The Work, Wealth and Happiness of Mankind* published in 1931. He himself thought that these two were just as good, if not better, than the original *Outline*. He was as astonished by their failure as he had been with the earlier success. He had had plenty of practice in taking these twists of fortune. It was said of one of Cromwell's generals – and HG had a real sympathy with them –that he came away from a victory as if it were a defeat, and a defeat as if it were a victory. With HG, this achievement was not a gift of temperamental composure. He could react to events furiously, and his enemies or friends could be shaken by the spectacle. But he often responded to the most wretched setbacks with a tremendous exhilaration and courage, and those who knew and loved him best – Jane, Amber, Rebecca, Moura – could see that, too.

* Jawaharlal Nehru, *Glimpse of World History* (1938). I owe this judgement to Professor Ralph Buultjens of New York University, who guided me back to Nehru's verdict – a most astonishing one on every count. Ashoka's reputation grows steadily, and HG was pointing the way to most of the other scholars.

NINE

The Magnificent Moura

And if she is a creature of impulses, the whole
quality of those impulses is fine and generous.
                    H.G. Wells in Love, p. 116

Writing was his trade. He had made himself an expert
craftsman, almost entirely by his own efforts. So the conditions
in which he was able to write were of capital importance to him
ever since he had acquired the upper room in Mornington Place,
Camden Town, in 1886. Of course he wrote too much, and the
more so in the later years when the offers and temptations
increased so spectacularly. Probably no journalist-cum-fiction-
writer had ever written so much since the days of Daniel Defoe.
And if all the work attributed to Defoe was validated – and most
scholars would question the attribution – HG still wrote more.
Of course, it might have been better if he had stopped or at least
slackened the pace. But if Defoe had followed that advice he
would have stopped before *Moll Flanders*, which HG came to
recognize as one of the masterpieces of that century. Maybe that
recollection, recorded in *Joan and Peter*, also drove him on.

But writing also became for HG the way in which he could

think afresh and discharge the duties to humanity which he also felt so strongly. And for all these reasons the women who best helped him to work might steal or consolidate an advantage over the others. Maybe this requirement in the later years was part of the trouble between him and Rebecca. Two writers under one roof is not the idyll which non-writers sometimes like to suppose. And in this respect HG's demands could become overbearing, if they were not understood and tolerated. Jane understood better than any rival for nearly forty years. Odette knew at Lou Pidou or in Paris, with a few tempestuous interruptions, for seven years, which is even more amazing. Even at the end of that turmoil he was writing, apart from major or minor journalism, what he himself called 'three good books'. And so they were: *The Shape of Things to Come*, *The Autocracy of Mr Parham* and *The Bulpington of Blup*. He had returned to Lou Pidou to complete them. One at least, *The Bulpington*, was dedicated to Odette, 'the critic of the typescript, gratefully bless her'. Good critics of typescripts were not easily acquired or dispensed with.

He had had some memorable nights before, but nothing to surpass the excitement and experience they brought to each other at that Stendhalian chance encounter which still transformed everything when he and Moura met again in Berlin. They did not swear eternal fealty; each might have laughed in the face of the other if they had. Or, rather, he might have asked it of her since, whatever his boasts about his support for equality of the sexes, he still did seem to demand, either in his novels or in real life, that the women should prove themselves more devoted than the men. Apparently, as the delirious days and nights came to an end later than the Reichstag organizers had intended, they exchanged assurances of freedom of action in the weeks, months, years ahead. Who knew when their next meeting would be? And Moura produced the perfect witticism to bring that curtain down – how she could wield that instrument in her own interest: 'Very well, my dear. As you will. If I happen to be faithful to you, that is my own affair.'

He returned to Grasse to take up the tasks which he had laid aside for the Berlin adventure. Apart from anything else, he must complete those three good books. Odette continued to help with them; she had her uses. *The Bulpington* was indeed dedicated to her, as *William Clissold* had been. But the renewed assurance with which he went ahead with these three extra-ordinary diverse projects owed something to the renewed spirit which Moura had given him. *The Shape of Things to Come* was not so unforgettable as its title, but it was an attempt to present in the form of a novel his whole extensive prophecy for the future. *The Autocracy of Mr Parham* was sometimes dismissed as a firework which never exploded; but it is much better than that. Conservative politics in those far-off, futile years of 1929 and 1930 is presented with the touch of a true satirist. *The Bulpington of Blup*, with a quite different hero and no real heroine (at least, none to compare with those when Rebecca was in charge), was aimed at a quite different target, and many readers have remarked how unaccustomed was the kind of success which it achieved. Theodore Bulpington is an aesthetic figure wedded to some Jamesian view of art and modelled on Ford Madox Heuffer, who fails to meet the challenge of the century – that challenge, in HG's eyes, still being the Great War of 1914 and its consequences, which so many of his generation were still shirking or dodging or disguising. The war, the last one or the next one: these were the twin nightmares which still dominated his mind. Theodore Bulpington still dodged those realities, too, whatever esoteric excuses they might devise for claiming that right was on their side. Even the pacifist and political objectors of 1914 might claim to have given a more directly honest answer. That was something for HG to admit. His scorn for them changed, not to an acceptance of their political conclusion but to an acknowledgement that they had given to the challenge a more directly honest answer than the Bulpingtons and all they represented. Of course, HG was influenced by the freshly virulent wave of anti-war feeling which swept across Western Europe – Berlin and Vienna no less than Paris and London – in the late 1920s and early 1930s. The poets and the playwrights were finding their true voices again. But HG had always had his own insights on these greatest questions, and he stuck to them, too.

Moura could talk and argue on all those subjects; she had an illumination of her own. She came to London and paid two visits to Easton Glebe just before he carried through his resolution to sell the place and move to London. One of those visits stood out in the mind of one interested but trustworthy witness – trustworthy rather on this point if on nothing else: the 17-year-old Anthony West. He wrote that he 'could not forget my first breath-taking sight of her as she sat talking to my father . . . Her fatalism enabled her to radiate an immensely reassuring serenity, and her good humour made her a comfortable rather than a disturbing presence.'* All percipient observers who ever set eyes on her were struck by that serenity; she seemed to make her particular form of it a quality all her own. Considering the hazards of her life, she had a special use for it; she was equipped uniquely to deal with HG. But, even so, and even after Berlin and Easton Glebe, and even after he moved to a flat in Chiltern Court, in London, where he 'could have Moura coming and going at her own sweet will', she never pressed her claim or extolled anything but their existing, sudden, wonderful companionship. After a while, and especially after the disposal of Odette, an arrangement was made that they should meet in Ragusa (or Dubrovnik, more properly called) where he was to attend a PEN conference, and depart together afterwards for a honeymoon without the formalities, in nearby Salzburg.

A new political row awaited him at the meeting of the PEN Club in Dubrovnik – quite a relief no doubt after the 'diabolical bitter parting' from Odette: according to her, not him. (If it is true, as claimed elsewhere in this treatise, that most of HG's lovers still lived on good terms with him after the various breaches, Odette was, in the strict sense of the term, the exception that proved the rule.) What happened at the Dubrovnik meeting was a shameful and stupid display of arrogant bad

* H. G. Wells: Aspects of a Life, p. 147.

manners by the Italian Fascist and the Nazi German delegations which seemed to be attacking the central idea of a PEN Club. Brutal Fascist operations had occurred previously along that coastline; it was there that Gabriele D'Annunzio had delivered his attack on Fiume even before Mussolini had seized power in Rome. At the Dubrovnik meeting, the immediate threat came from Germany. When HG insisted from the Chair that news of the persecution of writers must be heard, and some of the persecuted themselves, the Germans made fools of themselves and withdrew their delegates.

He naturally seized this opportunity to further the work of PEN for the protection of writers; and what he did, there and then, served him and that cause well in the years to come. To make a stand for free speech and free writing may not seem such an arduous or necessary task. But some observers were prepared to suffer or abandon altogether any exposure of what was happening in Mussolini's Italy, which is the reason why he exposed the matter in *Meanwhile* and returned to it with fresh satirical skill in *The Autocracy of Mr Parham*. Every scene in that book, the portrait of every victim, is sharpened when we recall the lengths to which Conservative-dominated London society had been ready to applaud or condone the brutalities of Mussolini rule in Italy. His book showed how British politicians were prepared to ape the methods successful there; how the English Parliament might be closed down as easily as Mussolini had performed the feat in Rome; how our Matteottis might soon be murdered in some London backstreet; and how such policies of appeasement – not that that word itself had yet been debased – could land the whole world into a new Armageddon. All these might be the consequences if, instead of marking out a much more adventurous, democratic path, we took the first steps on the road to Autocracy. Quite a number of people who should have known better seemed eager to make excuses for the Fascist antics at Dubrovnik. HG took his presidency of the PEN Club seriously. He thought that the protection of free writing was the clearest of all causes, and he wanted to play his part in carrying it all over the world.

Moura would have liked to have been there to witness his

revived spirits in Dubrovnik. She and the doctor who had diagnosed his diabetic condition can share the credit. The final tone of those good books was there to prove how substantial the improvement had been. But for the new honeymoon Salzburg had the honour of displacing Dubrovnik. Soon afterwards they returned together to London; a few weeks later they paid their first weekend visit together to Beaverbrook's house at Cherkley. He had some standing to be accepted as the unofficial best man at this belated, disorderly wedding feast. Just about a year before, HG had published *The Autocracy of Mr Parham*, in which Beaverbrook himself was a leading figure. All Cherkley guests must have read the book with an expert, anxious eye. Sir Bussy Woodcock was certainly seen everywhere as a satirical portrait of Beaverbrook himself and by no means a friendly one, despite the redeeming role allotted him at the end. Beaverbrook, for sure, would have read the whole book and would pounce on any guest who failed to show an equal assiduity. Even so, his renewed acceptance of HG as an honoured guest so soon after delivery of the attack, and while half of the above-mentioned London society at least was laughing at Sir Bussy's primitive Canadian manners and accent, is evidence of Beaverbrook's magnanimity. He had been given a minor role in *Men Like Gods*, and had been awarded not even the minor compliments offered to Churchill. But *Parham* was a more substantial affair altogether. He could have been offended. But maybe stealing Rebecca from the author had put him in a good temper or, more likely, above all else, it was Max's incurable curiosity which was his main motive.

He wanted to see Moura, as everyone else did. He would certainly have had a firsthand report from Bruce Lockhart. Tremendous tales about her were spread across that same London society: her beauty, her mystery, her poise. HG later described how he commissioned Roger Fry to paint her 'in the hopes that he would catch something of that Mouraesqueness, that makes Moura Moura'. But he failed, and it is indeed extraordinary and lamentable that in an age when both portrait-painting and the new photography were raised to a new standard nothing exists which even distantly portrays the real

Moura. All is a travesty – except HG's own pen pictures. And what she looked like in all her glory – say, in the later 1920s or the 1930s – is an essential part of the story. Especially in the light of all allegations made against her, while she was living and even more when she was dead, it is necessary to recall what she was like then and how much she chose for herself the course she wished to follow or the men with whom she would associate. She lived through times of peril and poverty and crisis, but whatever else happened she would not forfeit the *independence* of her mind and spirit. That was the word to which HG was forced back or forward in all his descriptions of her; that was the indelible part of the real Moura.

The wooing continued in London, Paris, Beaverbrook's country house Cherkley, or his London Stornoway, mostly from him to her; of course, not exclusively so, but he was not accustomed to such a one-way traffic. She had several old friendships which she still sustained. In the early 1930s the old flame with Bruce Lockhart still flickered: 'Friday 29 January 1932: Lunched with Moura. She showed me a letter from Gorky. He asks her to get all the English books on the history of English caricature. He signed himself "Yours sorely grieved, Maxim Gorky – Author – over forty, tawny-haired, bad tempered and overwhelmingly famous."* So Gorky had a sense of humour, for which he was not always given credit. He could also offer wonderful occasions when his charm could take control, and when the whole family gathered around him and especially the children, his own and other people's; they could taste the kind of recreations which HG had introduced in Easton Glebe in pre-1914 days. Gorky could carry that festive human spirit wherever he went. He did so most naturally in St Petersburg; but then, in the 1920s and 1930s when he thought he must move to Italy for his health, he created another Gorky home near Sorrento. Moura had often visited him there, stayed there indeed, and on one most notable and significant occasion she took with her, on his most pressing invitation, her 10-year-old daughter, Tania,

---

* *The Diaries of Sir Robert Bruce Lockhart* (1973), p. 202.

who had never been taken on such an expedition – at least, not by her neglectful mother. Tania had been brought up in her mother's native Estonia. The nature of her mother's neglect was something which Tania could only discover later. What she could never doubt was the common pride which they all had shared in the Russian language and the Russian culture which they were taught to love, especially when the old rulers of Russia had done so little to honour and protect it. Tania spent two months at the Sorrento home from home and never forgot the place and the man and the peculiar form of patriotism which they drank in – not exactly, in her case, with her mother's milk but at least with her rare benign approbation. What a place to be taught! 'He [Gorky] regarded every book as a valued friend and treated it with love and respect.'*

Some of that spirit which Moura and Tania could genuinely share, and which they had cultivated so memorably at Sorrento, she brought with her to London, and she would always establish quick links with those who shared it. One of these was the young Ivan Maisky, who was appointed ambassador in London in early 1932. He was still an untried man as a diplomat, but he quickly showed an aptitude quite beyond that attempted by foreign diplomats, especially Soviet ones. He knew the history of his country, as Gorky knew it and as Moura knew it. He would turn a discussion on to Pushkin rather than the latest shift in personnel on the Politburo. He came to appreciate English virtues, too, and these affections played some part in his judgements a little later. Whether HG introduced him to Moura, or who had taken the initiative, is not clear; but the friendships between all three became constantly closer, and beneficial for all concerned.

* Tania Alexander's *An Estonian Childhood* (1987) gives a splendid picture of the real Gorky, and much else besides. I suppose she knew Moura better than anybody, even HG; and, anyhow, the tales about Moura's alleged spying and everything else about her are much better dealt with in Tania's book than by anyone else. That anyone should write on these matters without taking full account of Tania's account is an outrage against both common sense and elementary decency.

Moura did not tell either HG or Bruce Lockhart exactly what had been her relationship with Gorky. She did not think that was called for by any code she accepted. She did tell Bruce Lockhart quite a lot about her relationships with HG and how they might be growing closer. For example, his diary entry for 17 November 1932: 'She is going with H.G. to Paris and then goes to Sorrento to Gorky. She showed me a correspondence card. On it H.G. had written in very small, neat handwriting: "Dear Moura! Sweet Moura." He sends her lots. Gives her presents.'*

He soon wanted Moura to go with him wherever he went, at least on his major political expeditions. He thought she could give him a new life, a new perspective, a fresh intimate reintroduction to the Russian scene in which he was especially interested, but a new guiding hand elsewhere also – in America, for instance. If she was to accompany him there, a further reason was supplied for getting properly married. And perhaps she would be better able then to share with him a little of that sublime serenity.

Some of these topics were tenderly if obliquely explored in *Brynhild*, the book in which he portrayed the next in his list of heroines. So heavy is the disguise that Moura cannot be unmasked as Brynhild, but her presence did give him a touch of equanimity. Meantime, another aspect of her nature became more prominent. She accepted without question the Wellsian principle that the purpose of both art and journalism was to discover the truth and to tell it. She would agree with the Priestley of that period that H.G. Wells was the most courageous defender of this faith, it was no small part of his charm and his greatness. She would never cease to honour him for his part in the crusade. And yet neither he nor she could or would apply the doctrine in private life. Moura, indeed, had developed her powers of dissimulation to such a pitch that the shield was always there, ready to be interposed if the conversation or the situation took a bad turn. Her readiness to deceive, almost reckless at times, might seem to conflict with her widely acclaimed

* *The Diaries of Sir Robert Bruce Lockhart* (1973), p. 236.

serenity, but anyone who sought to probe fairly the mysteries of her past could see that sometimes she could only protect herself, and maybe her friends or family, too, with an audacious lie, presented from those beautiful, firm lips. Tania might complain that her mother would rely too much on the facility or that she would expect her, too, to deal with importunate telephone enquirers, HG included, with similar evasions. Sometimes these confusions or prevarications would lead to concurrent embarrassments for both Moura and HG.

One such occasion occurred in November 1933 when he invited a distinguished party of his friends to the Quo Vadis restaurant in Soho to hear what they thought was to be the announcement of their wedding. But the Welsh harpist who was to play the famous Thomas Moore ballad did not turn up, and nor did Moura's acceptance. Some of her women friends were not surprised; she had told a few of them why she did not wish to marry again.* What happened or did not happen at that party was certainly never intended as a public slight for HG; Moura would never even talk of him disapprovingly. She loved him, and was learning to love him all the more. He had to leave soon afterwards for America where, alas, she would not accompany him. A little later, he still hoped, they would be able to make a fresh visit to their old haunts in Petrograd and Moscow.

President Roosevelt was a man after his own mind and heart, and the New Deal might almost have been framed in Wellsian terms. All American Presidents speak the language of Thomas Paine, although few of them know it. Some of those who surrounded the President in that first period had been trained also in that school, and HG himself wrote in his first report: 'I always have a sense that essential things are plainer to me in America.'† He continued to hail the President 'as a very strange

* Another explanation of the Quo Vadis fiasco, maliciously disseminated, was that Odette Keun was on the warpath threatening terrible ructions if he did not come back to her. But HG received warning of her dangerous intentions from a quarter which helps to sustain the exception-that-proves-the-rule theory cited above. The warning came from Amber Reeves, who heard rumours of it in her Downshire Hill home and took immediate steps to inform HG.
† *The New America: The New World* (1938), p. 24.

and great man, a recipient and resonator of all that is most soundly progressive in Anglo-Saxon thought'. That was his view at the earliest stage when the clamour against the President from people of his own class was reminiscent of the English landlords assailing Lloyd George. But much more now was at stake. 'No other country has the necessary freedom of speech and mind left if the conception of the new order is to be worked out.'

He returned from that visit to Washington, not quite his normal ebullient self, chastened a little perhaps by the absence of Moura. For almost two years his own mind had been made up. He wanted to form with her the kind of partnership which was most fruitful for his own mind. He had no doubt about her worth and fascination; and he felt all the more aggrieved when she told him that she would not be able to accompany and guide him on his projected visit to Moscow or in the visit he might make to Maxim Gorky who had moved from Sorrento to one of the dachas some twenty miles outside Moscow. He pleaded with her: 'You made me see Russia in 1920; why not now?' Once again, he pressed the idea of marriage, but again she resisted. She gave him the impression that Russia was somehow a barred country for her. Instead, they made the arrangement that she should go to her home in Estonia, as she claimed she often did, and await him there. Meantime, Ivan Maisky made the arrangements for his visit to Moscow and for a meeting with Stalin. Arrangements were also made for him and Gip to make the journey, if they wished, to Maxim Gorky, who was suffering some illness but would naturally be eager to see him.

In Moscow, one calamity followed another. He found himself at the mercy of Intourist guides and the whole atmosphere suffocating. Every comparison with what he had seen before seemed unfavourable: 'Then there was danger, hardship, heroism, hope, and a cause of limitless effort and adventure; now under the honest but uncreative fidelity with Stalin, cynicism and a widespread self-satisfied fatuity prevail.' He held his own in his conversation with Stalin, but concluded also that he had 'conducted himself clumsily'. He contrasted the atmosphere most sharply with the saving virtue which he had detected a few months before in the United States: 'Freedom of criticism is more and more desperately wanting, and the new Russia is clinging passionately to the persuasion that there is nothing more to be learnt. In no sense now is Russia still a revolutionary country; it has become a dogmatic country.'*

Halfway through that suffocating week in Moscow, he heard or overheard the devastating news about Moura. When he made some enquiries about her, he was told that she had been in Moscow or at Gorky's a little while before. When he raised the matter direct with Gorky and his interpreter, he got the confirmation. She had been there several times, although some care had always to be exercised about her movements, because it might embarrass her with her family in Estonia or Russian friends. It would be better to say no more. 'Obviously,' said HG, in response to some ignorant or overbearing Soviet bureaucrat.

At Gorky's he found himself involved in the furious, classic argument about free speech. No doubt, as he admitted, what he thought to be Moura's betrayal hardened his mind and heart for a while against all things Russian, but the transformation from what he had seen and heard in that same household, a bare fifteen years before, was tragic and complete. Every repression and suppression was defended. The language might not be so frenzied as that which he had heard from the Nazis or the Fascists at Dubrovnik two years before, but the message was the same. 'If that spirit was allowed to prevail in the Soviet Union, their leaders too, like all dictatorships before them, would deny themselves the means of escape and recovery.' He put the liberal case, what he defined as the true Socialist case, with all the power at his command. He could not be silenced on that subject anywhere. He wrote the words, just about the saddest he had ever inscribed: 'I did not like to find Gorky against liberty. It wounded me.'†

The other wound looked as if it would never heal. He told himself that week in Moscow that it was the most wounding blow he had ever been dealt by any human being before. And yet

---

* *The New America: The New World* (1938), p. 18.
† *Experiment in Autobiography*, vol. 2, p. 510.

he lived for another ten years, and almost all of them were shared with Moura. That was another story of true love recovered, to beat anything he had ever attempted before. *

Almost instantly on his return to London he found himself embroiled in a fresh and furious controversy about that interview with Stalin. He himself had thought that he had not put his own side of the argument as well as he should have done. However, when the *New Statesman* published the whole interview, each arguer could claim that he had been given the chance to put a powerful case. What they discussed primarily was the potent question upon which Socialists and Communists, across the whole continent of Europe and beyond, clashed: How was power to be achieved, and could the deed be done without the resort to force? HG accepted the reformist or democratic case, although he would always present it with his own variation or embroidery. Stalin elaborated the full Marxist class-war thesis: the capitalist class, in President Roosevelt's America or HG's Britain, would never surrender. Stalin presented his argument with considerable sophistication alongside his customary directness.

* When extracts from *H. G. Wells in Love* were published in the *Sunday Telegraph* in October 1984, Robin Bruce Lockhart wrote somewhat hastily to that newspaper to suggest that the light cast on what the headline called 'The mysterious life of Moura Budberg' was extremely sinister. The book confirmed 'for the first time, I believe,' that she had been lying when she constantly reiterated the claim – to Robert Bruce Lockhart, his father, among others – that she had never returned to the Soviet Union after leaving in 1924 until after World War II. No-one could deny that she did constantly spread mystifications about her travels in the Soviet Union and elsewhere, and the full scale of her row with H. G. Wells was revealed for the first time in print in *H. G. Wells in Love*. However, that volume, as I have indicated, also contains a whole series of other revelations about their relationship more significant than this. Once the Russian-spy theory about her travels gained credence – and that happened even before the publication of *H. G. Wells in Love* – the further, monstrous charges were made that she had been a Soviet spy all her life, even since the period of the so-called Lockhart plot. Robin says that he cannot give any credit to this last suggestion. Good. No-one who knew his father, few people who read his famous book, *British Agent* would accept that, either. But it would have been more gallant if he had not rushed in to suggest that Moura's affair with HG was not real; it was also one of the great love affairs of the century. Is it really so surprising when the same woman plays the same part with different men?

He thought he could quote Cromwell and the Chartists on his side of the debate; but HG had his moments, too. He steered the divergence between them at the end towards the question of free speech; he had an invitation which he hoped to deliver to the Soviet Writers Union to join the PEN Club. He had just time to mention the main principle which he still hoped to be able to discuss with his friend Gorky: PEN insists on 'free expression of opinion – even of opposition opinion'. Stalin then had the last word: 'We Bolsheviks call it "self-criticism", it is widely used in the U.S.S.R.'

What HG had not quite expected was the deluge which now descended upon his head, still bowed from other blows. He had produced a worldwide scoop, and the *New Statesman* was lucky to print it. But then the editor, Kingsley Martin, maliciously or foolishly, according to Anthony West, made the decision which reduced the journalistic achievement to the level of a left-wing joke. He invited Bernard Shaw to comment on the interview, and Shaw produced a dazzling explosion of wit, designed to fortify Stalin's exposition and to blow poor old clumsy HG to Marxist smithereens. It was just like those old Fabian times, when Shaw could usually outwit him in single combat, because he kept his temper better and unloosed his wit with such perfect timing. But on this occasion HG held his own at least. He was justly and bitterly offended by Shaw's reference to the PEN Club – 'The offer has struck Russia speechless' – especially since in the rest of the exchange Shaw made no effort to analyse the degeneration of standards which was taking place in the Soviet Union. HG had seen for himself what was happening, and on the grand disputed question of Karl Marx and his greatness he was able to summon better than any Daniel, a Bernard Shaw come to judgement. Only a few years before, in 1924, Shaw had written to the *Daily Herald*, in the period when that newspaper was the best Socialist newspaper ever published in this country:

From the point of view of English Socialists, the members of the Third International do not know even the beginning of their business as Socialists; and the proposition that the world should take its orders from a handful of Russian novices, who seem to have gained their knowledge of modern Socialism by sitting over the drawing room stove and reading the pamphlets of the Liberal Revolutionists of 1848–70, makes even Lord Curzon and Mr. Winston Churchill seem extreme modernists in comparison.

Unil Moscow learns to laugh at the Third International, and realises that wherever Socialism is a living force instead of a dead theory it has left Karl Marx as far behind as modern science has left Moses, there will be nothing but misunderstandings, in which the dozen most negligible cranks in Russia will correspond solemnly with the dozen most negligible cranks in England, both of them convinced that they are the proletariat and the Revolution and the Future and the International, and God knows what else.

I speak from experience; for this is not the first time that such international misunderstandings have arisen. For many years after the death of Marx, Friedrich Engels kept the German Social Democrats estranged from all the really effective English Socialists because he was unable to conceive that he and Marx, two old men living in the most jealous isolation from all independent thinkers, had been swept aside and left behind by the very movement they had themselves created. Nearly ten years elapsed before Liebknecht and Bebel woke up to the real situation, which was (as it still is) that the living centre of English Socialism was in the Fabian Society and the Independent Labour Party, and not in the suburban bourgeois villa where the survivor of the two great Pontiffs of the Communist Manifesto lived in complete political solitude . . .

The Russian writings which make the most favourable impression here are those of Mr. Trotsky: but even he has allowed himself to speak of Mr. H.G. Wells with a contempt which shows that he has not read Mr. Wells's *Outline of History*, and has therefore no suspicion of what an enormous advance on *Das Kapital* that work represents.

It is this amazing Russian combination of brilliant literary power and complete emancipation from bourgeois illusions, with an absurdly superstitious reverence from the early Victorian prophets of the London suburbs, that makes the literature of the Russian revolution at once so entertaining and so hopeless. When even a

mind and character as strong as Lenin's was so paralysed by this
superstition that when Mr. Wells laughed at the Marxian idols of
Moscow he seemed to Lenin to be not exercising one of the
elementary critical rights of a freethinker, but simply blasphemising
against a divine greatness that he was too 'petty bourgeois' to
realise, then what hope is there of any understanding for Mr. Sidney
Webb (another English writer who has gone far beyond Marx), or
for Mr. Ramsay MacDonald, or may I say for myself?

I think he says it there for himself plainly enough.

That was HG's last word in that particular controversy. When
the question of publishing the whole correspondence arose, it
was Shaw, not HG who wanted to hold back. What Shaw would
claim in conclusion was that Stalin was a better Marxist or
political strategist than Lenin; it was the theoretical corner into
which he had driven himself. Others might state the proposition
precisely the other way round.

Some of the fury which possessed HG in Moscow began to
abate a little when he could escape from the recriminating
exchanges with the new Gorky, so much a diminished man
from the one he had originally known and honoured. He felt,
in another sense, that his own judgements had been unfairly
hardened against Russian ways and achievements. But, apart
even from the meeting with Stalin and all other distractions,
he was striving to produce the proper climax to his own
Experiment in Autobiography upon which he had embarked two
years before. 'I need freedom of mind,' he had inscribed then
when he started on the enterprise in his introductory 'Prelude'.
Now he had reached the last section called 'Envoy', and he
wrote: 'I went by the train called the "Red Arrow", the Soviet
echo of the Flèche d'Or, from Moscow to Leningrad, and
thence I flew to Tallin. I am finishing this autobiography in a
friendly and restful house beside a little lake in Estonia . . .' It
cannot have been quite so restful. He still had a few bones to
pick with Moura – or, rather, a whole Russian anatomy to
dismember and put together again. But what he offered the
world, whatever the stresses, his combined judgement on

Roosevelt's America or Stalin's Soviet Union still radiates a peculiar Wellsian intelligence.

When he had started out at the foothills of that lonely mountain journey, it was almost an admission of defeat. His tone was apologetic or self-critical. 'I need freedom of mind,' he insisted in that first sentence; and then, a little later: 'I may do that major task that will atone for all the shortcomings of what I have done in the past.' And that was no false avowal. He could dismiss some of his own past work in terms worthy of Rebecca West. Some of it had been 'slovenly, haggard and irritated, and some of it as white and pasty in its texture as a starch-fed nun'. His aim was to say something he had never said before or at least in a way he had not attempted to master before.

But still the choice of the instrument, especially for him, was a strange one. He had once denounced the limitations of biography and, even more assuredly, of autobiography. True, his aim then – in his major essay on the subject in 1911 – was to extol the virtues and potentialities of the novel. But his condemnation of the other forms was none the less deadly. 'All biography has something of that post-mortem coldness and respect' – he had been particularly provoked by Lord Morley's recent *Life of Gladstone* – 'and, as for autobiography, a man may show his soul in a thousand half-conscious ways, but to turn on oneself and explain oneself is given to no one. It is the natural resort of liars and braggarts. Your Cellinis and your Casanovas, men with a habit of regarding themselves with a kind of objective admiration, do best in autobiography.' And, if that severe profile drawn by HG could not apply to all cases, even the very greatest such as Rousseau who had turned to this means of expression did seem to require an obsessive interest in themselves to make the achievement possible. Their motive power still seemed to be a colossal egotism. HG was not like that at all, as his preface to his new work freshly illustrated. He would constantly remind himself and others of his own weaknesses and of that other indication of his sanity, his awareness of his obligation to his neighbours and the world at large.

One defect in the biographical or autobiographical form of

writing he could not overcome, however much he tried. In the
'Contemporary Novel' essay, he had talked of being condemned
to leave out half the story. No doubt that was a false estimate of
the proportion which would have to be omitted; but, even if that
total could be halved and halved again, was not the impediment
still much too severe? In the *Experiment* he wrote: 'I suspect the
sexual system should be at least the second theme when it is not
the first in every autobiography, honestly and fully told.'
Certainly, in HG's case, few would have disputed that this was
the likely proper apportionment. He did his brave best, braver
than anyone else had done, even Jean-Jacques Rousseau,
according to such an expert witness as André Maurois. * And yet
it was still much less than the whole story. He had done more
than any other writer of the century to lead the way to the
fullest, freest discussion of sexual questions. It was a part of his
mission, and no small part. And yet he could not fully and freely
write on these matters without hurting his lovers or hurting
himself or both at the same time. Partly for this reason, he
contemplated returning to the form of the novel, and he did so
in some new and especially interesting instances. He was still left

* André Maurois, no mean judge in these matters, wrote in his *Poets and Prophets*
(1936) that HG's autobiography, published two years earlier, was 'so frank that
Rousseau's *Confessions* look cautious and maidenly in comparison'. He added, for
good measure, that for some years Wells wielded an intellectual dominion
comparable to that won and held by Voltaire in the eighteenth century. HG
would have been thrilled by both comparisons. But what would Maurois have said
if he had been able also to read the postscript to Wells's *Experiment in
Autobiography*, published in 1984 under the title *H. G. Wells in Love*? Of course,
these passages had been written partly in his own defence. They had been held
over for posthumous publication at his request. But they carried the confession
much further. Few writers in the 1930s had been so explicit and honest in seeking
to unravel the truth. Even today, in the 1990s, in these more relaxed times, few
writers with so much to tell have told it so openly. It was an essential part of H. G.
Wells's faith to write about the whole sexual system as openly and plainly as he
could; his courage in these matters was one of his shining qualities. In the 1900s
he had to incorporate these truths in his novels. In the 1930s he could compete
with Rousseau's maidenly confessions. In the 1980s his full story could take its
place with his own best. *H. G. Wells in Love* ranks with, say *Tono-Bungay* or *Joan
and Peter* or *Mr Britling*. Anthony Burgess, in his review in the *Observer*, saw the
point of it as well as anybody: 'This is a fine, moving, essentially comic book.'

241

with the question of how, on his own definition, he was to write a full and honest autobiography. His solution was to write two. Even while he was completing the *Experiment*, published in September 1934, he started to compile an elaborate postscript which eventually appeared as part of the volume entitled *H. G. Wells in Love*. It was certainly an addition of the first importance. His candour had been his special quality before; it was carried much further. The new *Experiment in Autobiography* and *H. G. Wells in Love* together constitute the bravest autobiography of the century – and yet the fact that he had to present his work in this manner vindicates the doctrine in that famous 1911 essay. Such are the restrictions on the autobiographical form that they can be outdone by the greatest novels – the Swifts and Sternes of his favourite century or the Joyces and Rushdies of our own.

Experiment in Autobiography was not the political success which he expected or the literary success which he deserved. He had a quarrel with his publishers, as he often had, about the manner of publication. A young Victor Gollancz sought to sell the two volumes separately, which is exactly what he did not want. He wanted the whole story to be seen together; it was the reason for his mighty climax which deserved a special acclaim of its own. No-one accused him of concealments or suppressions, and it would have been wretched if they had. He would still try to say more than anyone else in this form of writing, and he would plead forgiveness for his sins; how much he deplored his departure from his own sturdy atheism on the few occasions when it happened, and how eagerly he beckoned back all stragglers on to the straight and narrow path. Beatrice Webb read every page with fascinated approval and only the rarest reversion to the old doubts about his character. 'H.G. emerges from his autobiography a splendidly vital man: an explorer of man's mind, a critic, artist, deviser and visionary all in one in spite of deplorable literary manners and mean sexual morals. H.G. is to me a likeable and valuable man. He has been on the side of the angels . . .'[*] And she could see the beauty of his

[*] Beatrice Webb's Dairies, vol. 4, p. 344.

writing as well as its other more obvious virtues, and she wrote to him direct a letter of generous discernment.

Still, a belated, benign commendation from Beatrice was not exactly the prize to which he aspired. He wanted to be acclaimed for his political vision, and the constancy with which he had presented it to the British people and the world at large. Above all, he wanted his great warning to be heeded, and made the basis for action before the calamity came. The response which pleased him most came from a real man of action in the real world. President Roosevelt wrote in terms no less discerning than Beatrice. The two of them, HG with his new book and the President with his New Deal, were both teaching people to think – 'and your direction and mine are not so far apart; at least we both seek peaceable conveyances on our travels'. An excited reader in the White House: that was a triumph indeed. How much better chance there would have been of saving the world, if he had gained equally perceptive readers in Downing Street and the Kremlin, but Stanley Baldwin's favourite bedtime reading was supposed to be Mary Webb, and Stalin was still busy expurgating Maxim Gorky and even Karl Marx. It was to that great question of intellectual freedom which he would constantly return; and, on that test, HG sustained over the years an incomparable record, which he noted still quite modestly at the end of the *Experiment*: 'Exasperation [with his views] there had been; bans and boycotts from Boots to Boston; public school masters and prison chaplains have intervened to protect their charges from my influence, Nazis have burnt my works, the Catholic Church and Italian Fascism have set their authority against me . . .' But still he had been allowed to speak and write, which might help to show that mankind was moving in the right direction after all. 'I began this autobiography primarily to reassure myself during a phase of fatigue, restlessness and vexation, and it has achieved its purpose of reassurance. I wrote myself out of that mood of discontent and forgot myself and a mosquito swarm of bothers in writing about my sustaining ideas – My ruffled persona has been restored . . .' Without the inherent strength of those sustaining ideas, he could never have written his *Experiment in Autobiography*, especially its magnificent peroration in which Estonian trials could be subdued, like the mosquito swarms of three years before, to serve the highest Wellsian purpose.

With or without the postscript, his *Experiment in Autobiography* was one of the greatest literary autobiographies ever written. If there was no immediate acceptance of that verdict – as there certainly was not – it was partly due to the quarrels and debates which he continued to promote in so many different quarters. If he was so ready to entangle the work of novelists and journalists, why should they step forward to help him out? If he himself disowned the title of artist, why should anyone else be ready to restore it? He did try always in his writing to tell the truth, and the friends who knew him best – J. B. Priestley, Frank Swinnerton, Arnold Bennett – would always be eager to add their testimony to validate that claim. Without that, of course, the *Experiment* would have been worthless; but now, with its publication, after so much dedicated effort and so much acceptance of the views of some at least of his critics, he was still denied the accolade or the one that he wanted in the form he wanted it. It was partly a recrudescence of the old argument he had had with Henry James. Other more modern figures were tending to push him aside, although he still regarded his modernized views as a good deal more truly modern than theirs. He had always shown a respect for these others, even if he could not approve or understand their methods. He still believed that the greatest writing must capture the widest audiences, men and women. That was for sure still part of his Swiftian creed; he would never desert it. But Swift often turned to allegory to reinforce the argument or to bamboozle his accusers. HG had learned that habit from him, and in the aftermath of the comparative failure of the *Experiment* he turned to it again.

He wrote five novels in the next three years – *The Croquet Player* (1936), *Brynhild* (1937), *Star Begotten* (1937), *The Brothers* (1938), *Apropos of Dolores* (1938) – each of them in an original form, even if they had embedded within them some neglected Wellsian moral. All five were written with an individual charm and proficiency which disproved the common charge that he had lost his talent and his zest. The scale of the novella seemed to suit his latest moods and capacities better than the short story or the Sternean novel. No-one surely could read these five last fictional pieces which he wrote in the last three years before 1939 and make the charge either that he had merely revived his old uncritical optimism or that he had finally yielded to the blackest despair. Read altogether, the reader can still just be swept along by the humour and the narrative skill; they showed how near was the precipice. *The Croquet Player* was directly dedicated to Moura, and she must have received it with a peculiar pride. Sometimes she was also seen as the heroine in *Brynhild*, but this is surely a miscasting. She is much more like the Mary of *Star Begotten*, who preserved her slightly aloof serenity throughout the whole proceedings, but still understood him better than he understood himself. *Star Begotten* also contains a host of other delights and diversions: an exposure of a mind which might be at the end of its tether but which might still recover; a dazzling and deadly caricature of the most oafish press lord of that era, Lord Rothermere ('Marvellous how the press can make almost anything unbelievable'), a use of the term 'Big Brother' to expose the new methods of dictatorship, and finally, or not so finally, a Swiftian damnation for men who loved to be cruel, loved to conquer, loved to persecute – *Homo superbus*, who would set his own pride above the claims of all other creatures. *Star Begotten* was, as the author wrote, 'Dedicated on a sudden impulse to my friend, Winston Spencer Churchill', and no irony was intended. Despite their furious arguments in the past, they were moving on to some common ground. HG also used the opportunity to extol the supreme virtue of his favourite Winwood Reade: 'Whenever the mental going is a bit hard, whenever our intellectual eyes feel the glare of truth, we lose focus, and slither off into Ghostland.' Churchill himself had once recommended that flight from reality; it might be the only way to save Church and State, especially when the two were joined in unholy alliance. But as the world moved forward it was the recovery of a respect for truth which was the most necessary implement of salvation. That was the message of *Star Begotten*, as of almost everything else he wrote henceforth with Moura at his side.

Of all these, the most accomplished, subtle, serene almost in its Mouraesque conclusions, was *Apropros of Dolores*. Absurdly, but forgivably perhaps, this has been seen as his final word, and a most ungallant one at that, about Odette Keun. She saw it that way and threatened comprehensive legal action – as Dolores does in the novel itself – which would finally ruin HG altogether. It could have happened, and other commotions before and after in the London society of the time have tended to distract attention from the wonderful combined merits of the book itself. Dolores is the villain, for sure, but the battered Stephen Wilbeck is no hero. He mocks his own antics and conceits – even the delusions by which he was originally seduced. That particular passage is surely directed against him not her:

> I perceive a little chap who is still clinging to the assurance that he was something exceptional as a lover. It is nature's way with us. Few men, I suspect, can resist that dear delusion that the commonest of God's gifts is an outstanding distinction. Yet it is lavished upon the ordinary monkey far beyond our human portion. The facts of the case necessarily remain in decent obscurity but I think that in that particular respect my head was rather turned by Dolores.

Such ignoble confessions along with a whole range of topical revelations present an unexpected picture. He thought it necessary to ward off attacks in a prefactory note: 'Stephen Wilbeck is no more an auto-libel on the present writer than Tristram Shandy was an auto-libel on Laurence Sterne.' He promised his new publishers, Jonathan Cape, that he wouldn't take a libel action against them. And, if Moura had any anxieties, she made at last the most sensational of all her appearances, more ravishing even than the magnificent Moura of Moscow or Berlin: 'It was Aphrodite herself who saw fit to remind me that even in everyday sunlight, this universe has something profounder and intenser than its everyday events. I perceive I have as much of a vision as any of the saints. But of a different divinity.'* If the author of *Apropos of Dolores* had not to deal with his past reputation as an unconscionable reprobate, other readers, like Moura, have enjoyed the new work of art: a defence eloquent as ever of the 'stoical agnosticism which is the only possible religion of sane adults', or a portrait of Europe on the eve, to match anything on offer from the young contenders, the Evelyn Waughs or the Graham Greenes. It might have been better called *Apropos of Aphrodite*, and London would have better noted the new picture of Moura.

All of these last pieces were written at 13 Hanover Terrace, where he had moved soon after returning from Moscow. More than ever he wanted Moura to marry him, but he had to report: 'She will live with me, dine with me, sleep with me, but she won't marry me.' She did make Hanover Terrace the place first of all where he could write. Her methods were not the same as those of her predecessors, but they worked. *Magnificent* was the word he had selected to describe her fifteen years before; it still applied. As she pronounced it, according to Bruce Lockhart, the name sounded like Hangover Terrace. But she kept her head more beautifully poised than ever.

Moura supplied also the last touch required for the publication of the last major treatise which he wrote in 1939 – the volume which appeared in August 1939 with the title *The Fate of Homo Sapiens* – or, rather, Moura with the assistance of her daughter, Tania, who had found a job for herself in the office of Fredric Warburg, partner in the firm of Secker & Warburg which was finding the late 1930s a most anxious, testing period. Tania had adopted or adapted all her mother's attributes except one: beauty, high intelligence, a deep love of the Russia she had been forced to leave, and especially that Estonian enclave where she was born and brought up, but an awareness, too, of the terrible events in the new Germany which threatened the whole continent. The one attribute which she did not inherit or approve was her mother's chronic incapacity to tell the truth.

* *Apropos of Dolores* (1938), p. 328.

Tania herself could never quite unravel the reasons why her mother had developed this faculty to such a pitch. All she knew was the awkward consequences which this manner of living could cause for herself with her mother's suitors – especially HG as it happened – or the charm with which her mother could surmount the moments of exposure. Tania and HG in turn had charmed each other since they had first met or at least since they became better-acquainted in England. She was the ideal person to make the new introduction.

He could have terrible rows with his publishers, and in the interview with Frederic Warburg – a significant one in the history of English publishing* – it looked as if that experience would be repeated. Frederic Warburg was a principled but prickly man whose allegiance to those principles had come to the rescue of the tattered reputation of left-wing publishing in the 1930s – he would not bow to Communist pressures or blackmail – but who would have no chance of survival if he could not secure something like a bestseller from such a writer as H. G. Wells. But was he still a bestseller, even a potential one? HG naturally thought so; and, anyhow, of course, he was on the side of the authors against 'the men of commerce, honest for the most part, but greedy as a matter of course'. They should not dictate. 'I expect slavish obedience from them.' But soon he relaxed: 'My dear Warburg, I've heard a lot about you from Tania. She tells me you are quite a good publisher, considering what asses most of you fellows are, you should have quite a decent future.' But it was not all fixed even after that. Honest Frederic still had some moments of high anxiety and uproarious comedy. After all these commotions, it was the subject of sex which brought out the best in both of them. The publishing result was the appearance, no more than fourteen months later, of a beautifully printed volume of *The Fate of Homo Sapiens*. HG himself did not seem to care too much about the appearance of his books, unless like his *Outline* they could depend partly on the illustrations and maps or, like his Atlantic Edition, they did

* Recorded in J. R. Hammond's *H. G. Wells: Interviews and Recollections*, p. 97.

seem to underline his importance as a writer. But *The Fate of Homo Sapiens* was a thing of beauty in itself, a proper way for him to present his verdict on that epoch to the world. Authors can be excited when the actual volume comes into their hands, and the whole Wellsian–Warburg–Alexander connection could have a special celebration about this one. His success did help to save Secker & Warburg and a whole range of authors much needier than himself.

The Fate of Homo Sapiens was a comprehensive attempt to survey the moral and intellectual forces ranged against one another across the planet on the eve of the war which he and some others had done their best to avert at a time when successful prevention and cure might still have been possible: say, in the 1920s or the early 1930s. He was not a military expert, although thanks to his scientific self-training or his native intelligence he often proved himself more astute in these matters than the generals or the air marshals and, most especially, the admirals – he thought these last were an especially bone-headed breed. But a reader of this volume could see that it was the balance of moral forces and how they might reveal themselves, in political organization and action, which was the primary subject of his survey. He was deeply shaken by the displays of bestial conduct which had already been reflected in some of his recent novels: 'the spectacle of evil in the world during the past half-dozen years – the wanton destruction of homes, the ruthless hounding of decent folk into exile, the bombing of open cities, the cold-blooded massacres and mutilations and, above all, the return of deliberate and organized torture, mental torment and fear to a world from which such things had been well nigh abolished.' He was shaken, as every observer from civilized nations should have been shaken; *the past half-dozen years* he so exactly specified would take the reckoning back to cover atrocities committed in Fascist Italy, Nazi Germany and Fascist Spain condoned by a long list of statesmen in supposedly civilized states.

He had no doubt where the main menace came from: he called it 'the Nazi Religion which is, in its possibilities of destruction, the most urgent challenge the human mind will have ever had to face. Nazi Germany may well bring down conclusive disaster on our species . . . [If] the Nazi process continues upon its present lines, then the whole world must be given over to war preparation, at least until Nazi Germany ceases to exist.' Nobody could say that he had underestimated that part of the menace; he returned to face it again, but in that same passage he would deny 'a specific sadistic streak in Germans'. Even at that moment, he insisted that it was 'the specific sadistic' streak in the human race which clamoured even more strongly for our attention.

Since he had defined the menace which threatened universal destruction as a religion, it was natural that he should turn his scrutiny to other religions which had at one time or another made comparable claims to unchallengeable universal authority. The establishment of civilized standards, the recognition of individual rights for men and women, was a process which most other religions still resisted, the most notable example being the Roman Catholic Church and those who upheld the Jewish doctrine of the chosen people, especially if this last claim was to be translated into the establishment of an exclusively Jewish state in Palestine. He condemned Zionism as another evil outbreak of the kind of nationalism which the modern world must abjure. A little ahead of his time, he also condemned the use of some other religions to conceal the return to barbarism in Protestant South Africa or Anglican India or Shintoite Japan. He did have his own religion, and had sometimes caused a little confusion by an excessive use of the word. But in this particular testament he made it clear why he still looked to France for a special kind of inspiration. He saw allies there:

who will not suffer France to desist from her traditional task of world enlightenment . . . The achievement of the French Encyclopedists has always appealed very strongly to my imagination. Diderot and his associates had scented the onset of change . . . they did produce a new inspiring conception of a world renewed. They gave a definite form and direction to this confused and powerful impulse of their time.

That was no bad summary of HG's own political role.

And what of the forces of civilization still to be awakened? It was interesting still that he wished to state the whole question in decisive terms. The best hope came from America: 'The crisis discovered a great man in Franklin Roosevelt.' And that was no desertion from Wells's own abhorrence for any 'great man' theory. He did believe that Franklin Roosevelt represented a real nascent American democracy better than ever before, and such a voice at such a time could still tip the balance.

He looked to England but could see little but a tragic parody of her real greatness. The England he saw was not a democracy in action, but what he called the British Oligarchy, enrolling all forms of effective government into its hands and not merely blocking the path towards democratic development but blocking the essential steps to meet the Nazi threat. HG's British Oligarchy was a good name for what later became known as the Establishment or what William Cobbett even more expressively called the Thing. Its main characteristic was its resolve and power to do nothing but perpetuate itself. HG saw everything that was evil and dangerous in the system represented in the Prime Minister, Neville Chamberlain – 'essentially ignorant, narrow-minded, subconsciously timid, cunning and inordinately vain', and guilty in a special degree throughout the months of crisis since the Munich meeting in 1938: 'Most of the acts of Mr. Chamberlain since 1938 have been as irresponsible as those of any Dictator, equally unscrupulous and far more shameful.'

Yes, politics for HG and the British people was a matter of morals in the years 1938 and 1939 when he was writing *The Fate of Homo Sapiens*. If it had not been, Chamberlain and the British Oligarchy would have been able to pursue their chosen course till the end, and the Nazi march to the conquest of the world would have been complete. Totalitarianism came near to total victory. But HG was provoked to remark, with his English pride and English wit, that the philosophers and practitioners of totalitarianism do not always get their way: 'Even while Hobbes was preparing his book for the press, England decapitated

Leviathan in the person of Charles the First.' And even in 1939, thanks partly to HG's tuition, some English people were preparing the political decapitation of Neville Chamberlain.

TEN

Some Mind, Some Tether

If our sort can't think of something, nobody will
think of anything. We have to do something
about it. We! You and me!
Stella to Gemini, in *Babes in the Darkling Wood*,
p.23

The final chapter in the life of H. G. Wells might conveniently
start with the outbreak of war on 3 September 1939: the war
which he had prophesied or defined, along with Winston
Churchill, as the Unnecessary War. Wells's prophecies had
been more cataclysmic and more precisely accurate than
Churchill's, and the comparison is made without any disrespect
to either of our prophet-politicians. Each of them may have
made many individual misjudgements about the scale of the
coming catastrophe or the pace at which it was approaching; but
neither of them had been guilty of contributing to the corrosion
of the national will so insidiously instilled by the Baldwins and
the Chamberlains, the Simons and the Hoares. They had a
common vision in the sense that, despite all misapprehensions
and misconceptions, foreseeing the scale of the disaster, they
had done their best to warn their countrymen and the world.

Sometimes HG's enemies or critics would seek to reduce him

to the stature of an incorrigible optimist whose faith in the triumph of scientific truth and discovery encouraged him to dismiss the darker dangers which might still befall mankind. George Orwell came near to making this accusation in a fierce controversy with Wells in 1943, and since Wells himself had taken such precautions to define a different course it is easy to see why he was so deeply offended. But some of those who came to his defence, not merely concerning this particular item on the charge-sheet, but to repudiate the truly absurd general accusation of a facile optimism, sometimes nearly succeeded in branding him as one who had finally surrendered to a black despair. Anthony West seemed to reach this conclusion. Often he could be a perceptive critic of his father's writing, but it is also true that he shared only rarely the moments of exultation. He did not experience what V. S. Pritchett described: 'I have never read any book by H. G. Wells, early or late, which did not start off by giving me an exhilarating sense of personal freedom.'

The Wells of the 1920s and 1930s – and it provided him with his armour and sword when it came to the 1940s – was an artist-propagandist as well as a prophet-politician who could strike a proper balance between hope and fear. If he had wished to contradict the charge that he had abandoned any claim to be an artist to serve his own political purposes, he could at least have checked the flood which poured from his pen. But he believed his response was demanded by the mounting political infamies which he saw all around him. He thought silence or reserve would be craven and contemptible. So the polemical outpouring continued unstopped and unstoppable, and, for the most part, brilliantly apposite. But the artist was at work, too, piercing ever deeper. He would sail, if he could, with the Argonauts or the new adventurers; or he could peer, like Joseph Conrad, into the heart of darkness. He would never accept that the one activity must exclude the other; that had always been part of his own argument with Henry James. It would have been a strange moment to abandon his creed, in the 1930s and the 1940s, when the artists themselves or some of the greatest of them were being forced to pass their verdicts on the Gethsemanes and Guernicas.

H. G. Wells poured out his political pamphlets, old and new, some of them as deadly and passionate as any he had ever produced, directed, as they properly should be, at the guilty men. But, consciously and unconsciously, he also produced some works of art.

Why should the distinction always be drawn so sharply between the various categories, between the artist and the prophet? Three at least of Wells's chief mentors would never have seen it so. One of these prompted him to produce *Mr Blettsworthy on Rampole Island*, published in 1928 and dedicated to the author of *Candide*. Another was Laurence Sterne whose wayward diversions became more and more appealing to the Wells searching for new techniques. But the third and most inescapable influence was assuredly still Jonathan Swift. All his later novels (and much of the political pamphleteering) were Swiftian in the sense that no restraints were to be tolerated in the description of the horrors which human beings might inflict upon one another. They were Swiftian, too, in the preference for plain matter-of-fact writing; Swiftian in their readiness to design the most elaborate, even inscrutable, allegories. So was Swift an artist or did he impair his claim by the famous indignation which could lacerate his heart? Was Swift an artist also, by the way, when he became the Drapier, and resolved that every word should be so downright and deadly that everyone could understand? And yet, without the Drapier, there would have been no Gulliver. HG understood better than his critics how the Swiftian tradition, in all its glorious ramifications, should be properly and audaciously upheld.

He could not put a check upon his pamphleteering, even if he had wanted to obey some higher artistic summons. How he could rarely fail to give it some touch of his own originality was shown in the expeditions he undertook just before and after the fatal September. He had arranged to make a tour of Australia in the early months and had fixed to be back to deliver a lecture in Sweden for the PEN Club. He called the report on his Far Eastern tour *Travels of a Republican Radical in Search of Hot Water*, and his own choice of this title may be thought especially apposite in the light of the accusation against him that he was insufficiently democratic in his instincts. The accusation had always been wide of the mark: the H. G. Wells so avidly read, say, in the Workmen's Halls in Wales – their libraries were stuffed high and low with all types of his books – was no élitist. And he explained in that volume and doubtless also to those audiences why he loved and resurrected the old word *radical*. 'Radicalism', he wrote, 'carried a valid meaning in the United States' – where he also wanted to be understood – 'as well as in the British system, and it has none of the jejune, anti-Socialist individualism of the Lord Samuel type' ('Lady Thatcher type' would clearly be a more topical definition here) 'which has attached itself to Liberalism. The word carries us back to a phase of wholesome and hopeful social resentment before Hegelian claptrap, and the misconceptions of Marx and the solemn, disingenuous strategy of the Communists, clouded the wits of the rising generation of common English-speaking people.' A Radical line, he insisted, was better than the old 'Fabian term'. 'There never was a Fabian front. There was just a Fabian spray. They all wanted to get into Parliament in a hurry. Some of them did get in: can you name them?' But that was just a temporary irritation. What 1939 needed was a reawakening of true Radicalism. 'Radical is, I feel, far the best word for our present occasions. It suggests going to the root of things. It suggests digging and weeding. I wonder why the world has neglected that good, strenuous word so long.'

On his travels, he saw British imperialism in action in various guises, and hated what he saw:

> In Burma, as in India, the British Raj never explains and in effect it has nothing to explain. It is there, a brainless incubus. Its idea of education has been to give imitation European University degrees by written examination. This is supplemented by a strenuous censorship of subversive literature which stimulates every self-respecting Burman to read and distribute all he can of the forbidden fruit. One realises in this Eastern World how completely the existing Imperial system is a paralysis rather than a rule.

When he argued about the common interest which might bring Burmese and their English masters together, he received the reply: 'Our boys are learning more by striking, argument and reading forbidden literature than by sitting in classrooms. They are having to feel responsible for Burma. Perhaps that is right.'

Often he was frightened by the way old nationalisms seemed likely to take possession of the new world. 'Such nationalism', he would emphasize, 'was the purest artificiality, and is made by the teaching of history and nothing else, history taught by parents, friends, flags, ceremonies as well as by the persistent pressure of the schools, but mainly in the schools.' And this school-made nationalism injured the chance to take on the new nationalists as well as the old ones: 'You see only two sides to this world question, imperialism and nationalism. There is another: the free-thinking, free-speaking liberal world. Belong to that.'

A new kind of history teaching – that was part of the message he took round the world on that last journey. It could be made to sound simple.

We must tell the truth about human origins. We cannot afford to muffle that up in the interests of a few ignorant bigots . . . Never once should a civilised teacher talk of *our* tribe, *our* people, *our* race. The truth about that piece of doggerel is in almost every line. It is a foolish lie. So far from the southern coast of Britain being ours at the time of Caesar, we modern Britishers, as represented by our ancestral genes, were almost everywhere but there – we were in Gothland, on the Baltic coast, down the Danube, in Palestine, in Egypt – Heaven knows where. But wherever we were, our ideas, our arts, our power and range were progressing in an orderly intelligent manner. The history of communication, the history of implements, and the intelligent study of the consequences of this progress and extension of human mentality, is infinitely simpler than the old history. It is healthy food whereas the old race-and-nation stuff is poisoned food. Children like the unpoisoned stuff better.'

And often, when exposing old historical myths, he would

257

uncover the fresh challenges of the future. This was his new departure in the Canberra lecture of 1939:

What spendthrift ancestors we have had! What wastrels we still are! And all because history teaches us no better. Man burns and cuts down forests, he destroys soil, he acclimatises destructive animals. A map of the world showing the devastated regions, where devastation is due to mankind, would amaze most people. It ought to be put in every child's atlas. A history of the devastation of the world, due to planless exploitation is far nearer the reality of things than this amiable history some teachers want to teach. In the past two years you have seen great regions of the United States turned to sandy desert, you have seen Australia swept by fires, rick-burning and rabbits. You have seen a slaughter of scores of useful animal species, you have seen a monstrous destruction of natural resources and your old history-teaching does nothing, not *that* – to awaken the minds of the coming generation to the supreme gravity of this process. It represents the nineteenth century as a high old time for mankind under the direction of wise, wise monarchs and statesmen, whereas it was a phase of almost imbecile profiteering and competitive waste. The old history does not heed such things, it does not explain, it does not want to explain . . . If the young Hercules of a new world is to live, its first feat must be to strangle the tangled coil of poisonous old histories in its cradle.

That was the message he constantly proclaimed in the last months and weeks before 3 September. He had prepared another lecture to be delivered at the Annual Congress of the International PEN Club in Stockholm. Despite the declaration of war in London, he still went to Stockholm. The actual lecture was cancelled, but he could still publish it. His title was *The Honour and Dignity of the Free Mind*, and he was able to give an expression to the strand in his personal faith which was stronger and simpler than any other. 'Now there is a great darkening of the face of human affairs. . . .' All the more necessary was it to make the declaration; 'We hold we are here to assert, that the free-thinking, free-speaking intelligence is of more value than any political, racial or sectarian division whatever.' And then he translated these definitions into concrete terms: 'The authentic writer and artist and scientific worker are the aristocrats of the human community. There is nothing above them under heaven. They are masters. *Cher Maître* is no idle compliment to them. They work on honour and under no man's direction. They are subject to an inner necessity to do the utmost that is in them.' Then he would recite the names of the great princes of the intellectual world who had always spoken in an international language: Voltaire, Gibbon, Darwin, Huxley, Sigmund Freud, 'a cardinal modern figure in human thought' to take his place with the others. Charles Darwin, 'that gentle old man in his Kentish cottage', was one of his special favourites – perhaps because he also stirred Wells's own Kentish patriotism. But how was he seen in relation to the politicians of his time? They might be 'impressive figures, but the sawdust could be seen running out of them, when Huxley still stood on his pinnacle firmer than ever and the whole of his one world could see them'. And then HG delivered his own frontal challenge:

> Every disastrous thing that has happened in the past twenty years was clearly foreseen by a galaxy of writers and thinkers twenty years ago. The evil state of Europe to-day is traceable almost directly to the want of imagination, the self-protective cunning, and the deliberate breaches of faith made by our rulers during those eventful years immediately following the Great War.

And thus the new clash became inescapable.

> It is a conflict between gangster adventurers or dull politicians on the one hand, trading on old national jealousies and resentments, stale and decaying, and poisonous dogmas and fear, who are blundering us down to destruction. That is one side of it. On the other is the directive power of the fearless and unhampered human intelligence, expressing, educating and discovering. For this last, and for its supremacy, we of this P.E.N. Club stand.

The end for him and his world might have been a most

dispiriting one, when he returned from his Australian tour, in the summer of 1939, to face the certainty of a new war and the immediate collapse of all his best Wellsian expectations. When Beatrice Webb met him, she described him as a 'physical wreck . . . Poor old Wells – I was sorry for him. I doubt whether we shall meet again . . . We are too old and tired!'* His physical weakness might have affected his mind; he could have been overwhelmed by the combination of circumstances; the scale of the coming catastrophe and the pigmy stature of the political leaders called upon to deal with it. But something quite different happened.

His repeated theme about his twentieth-century world, at least since 1918, had been the race between education and catastrophe, and the arrival of the Second World War at England's shores, in such ignominious and dangerous circumstances, might have been expected to tip the scale in his mind towards the darkest conclusions. Instead, he displayed a fresh resilience, a reckless intellectual heroism. Thanks to his range of choice for the victims of his iconoclasm, his achievement during this period has rarely been acknowledged. But we can see it better now: it was partly a vindication of his prophecies, but much more a proof that he had lost none of his independent courage. If this was a mind near the end of its tether, it proved itself more resourceful, more responsive to the spirit of the age, than that of most rivals.

Some part of the credit for the restoration of his spirits must go to Moura Budberg. No-one could nurse his genius so well as she, although the use of the word 'nurse' may give a wrong impression about her particular range of ministrations. She was obviously a brilliant lover in the technical sexual sense, as he obviously was, too. Many of their most necessary and notable reconciliations took place in bed. But this was only one part of the mutual attraction which had survived two decades and blossomed into something more intimate still in the late 1930s and the 1940s, exactly at the time when he established himself at 13 Hanover Terrace for what he knew must be his last workshop and resting-place. He wanted her to move in with him and he wanted it

* Beatrice Webb's Diaries, vol. 4, p. 431.

passionately, obsessively. Her refusal, like her refusal to marry him, was part of the tempestuous quarrel between them described in the last chapter. What friends and enemies alike might fail to notice was how HG established, as he had hoped, a new poise at his Hanover Terrace house, and how much Moura's serene, commanding character contributed to it. She was one of the most considerable women of the century; she was at the peak of her powers; she had seen with her own eyes and felt in her own bones the tumult of the century, East and West, in two world wars; she never wavered in her resolve to keep her independence in an age when women were still not supposed to indulge such aberrations and that, of course, was the core of her dispute with HG. She insisted on the same independence for herself which he required for himself, and without that insistence she would destroy her own personality. She fought that battle and won. But what the outside world has sometimes failed to recognize is how he did achieve a domestic peace, a secure fortress from which he would embark on his last campaigns. Moura did that for him, and she kept her independence, too. She knew, even if he had taken so long to learn, that it was the essential condition.

'The colour of life is largely a matter of homes,' he wrote just as he was moving into Hanover Terrace. Homes had been very important to him, and so was Hanover Terrace with its bust of Voltaire in the dining-room. He thought he might be able to match the contentment of Voltaire at Ferney, offering his advice to the world without interruption. 'I hope my brain will keep hard to the end. My father's did; my mother's did not.' Even though world madness had broken out afresh, HG's brain certainly kept hard to the end, with Moura his wisest and most constant visitor – 'she has remained still the dearest thing in my affections. And so she will remain to the end. I can no more escape from her smile and her voice, her flashes of gallantry and the charm of her endearments than I can escape from my diabetes or my emphysematous lung.'*

* H. G. *Wells in Love*, p. 210. Enemies of HG and enemies of Moura often fail to notice the 'Last Phase' chapter of this volume which follows the section reporting their general quarrel. It is suffused with Moura's serenity.

Apart from her other qualities, Moura seemed to be an embodiment of the true internationalism which HG preached. Apart from her native Russian, she could speak four other languages perfectly and would lapse into any of them with beguiling ease. Her perfect French enabled her to hold a job on the journal *France libre*, a truly liberal newspaper which was soon challenging some of the seemingly authoritative tendencies of the office run by General de Gaulle. Her perfect Russian enabled her to move in all kinds of Russian circles, émigré or Communist. She would never conceal her pride in her native Russia, just as HG would never conceal his pride in his native Kent. Indeed, and quite naturally, when Britain and the Soviet Union became allies against the same Nazi enemy, Russian émigrés of almost every class could not conceal their glow of patriotism. Moura made no effort at this particular conceal-ment. If someone had told us then that all these were the calculated reactions of a KGB spy, it would have been impossible to believe, and one can measure what a torrent of historical revelation it would have let loose from her. She knew what agonies her people had had to endure in two world wars, with no respite in between, and she had her own idea of what the remedies might be which, naturally enough, were not so different from Wells's. And again the question may be posed: If she had been the woman of endless dissimulations, if she was the planted KGB agent, if she had not truly loved him, why should she not have accepted his constantly reiterated offers of marriage? She could have lived happily ever after or retired with the prestige and the money and the protection. Why did she refuse? The answer is that she loved him and she loved her independence, too. She would not surrender either; she insisted on both, and she persuaded him at last that this was the best solution for both of them. Here was the clue, or one clue at least, to the huge renewed intellectual exertion which he made in his last years. He had discovered something better than the lover-shadow he had always sought or claimed to seek: a new woman who had discovered a new independence, too. *

* One place where the Russians and their comrades, new and old, congregated

All Londoners who lived through those shameful times which led to the new war may first recall that the great deliverance started with a whimper. Instead of the cataclysm, nine months of 'phoney war' were interposed, before the rescue started. But there was no waiting and whimpering from Wells. His war started at once. Consulting with others but still placing upon it his own imprint, he wrote, produced and published, before Christmas, his new version of 'The Rights of Man' or 'What we are fighting for'. He had started the whole enterprise with a letter to *The Times* on 26 September 1939. One last-minute spur was supplied by the publication of the British Government's White Paper on the persecution of Jews in Germany. 'It is plain', wrote HG with his own emphasis,

> that *our Government has known for some time*, that such things were going on, and yet that up to a late hour it was willing to make peace with those responsible for all these tortures and murders the White Paper now substantiates. I suppose that if our Government had after all made that eleventh hour peace, then all that is in the White Paper, would have been hushed up. We should have sat down to our Christmas dinner thanking God for Mr. Chamberlain and ignoring the concentration camps altogether. And this incalculable Government of ours is still quite capable of sitting down in some sort of conference with the Nazis, the White Paper forgotten. We have no assurance that it will hold firmly to these common human rights for whose sake alone our people are willing to fight. And so we want our Government to declare for these rights unequivocally.

was 62 Park Street, Mayfair, where the ground floor and basement were occupied by Rose Herber, a Russian who could speak Russian and several other languages as well as Moura. She worked as a secretary for Sasha Galperson, a Russian Jewish film-maker, described in friendly terms in Bruce Lockhart's memoirs. Some time in 1942, I moved into the top flat at 62, and became overnight a friend of Rose Herber. Moura was her oldest friend and most constant companion in London, and I renewed the acquaintance I had first made with her at Beaverbrook's country house, Cherkley, in the winter of 1938. All three of us had plenty to talk about, but HG was always top of the agenda.

His continuing suspicions of the Foreign Office cut deep indeed, and could often involve him in quarrels with his friends. Storm Jameson, one of his old admirers from pre-1914 Fabian controversies, had taken over the presidency of PEN, one of the causes which was truly near his heart. He might accuse her and others who came within range of his invective of having bowed to the whims and wiles of the Foreign Office in the conduct of PEN business. At first hearing this she would be suitably outraged. Next week she might cool her annoyance only to provoke another outburst from him. Then, at the eleventh hour or later, he would repair all hard feelings with the sweetest of smiles.

He produced three works of fiction during this period; the precise dates of their composition and publication are significant since he was always absorbing the momentous nature of the world events which crowded in upon him and still seeking as adventurously as ever to interpret and reinterpret them. The first, *All Aboard for Ararat*, written in the early weeks of 1940, should have attracted as much attention as *The Croquet Player*; it was not actually dedicated also to Moura, but it could have been. The opening sentence seemed to portend a final doom, as *The Croquet Player* had done, but the mood was quite different: 'It seemed beyond dispute to Mr. Noah Lammock that madness had taken complete possession of the earth and that everything he valued in human life was being destroyed. Courage, devotion, generosity, still flamed out amidst the tragedy, but they shone only amidst a universal defeat. They were given no chance.' But Noah argued with God Almighty, Maker of Heaven and Earth, and the point of the argument was how to make a better show next time of the expedition of salvation. The God who appears in *All Aboard* certainly endears himself with his diffidence; it was always somebody else, mostly interested priests and preachers, who wanted to attribute infallibility.

'I have been called the "Great First Cause, but that "Great" is a vulgarity . . . While I exist, I am not omniscient. How can I be? Theologians have been very stupid in declaring I am. Vulgar artificial glorification. It flies in the face of commonsense. My original idea was of an immense responsive universe with a delightful garden at the centre pervaded by a sort of appreciative exaltation called love . . . But people read their Bibles in such a slovenly fashion. You can hardly call it reading! They bolt the stuff in a state of pious awe. I did so hope they wouldn't. I *hate* pious people . . .' But he could not suppress altogether his pride in that *Bible*: 'Taking it by and large, that Book of mine is wonderfully trustworthy. You will never never get a better universal history . . . The statistics may be loose; but you see I have always dealt in general ideas, always realised, since every single thing is really unique, the underlying fallacy of counting. I treat figures with a certain offhandedness . . . From first to last, my fault has been trustfulness. I am the Eternal Optimist. People say "God is Love". Far truer, that "God is Hope".'

And God persists, Noah is charmed,* and God explains his own disappointment with his Chosen People:

'Then He tried the Messiah idea. Saul of Tarsus put that askew in a brace of shakes. And then again at the eleventh hour I had found a really upright man who could not fail me. *Now*, I thought we shan't be long. I have said: "Let there be one more New Deal. Just one more. I was going to rain destruction upon the whole breed of *Homo Sapiens*. I was going to flood and stifle the whole earth under a torrent of German mud, blood and Ogpu, and have done with it . . ." But then each relented and pleaded with the other. Don't go on arguing about what I am or have been in reality, consider what I am now in men's imaginations. Consider my publicity value. A great majority of mankind has heard of the Lord God Almighty, the Heavenly Father, the Eternal Friend, but who has heard of Mr Noah Lammock, and his modern ideas? They don't bring up the Old Testament against me as you do . . . It passes over their minds like a fairy tale or a nursery rhyme. They don't believe that the whale swallowed Jonah any more than they believe that the dish ran

* Another of his references here is to 'Madam Rebecca and her double-crossing son'. And another mother and son could have taken some offence – or maybe it just proved how well Wells knew his Bible.

265

away with the spoon. Yet all the same they believe in a Heavenly Will for Goodness, and it is a great inspiration for them . . . I may have been an excuse for priestcraft and tyranny but also I have sustained the prophets and reformers. Don't turn me down altogether yet.'

And, of course, the new Noah responded: He, too, wanted to discover what was the real nature of this worldwide relapse. 'What is the real significance of this stupendous inundation of force and cruelty?' But they, God and Noah, soon stumbled on an even closer intellectual kinship. Each had his vanity as an author, and it was God who first broached the subject. That idea – 'that important idea of yours, the Museum Encyclopedia, dusty and derelict, is in your *Time Machine*, for example. Why pretend? The same idea is the framework of your *Work, Wealth and Happiness of Mankind*. It is *World Brain*. It crops up more and more frequently in your books as you get older and repeat yourself more and more.' And, as Noah vainly protested again, the flattering God pressed home his advantage: 'Even your boasted Professor Huxley, the old Huxley I mean, praised me with scarcely a qualification. For centuries, the literary side of my Book, at any rate, has been the marvel of mankind. It has been the treasure of the humble and the handbook of the mighty. No-one asked what books he would like to have on a desert island, has dreamed of omitting it, no-one.' And there was something very endearing about this irascible Divinity, entranced by his own creation, now that one met him face to face. He was, Noah realized, 'first and foremost as an Author, a great Author, that the world knows him best, and the vanity and self sufficiency of Authorship is innate and incurable'.

And for a while, it must be admitted, the old man more than held his own. But Noah skilfully steered him back to modern times.

Is it the old world we want to save and restore, after it has been properly overwhelmed for its sins and corruptions, or are we proposing to make an entirely new world, when this last frightful flare up of war and the conflicting sovereign states and all the bad old traditions are over? Do we intend to go *on* with the modern ideas, or do we intend to go back with those perfect Christian gentlemen, Franco, Halifax, Daladier, Pétain, Bushido – if you can call that a Christian gentleman – all the shattered hosts of reaction.

At which the Lord protested at the turn this conversation was taking: 'Need we talk politics?'

But it was real politics, the mixture of ideas and action, which always fascinated Wells, and his Noah would even flatter this God for a while in order to probe a little deeper: 'When you are put to the test, Oh Lord, you are never for the priests and conservatives, you are always for the prophets. You are the invincible Revolutionary. The Bible is the record of your Revolution which is where I fall out with these people with whom you seem to propose to tie me up, with this World Encyclopedia, World Brain idea etc.' – meaning, of course, Wells himself in his more exclusively ideological mood. No doubt the French Encyclopedists did their job in their century: 'They gave the French Revolution eyes.' But something even more adventurous must now be attempted; that was the true mood of 1940.

And beneath this piercing searchlight Noah was even prepared to take a fresh look at one of his favourite Great Men:

You see, the idea that a man might be saying something fundament-ally important without flourishing about with a damned hat, a damned great cloak, a damned great beard, a mop of hair and an excessive personality was inconceivable to the Victorians . . . What man of Science is there now, who believes that in his utmost work he is any better than a bearer, entrusted for a little while with something greater than himself which he too must hand on to equal or better men? But so it was that Marx, quarrelling, dogmatising, jealous of any infringement of his Greatness, sponging on his infinitely finer admirer Engels, had to be what he was. He could not escape it. He knew no better and stamped these paralysing limitations on to the developments of Socialism for a century.

But the revolutionary moods, the revolutionary spirit, did not fail. 'That first French Revolution was an attack upon the suffocation of human hope and possibilities by aristocratic privilege and clerical imposition, and it effected immense liberations.' For the mass of people all over the world, the hope was that immense liberations of equal consequence could be unloosed, but some of those movements lost their way. 'The inner control of the movement fell more and more into the hands of the little, over-loyal, second-rate, doctrinaire, useful ass, and into the hands of those who crave to exercise power.'

So the blueprints for the new Ark mixed with a reminder of the kind of men needed for the task; the messengers mixed with the message: 'I am all for those people who want to unite popular movements throughout the world upon a new Declaration of the Rights of Man. Such Declarations have worked great things in the past, keeping men erect and alert.' But some people also resolved that 'the common man shall not be hoodwinked and betrayed again, a slightly disgruntled critical wing of the élite itself, Voltaires, Montaignes, Shaws and Samuel Butlers.'

And then again:

This new born religion, *this religion of the perpetually increasing and renascent truth*, carries with it an inner compulsion to live, or if need be, die, as it dictates, directly its apprehension becomes complete. Do you get that? Enquiry replaces dogma. You grow. So that there is no possibility of a heresy hunt upon the Ark, any more than you can have a heresy hunt within the Royal Society. Our first duty is to maintain our own complete liberty of speech and publication. Freedom to grow.

And, by some quirk which Noah or Wells also respected, the English, even the English aristocracy, produced some rare and indispensable specimens.

'I cannot man my Ark without this superb you-be-damned to all mental controls, towards all inquisitional authority. From Byron to Bertie Russell, there has been an immense variety of individuals in our world, for the most part extremely exasperating outcasts, who rebelled and said the things that came to them plainly, though their heavens fell . . . And because of their own mental freedom, they have also enabled bold writers, artists and thinkers to say what they pleased and share their immunities. My Ark cannot be manned without free-spirited gentlemen, saturated with Pride. How am I to get hold of them now? And how sustain their intellectual insolence – on nothing? Or will they evaporate with the rest of their class? . . . Wanted: Gentlemen with strong brains mounted on stout backbones . . . Can we find any Shelleys for our Ark today? If there had been a Communist Party in his day he would certainly have been an active member, at any rate for a time before he set about knocking the Party to pieces.'

So Shelley, Byron, Voltaire and the whole of the great company which Wells could summon to his aid contributed to the mood of 1940. His eagerness to secure Byron's company on that last voyage of salvation was a peculiar favour; hitherto something in his manner had been allowed to alienate HG's affections, although Shelley had been a constant companion almost since his Bromley days. Altogether the tone and temper which he achieved in *All Aboard for Ararat* suggest that he was already touched by the first signs of the real deliverance which came just a few weeks later with the overthrow of the Chamberlain government in the Norway debate of 14 May 1940. Indeed, the very last chapter clinched it. Summoning another biblical tale to his assistance, Jonah, the most unspeakable character in the whole presentation, attempted to come on board, with the most hypocritical appeal. The author offered his candidates for a more modern list – Franco, Pétain, Hoare – and then a space was left for the reader to select his own preference for the prescribed list of traitors to the human cause.

All Aboard for Ararat, published in that bright but fateful spring, advertised his *Babes in the Darkling Wood* to appear that autumn. This was a more ambitious work of fiction covering the period just before the war, but mounting to that same 1940 climax. Indeed, he called the *Babes*, in a rare belligerent preface defending his own art, 'the most comprehensive and ambitious dialogue novel I have ever attempted'. He took a glance back at his own *Ann Veronica*, the young woman whose soliloquies and rhapsodies, revealing the idea of the younger intelligentsia in 1910, he had found so interesting: 'Before then no-one had realised there was an English intelligentsia. The book is not a dialogue, simply because no-one answers Ann Veronica. It interested a number of people who did not realise fully what bad taste they showed in being interested.'

His new babes were just as splendid a pair of young lovers as any upon whom he had ever bestowed his blessing: adventurous, inquisitive, utterly absorbed in each other but intelligently responsible to the world around them, revelling in every new discovery of sexual freedom, ecstatically celebrating their own moral conquests but preparing for fresh conquests across wider fields. No reader could suppose that there had been any final weakening in the Wellsian confidence of what mankind and womankind could do for themselves if they had the courage and the wit and the recognition of the other old Wellsian conditions, and yet he would still be ready to stare the real perils in the face and deliver his world-shattering warnings. This piece of writing might have been not much more than an old man's lament for the stupidities and the cowardice which had brought the catastrophe upon us, but, with him, even at the darkest hour of 1940, these fears must yield to the passionate, irresistible demands of the new generation.

The exact moment when he wrote was of some significance: the lovemaking and the first adventures of his young hero and heroine covered the period from the fresh surrender to the Fascist onslaught in the early months of 1939 to the ending of 'the phoney war' in May 1940 when Hitler's tanks broke through the Ardennes and, at last, a new government in Britain appeared to face the real menace. It was the most perilous moment in British history – and, maybe, in world history, too; the forces of barbarism were nearer to victory than ever before, but the forces of freedom stiffened their sinews at the last decisive opportunity. *Babes in the Darkling Wood* was an honourable contribution to that debate. His new breed of babes defied the darkling wood and cut out for themselves, as if wielding some all-powerful scythe, an intelligible route for the future.

Some of his outbursts during the phoney war itself had a poignancy all his own. He could not help hearing the sermons which still came from the pulpits. He had his own peculiar perspective on these high matters, and it was by no means one to be dismissed.

> The old Anglican tradition hangs on here, scotched but not killed, during the whole period of English liberalism, and it wriggled back to political power in this last monarchist and clerical counter-revolution of the Frightened Thirties, which has recaptured our poor fly-blown Empire, to steer it now rapidly, so rapidly now it terrifies one, towards military and economic disaster. Think of Lord Halifax with Lord Lloyd behind him at the Foreign Office, think of our triumphant archbishops and our stupid broadcasts, read *The Times*, watch the confident smiling and bowing and posturing of the Court, listen to the wartime buzz of the pulpits, the press, the streets. One might think of all our once great and mighty England dead and decayed beneath these crawling, swarming Anglicans. Where is God's Englishman now? Where is the England of Milton and Newton, Gilbert and Bacon, Darwin and Huxley, Cromwell, Nelson, Blake? It is not only you youngsters who are baffled. The whole country is baffled to hear the voices that claim to speak for it now. The world is baffled by the awful legacy of those teachers who would not learn. *

And some side-glances at 1939 and 1940 enabled him to give a discerning view of the Soviet Union or the old Russia, if you like, which he always studied with a special interest and insight. The Soviet invasion of Finland destroyed one band of Communist idealists who had never believed their chosen state could be guilty of such a crime. 'It exposes the fact', his

---

* *Babes in the Darkling Wood*, p. 327.

instructor insisted, 'that while Russia is human, all too human, your crowd of young people began by over-believing in it and refusing to hear any criticism of it, and now most of that bright red youthfulness in you is slumping over on the other side. You have been betrayed, you little dears, and that absolves you from everything.'

Or this one – another ineffable glimpse of the English people in 1939:

'Kalikov? Oh! He's interned. Yes interned.'
'Interned!'
'Naturally.'
'But he's a Bulgarian! We're not at war with Bulgaria.'

And a few minutes later.

'But to intern him!'
'We can't be too careful. After all, we are less than twenty miles from the coast. And I'm not certain he wasn't more or less of a Jew. All that hair of his.'
'But we're not at war with the Jews. And Kalikov isn't a Jewish name.'
'There are Jews and Jews and they take all sorts of names. They are really all alike,' said the vicar, and dismissed that increasingly difficult topic. 'Anyhow, he's interned.'

He sent copies of *Babes* to Bernard Shaw, among others, who generously replied: 'You are not dead yet (I am, unfortunately); there are luminosities and subtleties that are newly born as well as the old Wellsian faculty.' But any serious compliments were still suitably barbed, since Shaw accepted that some part of *Babes* (no doubt the powerful anti-Stalin, anti-CP sections) was directed at him. But HG had a strong case now, although Shaw found it impossible to admit as much. He protested about 'the insufficiency of H.G.'s Rights of Man propaganda: it did not get down to brass tacks'. A few weeks before, he (Shaw) had been complaining to another of his old correspondents, Beatrice

Webb: 'The Wells Bill of Rights left me out of all patience with abstractions on which Stalin and Lord Halifax are perfectly agreed.' True enough in one sense, but it should also be noted that HG took precautions to deal with his special *bête noire*, Lord Halifax, by other means – and Stalin, too, for that matter. Shaw still called Stalin 'the greatest living statesman', while HG was achieving the fresh luminosities on all these personal and political questions which the times required.

Another near-contemporary view of the England and the Europe of the early 1940s – and by no means an orthodox one – was given in *You Can't Be Too Careful*, published in the autumn of 1941. His supposed hero, Mr Edward Albert Tewler, had no heroic qualities, and he suffered from all the deficiencies of his upbringing, the standard education of an Englishman of the lower middle class reared in our century. He had to face all the horrors with nothing to protect him but Anglican prayers, *Times* leading articles and Chamberlain's strategies. World War? 'No affair of ours,' Tewler would insist, as he had been taught up to the twelfth hour and beyond.

'One thing we must never forget about Mussolini,' said the vicar of Casing to Mrs. Rooter in an earnest friendly talk at Harvest Thanksgiving. 'Mustard gas or no mustard gas, he did put back the crucifix in the schools. I could forgive him many things for that.'

And then Tewler adapted himself to the pressures of the phoney war.

So that when at least Mr. Neville Chamberlain gave up appeasement, in a fit of exasperation at the unendurable mockery of his umbrella, and declared war, Edward Albert, in common with a very considerable number of his comfortable independent fellow citizens, made no attempt whatever to join the fray. Throughout the later months of 1939, Tewler England and Tewler France did not so much wage war as evade it. They potted at the enemy from behind the Maginot line and left Poland to its fate. They watched Russia re-adjust its frontiers in preparation for the inevitable struggle against the common enemy with profound disapproval. That Prince of Tewlers, the young King of the Belgians, obstinately refused to prepare a common front against the gathering onslaught. He was neutral, master in his own country, he insisted, and nothing could happen to him. He uttered a squeal for help when his frontier collapsed and vanished from the scene, and all the King's horses and all the King's men will never restore a Europe that will have any role for him again. The military science of France and England required that when an army is outflanked it should either retreat headlong or surrender. When confronted by a pincer like movement, a soldier and a gentleman abandons his men and materials and bolts home, ascribing his defeat to the decadent morals of the time. The British tradition was a Day of Prayer. But wars are won by ungentlemanly persons who break the recognised rules of war and swear freely. The reactions of Almighty Providence to these Anglican praying bouts was ambiguous. The English and the French strategists got themselves soundly licked by tanks, planes, and this professional horror of nippers, and they were rather scandalised by the obstinacy of their men who insisted upon going on fighting until disaster took on an appearance of glorious retreat. Goebbels had only to say 'envelopment' or 'penetration', and the confidence of the American and English military experts ran out at their heels. Pétain surrendered France. Until that happened, Morningside Prospect had seemed a whole world away from bloodshed and violence. But the French collapse sent a shock through the villas. Newspapers fluttered at the garden gates and men sat in the golf club house with grave faces and stopped to talk war upon the tees.[*]

But then at last Britain did awake, and HG proposed a proper negotiating position. 'We can make no terms with falsehood.' He despatched a copy of *You Can't Be Too Careful*, Christmas 1941, to Beatrice and Sidney Webb with the comment on the page: 'outrageous but true.' And he did have the right to say it.

Hanover Terrace was the scene of most of his wartime trials and triumphs. He took pride in the fact that once the bombs really started falling on his beloved London he would not seek

[*] *You Can't Be Too Careful* (1941), p. 248.

any escape, especially the pressing invitations which he received to escape altogether across the Atlantic. He did make a few weekend excursions with Moura and Tania to Great Haseley in Oxfordshire, and Tania graphically recorded how some of these excursions coincided with the most notable developments in the war itself. One of these, and the most significant of all, was the bright Sunday morning on 22 June 1941 when the news came through that Hitler had committed the historic Napoleonic crime and folly of invading Russia, and when, no less momentously that night, Churchill embraced our new allies, and a real new prospect of actually winning the war was suddenly presented to us. HG and Moura had a special right to rejoice; the prospect for both their countries was transformed beyond all reckoning. HG and the others hastened to join the festivities in the Oxfordshire village where they were staying, and particularly reassured the local vicar who handed him the microphone that his name was Herbert George Wells, as English as they come, but that Russia could help us win a war and build a new world. And when Churchill spoke from 10 Downing Street that night in the same sense no-one had a better right to greet him than HG – or, rather, there was another claimant to join the rejoicing, Ivan Maisky at the Soviet embassy. In the darkest days of 1940 when not so far away an American ambassador was reporting to Washington that Britain could not survive, Maisky reported in the opposite sense to Moscow. His country, Moura's country, was now to endure the most terrible human slaughter ever recorded in the annals of war. Yet her country, her people, would survive, and it could be properly claimed that Ivan Maisky's diplomacy and HG's foresight and Moura's love all made their contribution.

He had an equal right to acclaim the further transformation in the world's fortunes which followed the Japanese attack on Pearl Harbor and the belated mobilization of American power to help settle the issue, East and West. No-one could accuse him of having indulged in a febrile anti-Americanism, such as the Chamberlain administration did exhibit as late as 1938. They dangerously, wickedly almost, misjudged President Franklin

Roosevelt. If they had accepted HG's firsthand reports, they could have formed a much wiser foreign policy to meet the tests of the late 1930s. Indeed, if some Americans had listened, they could have saved themselves the humiliation of Pearl Harbor; that was one of HG's prophecies way back in 1920. Indeed, he had formed a view of what would be 'the American century' way back in 1906, soon after his meeting with Theodore Roosevelt. Even more exactly, it was his Mr Britling who understood the American role in that first world war better than any other imaginative writer and who could have helped stop another one. Anyhow, the American President who had read his books seemed better-equipped than the British Prime Ministers who had not.

Desperately slowly, as all who lived through it can remember, the fortunes of the Grand Alliance changed. It did not come swiftly, even after the colossal misjudgements by the Germans and the Japanese. But HG and Moura did have plenty to celebrate, and sometimes these happy occasions were staged in Tania's presence at Great Haseley. But on one occasion Rebecca West was among the guests, and Tania records of her mother that it was 'the only time that I ever saw her at a loss for words'. Strangely, it may seem, she did not discuss the matter with her mother, but she offered the verdict: 'Moura was unusually subdued and silent and I realised then the cause of her discomfort. Rebecca West was a woman with a lively, and above all, disciplined intelligence. Moura was, I think, rather afraid of her, and uncomfortable in the presence of such a woman.' A younger HG – the author, say, of *The Passionate Friends* – might have referred the matter to his Assize of Jealousy, or maybe that court had long since outlived its usefulness.

The most important of all his wartime writings – a book with some claim to be the most powerful of all his journalistic compilations – was what he called his contemporary memoir, *'42 to '44*. The volume has often been neglected or derided, and Wells himself must accept part of the responsibility for this absurd misjudgement. Two casual references to *'42 to '44* which appeared later in his *Mind at the End of Its Tether* seemed to dismiss the book, or at least to give his enemies the excuse not to read it. This was just another example of Wells's disparagement of his own achievements, his adoption of the Swiftian posture of the hypocrite in reverse which his bitterest enemies, like Swift's, would seize upon for their own wretched purposes. In the case of *'42 to '44*, the self-injuries were all the more deadly since little time was left for the remedy to be applied. If Wells himself was able to confess that *'42 to '44* had blemishes, why should anyone else step forward to challenge the verdict? But the modern reader can judge for himself: *'42 to '44* stands on its own merits. It was English journalism at its best and bravest, at the height of the Second World War.

What HG thought of it himself at the time of its actual publication (March 1944) has some persistent interest. He called it 'A Contemporary Memoir upon Human Behaviour During the Crisis of the World Revolution'. It was dedicated 'to the Eternal Memory of John Ball', but contained also in that same dedication a reference to Nietzsche. To embrace together the ancient founder of English Socialism and the modern European exponent, as some would say, of the gospel of force might be cited as an example of Wells's intellectual perversity. Such complainants should read the quotation more patiently. It is Nietzsche, the seeker after knowledge, who had helped to awaken Wells's own mind, and he would always honour his debts:

DEDICATED TO THE ETERNAL MEMORY OF JOHN BALL.
And all my thought and striving is to compose and gather into one thing what is a fragment and a riddle and a dismal accident. And how could I bear to be a man if man was not a poet and a solver of riddles and the saviour of accidents.
NIETZSCHE – *THUS SPAKE ZARATHUSTRA*

Then, in his preface, Wells adds his own estimate: 'It is all I have made of things, my ultimate philosophy, copious and complete . . .' But he hastened to add his own qualifications: 'a philosophy must be a poor, pretentious, incomplete thing that cannot comprehend the trivial. Come with me to my base behind the battle-front, if you will . . .'

Sometimes he would launch from the base furious, calculated assaults upon selected enemies. Several of these were published in the *Evening Standard* at the time when the present writer was the editor of that journal. He was happy to publish everything Wells wrote and to print it in the manner Wells required. That in any case was the condition Wells himself laid down. Headlines, paragraphs and punctuation had to be followed exactly as he had prescribed, but these were only some of his conditions and not the most awkward. All the articles had to be taken together if they were to be taken at all.

Wells himself knew, none better, who was likely to be offended by particular assaults, and how the whole series might thereby be jeopardized. When the series reached us at the *Evening Standard*, I believe they had already been hawked around Fleet Street by Wells's agents. Wells's old friend and enemy Lord Beaverbrook, the proprietor of the *Evening Standard*, might have been expected to be especially offended by some of these pieces, and no-one knew better which they might be. However, all were printed, according to Wells's insistence, and Beaverbrook himself seemed to enjoy the cries of outrage from other quarters sufficiently to suppress his own qualms. Anyhow, the whole of '42 to '44 was a *tour de force*, mixing immediate necessities with fresh excursions, testing the Wellsian imagination to the limit.

The first part of the whole book, 'The Heritage of the Past', presents as the central question a full-scale examination of the psychology of cruelty: an attempt to outline together the science and the history of the subject. He glanced back to his first biological studies under the great T. H. Huxley: 'In those stable times all ideas of change had to be broached with a sort of proprietary facetiousness . . . The British mind was stagnating in contentment.' But Wells had never been content with such excuses: the phenomenon of human cruelty was present in some of his own first publications in the complacent 1890s. Strange, indeed, that the Wells who exposed the mind of Dr Moreau should have been accused both of sharing the evil tastes of the doctor and of refusing to recognize how deep was the phenomenon and where it came from. But Wells was always facing it! 'It is distasteful to face the fact that the human animal, by reason of its intelligence, can be the most deliberately cruel of all living things. Exceptionally so. Above all other creatures.' He would persist in his analysis and permit no mitigation or qualification of the charge: that would be to suppress the truth. 'One thing we are not permitted to shirk any longer is this reality of cruelty, and how cruelty begets cruelty, and how it is our business to discover the nature and origin of this reciprocating cruelty: how essential it is to find a solution to the human martyrdom we call civilisation.' This was the greatest of all Swiftian questions, indelibly inscribed on the walls of St Patrick's Cathedral. Nothing about God there; everything about the human cruelty for which there should be no forgiveness.

But then, in '42 to 44, Wells offers his sensational response to the mighty theme, one which he himself had been presenting in different forms since those far-off Victorian times or at least since the publication of In the Days of the Comet in 1906, and which should certainly have commanded attention at the height of this revolutionary war. 'Socialism dawned in Kent,' was his retort to those who attempted to suggest that there might be something unpatriotic in raising the demand for revolutionary changes – not least in property relations – in the midst of the war itself.

> The vague indignation of popular common sense found expression in the preaching of one whom the courtly Froissart called 'a mad priest of Kent', John Ball. 'Good people,' cried the preacher, 'things will never go well in England so long as goods be not in common, and so long as there be villeins and gentlemen. By what right are they whom we call lords greater folk than we? On what grounds have they deserved it? Why do they hold us in serfage? If we all came of the same father and mother, of Adam and Eve, how can they say or prove that they are better than we, if it be not that they make us gain for them by our toil what they spend in their pride? They are

clothed in velvet and warm in their furs and their ermines, while we are covered with rags. They have wine and spices and fair bread; and we oat-cake and straw, and water to drink. They have leisure and fine houses; we have pain and labour, the rain and the wind in the fields. And yet it is of us and our toil that these men hold their state.'

And so to the plain challenge of

> When Adam delved and Eve span
> Who was then the gentleman?

The French Jacquerie was simultaneous and all of a piece with the primordial socialism of John Ball. As a matter of fact, Kent and the south-east of England were far more closely linked in thought and social life with the north-east of France than with the lands behind either region. There were parallel movements in Flanders, and especially Ghent and Bruges and Ypres. The Ghent weavers were the stoutest.

How Wat Tyler was murdered; how John Ball was executed in the sight of Richard II; how that tragic and inglorious king lied and cheated his way out of the Peasant Revolt, how the people trusted him and were massacred for their touching disposition to accept the word of a gentleman; and how, after a phase of alleviation, due to the fact that the more they were butchered the rarer they became, they increased and multiplied and were economically debased once more, all that is to be found in any history. But the spirit of that Kentish revolt did not die.

How at last, from nonconformity and dissent and radicalism, the idea of a lucid world socialism was created and how with it grew the awakening self-respect of the common people, all these strides along the road of progress were described. His streaks of lightning lit up the path, until at last came the thunderous climax: 'You may murder world socialism now and hide it in the cellar, and when you go upstairs again you will find it astraddle your hearth.'

So the patriotic mood of 1940 still gave its resonance to the whole national and international debate. And HG could be excused his own 'Patriotic Digression':

I am often accused of being anti-patriotic, the friend of every country but my own. So far as declaring that our present monarchy is something exceptionally lovely or wise, or echoing the Anglican 'loyalty' of that queer American born artifact, T. S. Eliot, or responding to Kipling's chi-chi imperialism, or adoring the 'stately homes of England', or believing that the Union Jack is anything but a patchwork rag, I am passionately unpatriotic. I detest all that Hanoverian stuff. Pope's *Dunciad* was plain prophecy. I prefer Cosmopolis and mankind. It is in the nature of any real Englishman to do that.

I prefer Cosmopolis and mankind, it is true, but here I am going to confess to a profound pride in my own people. Frankly I do not think that Cosmopolis can dispense with us. I am a Cosmopolitan patriot; let men of other nations be the same according to their birth. I have my home-bred perspective. I find a profound satisfaction and inspiration in Milton's phrase 'God's Englishman', as the resilient, competent and obdurate servant of mankind. Consider the men who have sprung from this little island to fertilize the world!

Roger Bacon and Francis Bacon, William Gilbert, Isaac Newton, Erasmus Darwin, Charles Darwin, T. H. Huxley, Cavendish, Dalton, Joule, Faraday, Bateson, Bragg . . . and so on to Lord Rayleigh, Gowland Hopkins, Rutherford, a tremendous galaxy . . . And if now scientific work is the most universal thing in the world, none the less it was the pedantically methodical Francis Bacon, inspired by Gilbert and his posthumous child, the Royal Society, who first put research and mutual publication into working order.

Then the first of socialists, John Ball.

Then the subtle and obstinate Wycliffe, who denied Trans-substantiation and split off a living and progressive Protestantism from an ever more reactionary Church, who had the Bible translated into the vulgar tongue, and, together with his pupil, Jan Huss, begot the Reformation.

Then, as the finest spirited of administrators, Sir T. Stamford Raffles, most foully treated by the East India Company, which sued his widow for damages because he had liberated its slaves prematurely . . .

Then, as destroyers of monarchy and oppression, the Puritan regicides and in particular Oliver Cromwell, who gave mankind the new and illuminating idea that a king could be guilty of, and be tried and beheaded for, treason to the people.

As for other republicans, George Washington, Jefferson, Tom Paine, Abraham Lincoln – he too was good English – William Blake, Godwin, Shelley, the Tolpuddle Martyrs . . .

I will not expand about our poetry and literature, for here is a realm of special values, from Shakespeare who shone out in such plays as *Henry V*, *Macbeth*, *Hamlet* and *A Midsummer Night's Dream*, to such extremes as Bunyan, Pope of the *Dunciad*, Tennyson – a vast and vastly varied multitude.

These are some of the deeds and names upon the English roll of honour that begins with Roger Bacon and John Ball. Maybe they loom larger in perspective because they are nearer to me, but can any other country or tongue produce a brighter constellation?

He described how the English revolutionaries, often giving the lead to their American or French comrades-in-arms, carried forward the common cause until the crisis of 1940 or, even more precisely, Christmas 1942 when they were actually penned and when the next stage was to be set. He could not resist a final side-glance at the English enemy now being shunted from the stage:

The smouldering discontent of the privileged and advantaged with the development of liberal equalitarianism has been seeking a method for countering this drift. That abundant creature in our social complex, the little snob-cad, has found his advantage in over-expressing the secret desires of the upper classes, and the political adventurer has found an abundant following at this social level, needy, yet passionately eager to feel a 'bit superior', combining social pretentiousness with a profound cacophony.

Anyone who beheld the Mosleyites running like the wind down Regent Street from the Jewish prize-fighters, who used to break up their demonstrations, knows the real quality of this weedy reactionary riff-raff. It was bred abundantly in those peculiar British establishments, the private schools. Abroad the cad snob is drawn from a slightly different stratum, in which the minor functionary plays a larger part. The Empire has contributed its quota of offspring from minor officials and business representatives, not always innocent of a chi-chi accent. A congenial ideology appeared in Kipling's *Stalky and Co.*, in which the idea of nasty little quasi-upper-class boys taking the law into their own hands was glorified.

But the real drama, better than any Marxist presentation, better than any essay in the materialist interpretation of history, was to be staged, a fresh study in this drama of John Ball and Richard II in modern dress.

One part of the coming struggle must centre round the new Declaration of the Universal Rights of Man. That was one firm ground on which the future might be built. Bernard Shaw and others might deride them as platitudinous and opaque and much too little ambitious for the fulfilment of the major tasks ahead. But they could be understood in every language and across every continent, and they soon were. Wells appreciated better than Shaw had ever done the lasting appeal of Thomas Paine and Thomas Jefferson, and he was soon to add a fresh appreciation of Jefferson's greatness to his own historical understanding.

Next he launched his *Evening Standard* series. The first was called 'Idiot's Delight' (his own unchangeable title, of course), and it appeared to be addressed to some of his old opponents in the Foreign Office who thought that their way to prepare for the new world was to redraw some old maps. The next was called 'The Plain Truth about the Communist Party'. He likened the thought processes of the British Communist Party to that of the Roman Catholic Church, much to the fury of both: 'Each embodies a moribund philosophy and a control of thought and knowledge. But how can there be a world community without a

283

common world-wide philosophy to hold it together, and a free-growing body of knowledge under the symbol of the incessant "L" to keep it alive?'

Then in his series of *Evening Standard* bombshells he planted one on racism in South Africa directed precisely to Field Marshal Smuts, at that time a highly respected member of the British War Cabinet. To taste the dish properly, modern readers need to be reminded how high was Smuts's reputation across the whole political spectrum. He was a liberal South African who had never subscribed to any doctrine of apartheid. Indeed, the word had not been invented then, although the practice had long prevailed in many varying and humiliating applications. So Wells was not afraid to deliver his worldwide warning: 'I ask you, when all the world is made equal and free, how can the petty white tyranny of your system escape a convulsion?' Beneath such an assault Smuts might have a grievance that it was impossible for him to answer. And that Wellsian prophecy reached its fulfilment only fifty years later.

Two more domestic or near-domestic questions figured in that series; they might sound comparatively trivial half a century later, but at the time they were explosive. One was a direct assault on the competence of the First Lord of the Admiralty, A. V. Alexander, who happened to be a close friend of our own publisher, Beaverbrook. Another was an attack on the Irish government for the way it conducted its affairs, much to the injury of the cause of human rights everywhere: 'God, of course, is Minister without Portfolio in whatever Cabinet happens to be in power . . . Awkward problems can always be referred back to Christ or Cromwell . . . Yesterday is continously being shoved in front of the public eye to bamboozle them about the problems of today.' And then two others to add to his 'Specimen English Statesmen', each of them also constant guests at the Beaverbrook board. First Sir Samuel Hoare,

> one of those rulers of whom the British seem unable to get quit . . .
> It is appalling that this blinkered, pleasant, gossipy, gullible snob,
> after being Air Minister, Secretary of State for India, Foreign

Secretary, First Lord of the Admiralty, Home Secretary and Lord Privy Seal, should have been installed at last in Madrid, as spokesman of the democracies . . . The world needs a free liberal Spain in a federated world. There can be no place in any tolerable human future for a man of Franco's type, with treachery in his heart, victims still in his clutches, and blood upon his hands.

And then another, the first Baron, Lord Vansittart: 'It is a terrible thing to say of any public figure, but I was provoked to class him with Sir Samuel Hoare.' That charge is never clinched. How could it be? Vansittart was inspired by a deep and indelible hatred of Germany and all its works, and that might at least be supposed to acquit him of some of Wells's strictures. He could be anti-German, too; but, contrary to the libels often unloosed against him, he never turned it into a racist accusation. But Vansittart was always allowing himself to be led astray by his ill-concealed contempt for the follies and vulgarities of democracy. And that had led him, too, to be a party to the great betrayal of the Spanish Republic. Fascism and Nazism could have been defeated on Spanish battlefields, and a continent could have been saved.

More revealing still of Wells's true wartime insights was his full-scale examination of Anglo-American intelligence, his answer to his own question: what can one forecast from America, the great problem-child of humanity? He had made some notable visits across the Atlantic, in 1906 at the time of Theodore Roosevelt's presidency, in 1934 soon after Franklin Roosevelt embarked upon his New Deal, and most recently in the winter of 1940, just after the Battle of Britain and before America's entry into the conflict. He had a ringside seat at the 1940 presidential election, and was amazed by 'its out-and-out baseness. I can use no other word. The deliberate falsifications, day after day, of an almost unanimous anti-Roosevelt press were abominable. At present there is still a great light of liberalism shining in America, but it does not shine in bank parlours, business offices and editorial rooms.'

HG had long since been impressed by the deficiencies of American society; he could put them in perspective.

A vast majority of these multitudes, amounting to well over 200 million, have a satisfaction about their character, their social wisdom and their superiority to the rest of mankind, only to be paralleled in history by the self-satisfaction of China in the days of Mandarin rule. There is nothing more they have to learn. Upon them falls the grave responsibility of leading what seems to them to be an incurably inferior world. They have as a mass no philosophy whatever; their education is limited and dismally inadequate, their knowledge of history, if one may call it knowedge, is a training in patriotic bragging and lying. Their religion so far as America goes is a sincere worship of the dollar as a source of power, freedom and the pursuit of all the good things in life. In the British system this money worship is complicated by a genuine and earnest snobbery; in both cases nowadays, it is camouflaged by a coarse veil of Christian cant.

It might be that he would be misled by this analysis, but then he recalled his own visit, five years earlier – a bare five years, it was fascinating to recall. What mighty events and conclusions had intervened?

When I visited President Roosevelt in 1935, things were asway and rather confusing. In 1937 they were clearer. The New Deal had been a magnificent promise, and it had evoked a mighty volume of hope. Now that hope was dissipated. Mass-hope is the most wonder-working gift that can come into the hands of a popular leader. The mass-hope of world peace at the end of the Great War, the mass-hope of the Russian Revolution and the mass-hope of the New Deal were great winds of opportunity. But these great winds of opportunity do not wait for ships to be built or seamen to learn navigation. If ships are not ready for them, they blow themselves out. They pass; they are not to be recalled.

We might intervene here to recall the attacks sometimes unloosed on Wells for failing to understand or respect 'the masses'. Sometimes the attack might come from Marxists or from politico-philosophers of other brands. The most recent of these was the one contained in John Carey's *The Intellectuals and the Masses* (1991). Here Wells found himself in the strange company of Henry James, T. S. Eliot and Wyndham Lewis, attacked for his élitism and his constant contempt for the masses. Wells himself would have been amazed both by the accusation and by the literary company he was alleged to be keeping. If John Carey had troubled to read Wells's *'42 to '44*, he could have saved himself from such a collapse into absurdity. Wells himself did not often use the term 'the masses', perhaps for the very reason that the Marxists used it so crudely. But he did understand the great popular movements, the revolutionary convulsions, which had been the governing events in past times and would prove so again. He rightly saw the performance of Franklin Roosevelt in the 1930s as one of these periods of mass hope, and believed they would come again.

And, for all the lying and the indecency of the 1940 election, he returned with his hopes for a better world reawakened. He would not make obeisance before any Great Man interpretation of history: never had done and never would. But he came back also with a fresh appreciation of what political greatness might be. As he travelled across the country in 1940, and read its history afresh, he discovered who was the greatest of all American Presidents, intellectually greater than Washington or Lincoln or Theodore Roosevelt or Franklin Delano. Thus, HG had his full introduction to Thomas Jefferson, and the matter which clinched the association did credit to them both. Someone showed him the page in a book in which Jefferson had written: 'I never will, by any word or act, bow to the shrine of intolerance, or admit a right of enquiry into the religious opinions of others.' Upon that rock, free thought in the United States of America was founded. But Jefferson had many other strands in his mind and character which Wells would especially appreciate: his scientific training, his deep-seated scepticism, his uneasiness about the rejection of unforeseen possibilities, his magnanimity, his allegiance to his real friends like Thomas Paine, his understanding of *Rights of Man*: 'Wherever the history of the English-speaking peoples is studied, Thomas Jefferson, the real Jefferson, and not the begetter of that dreadful offspring, the secessionist democrat, should be an outstanding figure.' That was the homecoming HG early in 1940, and they would accuse him of pursuing some personal themes or vendettas. He himself had a touch of Jefferson's magnanimity.

He was aghast again to see how so many people – yes, masses indeed – were cheated of their just expectations.

> Our human heritage is a devastated estate of undeveloped or distorted possibilities. One can only guess what proportion of human beings in the past missed the slightest chance of development, how many mute inglorious Miltons died in silence, how many potential Miltons never learnt to read. There are claptrap phrases about backward races and inferior peoples. These are the excuses by which those who still hope to go on at an advantage over their fellow creatures camouflage their own base dreams. There are no backward races!*

That, too, was the message for the world which Wells brought back from the United States.

On his last visit to New York he met for the last time another English writer who had almost matched him in popular appeal as both novelist and short story writer, although their temperaments might be thought entirely uncongenial. But each spoke well of the other whenever they got the chance. Somerset Maugham wrote how the HG who came to lunch 'looked old, tired, and shrivelled. He was perky as ever, but with something of an effort.' His lecture tour had been a fiasco, since his voice had become even thinner. But he had had that experience before and taken it in his stride. What nothing could efface was his humour, especially when it was turned on himself.

> Notwithstanding HG's immense reputation and the great influence he had on his contemporaries, he was devoid of conceit. There was nothing of the stuffed shirt in him. He never put on airs. He had naturally good manners and he would treat some unknown

---

* A *Contemporary Memoir* (1944), p. 98.

scribbler, the assistant librarian, for instance of a provincial library, with the same charming civility as if he were as important as himself.

It was Maugham also who recorded the answer some others extracted from Moura:

I once asked one of his mistresses what especially attracted her to him. I expected her to say his acute mind and his sense of fun; not at all: she said that his body smelt of honey. *

Another general encounter on that last New York trip seemed to belie the idea of an old man sinking into intellectual decrepitude. His old friend, Somerset Maugham, could revive him, but so could a new one, a near-namesake, called Orson Welles. A few years before – on 30 October 1938, to be precise – Orson Welles had caused a sensation and near-panic across a substantial area of the eastern United States, by reading passages about the arrival of the Martians from Wells's old classic, *The War of the Worlds*. It was so realistic that tens of thousands of his hearers thought it was real. At the time it was reported that HG had not been amused by the incident. But any animosity soon vanished when the two men actually met. HG remarked: 'I've had a series of most delightful experiences since I came to America, but the best thing that has happened to me so far has been meeting my little namesake here – Orson – I find him most delightful – he carries my name with an extra E which I hope he'll soon drop . . . I've known his work before he made this sensational Halloween spree – are you sure there was such a panic in America?'†

Soon after his return, and at the very time when he might have taken some credit for himself in keeping his political vision up to date and enlarging it to embrace the Anglo-American future, he found himself thrust into an argument, and what

* Maugham, *The Vagrant Mood*, pp. 211–12.
† The exchange is described in Arthur C. Clarke's 1994 introduction to a new edition of *The War of the Worlds*.

developed into a bitter one, with a young writer whom he could regard as a pupil and who was certainly ready to acknowledge him as his master. George Orwell eagerly confessed that he had been brought up on the writings of H. G. Wells, and that for him to deliver an attack was a kind of parricide. Provoked by some of the articles by Wells about his American trip, in which allegedly he had underestimated the continuing strength of Hitler's assault, he transformed the criticism into one of his general attacks on the English Left and the manner in which their weaknesses and waywardness had helped to feed the strength of the Nazi giant both before and after the outbreak of the actual war in 1939–40. This became more and more a common strand in the Orwellian theme. However, any ill feeling left by this first assault seemed to be dissipated at a dinner-party held at the house of their mutual friend Inez Holden, with William Empson, the critic and poet, acting as the slightly inebriated chairman. Wells defended himself, Orwell offered no apologies, each appeared to have profited from the argument. After several hours, they all staggered out into the blackout of wartime London, all seeming to follow the example of the chairman. Wells, according to Inez Holden's testimony, had enjoyed the whole evening; he had some reason to believe that any soreness between them had been removed.

But the sequel was more serious. Six months later Orwell returned to the subject, and to deliver an even more comprehensive and wounding assault. Indeed, his talk entitled 'The Rediscovery of Europe', and reprinted in *The Listener*, could be regarded as one of the most important essays on literature which he had ever attempted. H. G. Wells was not the only victim: almost all the other writers of his generation – Shaw, Housman, Hardy, Bennett and the rest – were criticized for their 'complete unawareness of anything outside the contemporary English scene'. It had been left to the new generation – Joyce, Eliot, Lawrence – 'to rediscover Europe and to rediscover too a sense of tragedy, a better awareness of the processes of history'. Poor HG was especially arraigned for the way he 'looked at the past with some sort of surprised disgust as a civilised man contemplating a tribe of cannibals', as the leading exponent of the view that, if reason was allowed to rule, science could bring unqualified, incalculable benefits for mankind. Wells was 'too sane to understand the modern world; he could not see or would not see that the barbarian had taken command'.

Each part of the indictment must have added to HG's sense of grievance. Maybe what came nearest the bone was the revival of the suggestion invoked once by Rebecca West that he did not understand the new generation of writers, the greatness of James Joyce in particular. That might be near the truth, although HG, with his customary generosity of spirit, as we have seen, had done his supreme best to help Joyce at his most severe hour of need. But, for the rest, most of the accusations seem especially harsh, especially in the mouth of Orwell. How could the reader of *The Island of Dr Moreau* – Orwell had just been rereading it – convict him of a puerile optimism about the future conquests of science? Why should he be told that he was a poor student of history when he had taken as one of his chief instructors the same Gibbon whom Orwell so justly honoured? Why should he be lumped with those who had presented a rosy view of the rise of Fascism when at each opportunity dating back to Mussolini's first appearance he had delivered his warnings with such passionate scorn? He had been quite as consistent an opponent of Fascism in every form, in Italy, Spain, Germany or Britain, as 'the Trotskyite in the big boots', as he would call Orwell. And was not some part of the estrangement due to the fact that Orwell and some others had not troubled to read what Wells had actually written about their common deliverance in 1940, the sense of exultation which they were all entitled to share? The irony was that three writers on the English Left had performed that task best: one was George Orwell himself in *The Lion and the Unicorn*, published in December 1940, the second was Rebecca West in *Black Lamb and Grey Falcon*, which added her tribute to English patriotism in that same autumn, and Wells himself who wrote the passages in his *Babes in the Darkling Wood* at the same time or the descriptions of the same events which appeared a year later in his *You Can't Be Too Careful*. At least Wells had a case. But Orwell's wartime diary for 27 March 1942 had the gruff entry: 'Abusive letter from H. G. Wells who addresses me as "You shit", among other things.'

Most infuriating of all must have been Orwell's attack on Wells's sense of history. He prided himself that he had done something original here at least in the field of popular education. Orwell seemed to conclude that this achievement counted for nothing, and his dismissal of Wells's labours was performed with just the arrogant flourish which might have been expected from the legion of enemies whom he had made in the university world. The Orwell who aspired to raise the standard of popular political writing should have paused to consider what Wells had accomplished in the writing of history. They were in the same trade, and they would acknowledge the same masters. Orwell insisted that Edward Gibbon with his readiness to pass sweeping moral judgements was the kind of historian needed to describe the modern age of crime and horror. But Wells had long taken Gibbon as his model, and Jonathan Swift had inspired them both. Their common heritage in so many fields should have helped preserve the decencies.

In the field of writing history, a third, less well-known name is Winwood Reade, the author of *The Martyrdom of Man*. Orwell could not quite match Wells's enthusiasm here, but it was significant that Wells himself included a fresh appreciation in the final pages of *'42 to '44*. Nietzsche, innocently quoted at the beginning of *'42 to '44*, laid down the great condition – *if man was not a poet*. If man was not a poet, the story might sink into bathos or torpor or contempt. But Winwood Reade was a poet, and so was HG. He inscribed those words at the beginning of what he thought might be his last testament, and returned to them in another favourite form at the end even before he presented his own scientific thesis. He quoted J. M. Robertson's introduction to Reade's *Martyrdom of Man* insisting that Reade was essentially a poet writing not a scientific treatise but an epic of history. And then, to clinch the claim of poetic insight, he quoted:

While the men of mind were battling with the forces of Nature, a contest of another kind was also going on. Those who dwell on the rich banks of a river flowing through desert lands are always liable to be attacked by the wandering shepherd hordes who resort to the waterside in summer, when the wilderness pasture is dried up. There is nothing such tribes desire better than to conquer the corn-growing people of the river lands, and to make them pay a tribute of grain when the crops are taken in. The Egyptians, as soon as they had won their harvests from the flood, were obliged to defend them against the robbers of the desert, and out of such wars arose a military caste. These allied themselves with the intellectual caste, who were also priests, for, among the primitive nations, religion and science were invariably combined. In this manner the bravest and wisest of the Egyptians rose above the vulgar crowd, and the nation was divided into two great classes, the rulers and the ruled. Then oppression continued the work which war and famine had begun. The priests announced and the armies executed the divine decrees. The people were reduced to servitude. The soldiers discovered the gold and emerald mines of the adjoining hills, and filled their dark recesses with chained slaves and savage overseers. They became invaders; they explored distant lands with the spear . . .

It would not have been altogether amiss if Wells's own writing had ended there. He had always been eager to acknowledge his debt to those who had blazed the trail before him and he hailed Winwoode Reade, 'that great and penetrating genius', more eagerly than ever before. HG knew as well as Nietzsche that if man was not a poet he might fail altogether. He knew that the story of mankind and humankind was an epic which could only be properly recited in those terms. In the face of all trials, he was resolved always to tell the truth about the human condition. So this could have been his final word.

His own dearest single achievement was *The Outline of History*. If it had not been for all his other diversions and antics, this might have been better recognized. A. J. P. Taylor had a temperament almost as generous as HG's own when it came to the question of repaying real debts. Celebrating HG's centenary in a 1966 lecture, he not merely remarked on how *The Outline* was still read, but how it was 'still the best general survey of man's history that there is', insisting also that he himself, as a historian, owed more to *The Outline* than to any other single book. This was praise indeed, since Alan had a positive distaste for universal histories, and since he had remarked in the same lecture that most other great political prophets had seemed to concentrate their message into single volumes – Rousseau's *Social Contract* or Darwin's *Origin of Species*. Wells, on the other hand, was always dissipating his energies into fresh diversionary channels, and inviting his excited readers to await his next, final revelation in whatever form he might choose for it. The Taylor accusation had some justice in it, and might be said to apply in an especially cogent sense to the point he had reached when he put the finishing touches to his considered *'42 to '44* volume, and had the supreme example of Winwood Reade's masterpiece there before him. His own *Outline of History* still stands as one of the great books of the world. But HG, even in December 1944, still plunged forward; he was not quite sure where.

Anthony West suggested, without any malevolence towards his father but with most injurious consequences for his reputation, that his mind weakened from about 1942 onwards, and sometimes he would fix the date of the deterioration even earlier. Once the impression had been given, it became ineradicable. Like Dr Johnson's accusation of madness against Jonathan Swift, it seemed to acquire the validity of folklore. Eventually the whole period became associated with one of his last published works, *Mind at the End of Its Tether*. One kindly Christian critic changed the title with intended damning effect to *Man at the End of His Tether*. It did look as if HG had lost some of his dauntless human spirit, his normally irrepressible insolence and courage. His enemies pounced; even his friends might be nervous.

But the Anthony West diagnosis had no firm foundation. Maybe throughout the war years he was losing a little of his natural intellectual sprightliness, but he still retained a good deal more of it than most ordinary mortals and he ceaselessly sought to apply it – as we have seen in the reports of his literary contributions between 1942 and 1944 to the world all round him. One proof was given in the continued high standard of his journalism.

Sometimes he wrote for *Tribune*, in response to invitations from the editor, and the article which appeared on 28 January 1944, under the title 'The Pious Butler and Religious Complex', obviously gave him special delight.

> A story the pious Butler should read is *Candide*. He should compare himself very carefully with that other distinguished educationist, Pangloss. There is a warning for him in that gaily tonic story he might well take to heart. I doubt if mankind can afford much more Cant now . . . There is no power above the power of unflinching truth. The universe may destroy you, but never can it prevail over the unbending spirit of righteousness and that in itself is victory, whether men live or die.

And that, too, might have been his last word.

But sometimes also he would write for *Tribune* for the simple reason that it was the only paper which would print his views, so little had he lost his old magnificent iconoclasm (Beaverbrook's *Evening Standard* was now, alas, under new and less liberal management). *Tribune*, on 15 December 1944, published an article headed 'Churchill Must Go' which the editor printed without necessarily agreeing with all its ideas. H. G. Wells and Winston Churchill, as we have taken proper pains to record, had had a strangely changing series of relationships throughout the century. Sometimes they seemed to approach national issues with an unexpected common interest or sometimes a period of fruitful association, fruitful for the country no less than for themselves, might be shattered, most probably by one of Churchill's sudden excursions into folly or worse. The most wretched example was their estrangement at the time of the Russian revolution and the abortive Churchillian exertion to start a new war. It looked as if the Churchill of 1944 was imagining that he could re-enact that scene. HG's conclusion was clear:

> There can be no doubt of the feelings of the common people of England and the rank and file about this ugly business in Greece and other countries under the heel of slapdash British Toryism. As people have made enormous sacrifices to produce munitions for a united national effort, what is to prevent a working man asking: Why am I overstraining myself to equip our usurper government which has long outstayed its mandate to suppress my fellow workers? What are these guns and shells going to do? In the midst of a still uncertain war, this ineffable Prime Minister of ours has precipitated us into the class war – and on the wrong side. If we do not end Winston, Winston will end us.

The invocation may sound hopelessly out of touch, but observant readers may recall that, six months later, the English people did, after their own fashion, end Winston, even if the reprieve came too late to prevent the inflicting of deep wounds in Greek society, which have hardly yet healed and which injured especially some of the people who had been our firmest friends in resisting the Fascist conquest of their country. HG was sometimes accused of having an obsessive hatred of royalty, and there is plentiful evidence for the case in this article. But in Greece and Italy, too, the mass of the people at that stage in the war were on HG's side, not Churchill's. He could summon Voltaire to his side to dismiss Butler and a wiser Churchill to subdue Churchill. Whatever else it was, it was not the work of an 'enfeebled mind'.

Two other of his last journalistic contributions he offered to the *New Statesman* and the *New Leader*. 'Any tendency towards what he would have called flunkeyism', Kingsley Martin, editor of the *New Statesman* noted, 'stirred Wells to righteous wrath.' That may have been the reason why he so hated monarchy – the fountainhead, he thought, of snobbery. His last two newspaper contributions were letters attacking the British monarchy. He asked me during his last illness to publish an attack on the

Crown, which I did – though I felt it strangely irrelevant in December 1944, maybe more relevant in the 1990s.

Yet the same Wells did write *Mind at the End of Its Tether*. It can be read, has been constantly read, as a full-scale repudiation of all his own roseate prophecies about the future of mankind. It is truly a bleak and terrible forecast about how catastrophe wins the race against education. It is written with much of the rhetorical force which he could bring to bear in his greatest arguments. It is no trivial discussion; it could be his last word.

Anthony West himself has argued that the final deep note of pessimism should not have surprised his readers; it had always been there, at least since *The Island of Dr Moreau* or even *The Time Machine*. Wells had never been the blind believer in the perpetual triumphs of science for which he had been given credit or discredit. No-one could read such a later piece as *The Croquet Player* and reach so misleading a conclusion. The claim is just, irrefutable. Yet Anthony West, with his knowledge of more modern (or modernist) debates, and with a final blank mis-understanding of his father still colouring his verdict, presses the argument too far, and would remove from the reckoning the other Wells who never lost his taste for the human adventure. It should never be forgotten how much Wells himself balanced these conflicts and ambiguities and could offer his own brilliant synthesis. He had been trying his own practised hand at this task with some success, say, since *The War of the Worlds*, published in 1898. * If Anthony could insist that it was always absurd to dismiss Wells as a crass believer in unlimited technological progress, it was hardly more excusable to forget the occasions when his heroes refused to surrender to their wretched fates. Mr Polly, against all odds, could show them how to do it. And had he not constantly sought to re-create Mr Polly, and was not that another of the charges against him?

* See Patrick Parrinder's *H. G. Wells and the Fiction of Catastrophe* (1991). And this is only one of the original Parrinder contributions to Wellsian knowledge soon to be added to a fresh collection of essays. His treatment of Mr Polly in his H. G. Wells Writers and Critics series (1970) still stands as one of the best written on the subject.

Moreover, Anthony West cannot be taken as an infallible witness – especially, it might be argued, in this last phase. What he records is how they increasingly argued and how his father increasingly failed to understand him, and said so. This was not exactly the mood in which Anthony's own judgement would be best exercised, and he in fact made no effort to follow the particular divergent paths which his father's thinking followed –as we have sought to do in these pages. And one of the matters on which father and son found themselves at loggerheads was the fighting of the war itself. Anthony did not share the common exultation of HG and Rebecca in 1940; he did not seem even to share the common hopes of victory which infiltrated Hanover Terrace. Considering how close they had been in years gone by, this development must have been painful and inexplicable. 'I just don't understand you,' his father kept repeating.

However, even *Mind at the End of Its Tether* contained some other particular enlightenments which we were not supposed to neglect – some human asides which one would not stumble upon in other such prophecies of total annihilation, such as the Book of Revelations or Dante's *Inferno*. Even amid the din of Armageddon, HG heard another voice:

> 'One of the most sensible suggestions', said Aesop, 'I have heard for a long time, far too sensible for your world to adopt, is the total banishment of the jackboot and indeed of any sort of hard footwear from the world. You cannot trample on your fellow creatures in slippers. You cannot dream of kicking them, if you have any respect for your toes.'

Slippers, he had to admit, were not a complete panacea; they could not answer all problems. But if some of Wells's most apoplectic Christian critics had transcribed this passage they would not so furtively have been able to portray him as the Arch-Infidel condemning whole races to perdition.

Bleak and barren as were the conclusions of *Mind at the End of Its Tether*, the tone of the actual presentation derived more from old Aesop who was double-crossed and murdered and finally caricatured by the Delphians. Wells must have expected the same fate. So he took the precaution, not always noted by even his admirers and not, alas, by Anthony West, that some other benefaction would be offered to us. Two other pieces of roughly the same length were left in drawers by him. Each had as good or bad a claim to be regarded as his last testament. They might best be lumped all together and apportioned equal prominence, which is the method of publication he himself had sometimes chosen in previous periods of his life. The two neglected volumes show him laughing at himself as well as at everybody else. 'To laugh is to awaken'; he never lost the gift.

He journeyed off in *The Happy Turning* into 'the delightful land of my lifelong suppressions'. Some were gay and some were grave; they gave him a taste for blasphemy which he went on cultivating further to the end.

But I remember a considerable number of quite frightful dreams that came before my teens. I read precociously, and I was pursued implacably, to a screaming and weeping awakening, by the more alarming animals I read about. An uncle from the West Indies describes some frightful spiders that scratched and crawled. I was then put to bed alone in the dark in the upstairs bedroom of a strange house, and I disgraced myself by screaming the house down. I had horror dreams of torture and cruelty. One made me an atheist. My mother was a deeply religious woman, but she did her best to conceal the Devil from me; there were pictures in an old prayer book showing hell well alight, but she obliterated these with stamp paper which I was only partially successful in removing, so that until I held the page up to the light, hell was a mere suspicion and one day I read a description in an old number of *Chamber's Journal* of a man being broken on the wheel over a slow fire, and in my sleep it flared up into immeasurable disgust. By a mental leap which cut out all intermediaries, the dream artist made it clear that if indeed there was an all-powerful God, then it was he and he alone who stood there conducting this torture. I woke and stared at the empty darkness. There was no alternative but madness, and sanity prevailed. God had gone out of my life. He was impossible. From that time on, I began to invent and talk blasphemy. I do not like filth. Merely dirty stories disgust me, and when sexual jokes have an element of laughter in them, almost always it is dishonouring and cruel laughter. But theology has always seemed to me an arena for clean fun that should do no harm to any properly constituted person. Blasphemy may frighten unemancipated minds, but it is unbecoming that human beings should be governed by fear.

He had been constantly entertained by the Holy Carnival.

I have had some very entertaining divine conferences. The gods men worship are difficult to assemble and impossible to count, because of their incorrigible habit of dissolving spasmodically into one another. I have remarked already upon the permutations and combinations, if those words are permissible, of Isis, the original Virgin Mary. Cleopatra's infinite variety was nothing to it. The tangle of the Trinities is even more fantastically versatile. There is the Athanasian Trinity, and the Arian Trinity, the Catholic and the Orthodox, the Logos and that ever-ambiguous Virgin. There is the Gnostic Godhead, which makes Jehovah out to be the very Devil, Pope's consolidated Deity:

'Father of all, in every age, in every clime adored
By Saint, by Savage and by Sage, Jehovah, Jove or Lord'

The vast theogony galumphs about in an endless confusion.

They pour endlessly through the streets of my dreamland; striking strange symbolic attitudes, some with virgin beards, some grotesquely shaven and shorn, hunchbacked with copes, bellowing strange chants, uttering dark sayings – but always incredibly solemn. They tuck up their petticoats, these grave elderly gentlemen, and one, two, three, leap gulfs of logic.

I noted the present Primate, Chief now of the English order of primates, his lawn sleeves like the plump wings of a theological Strasbourg goose, as, bathed in the natural exultations of a strenuous faith, he pranced by me, with the Vatican a-kicking up ahind and afore, and a yellow Jap a-kicking up ahind old Pope. I had a momentary glimpse of the gloomy Dean, in ecstatic union with the Deity, yet contraceptive as ever, and then, before I could satisfy a natural curiosity, a tapping delirium of shrilling cymbals swept him away, 'Glory! . . . Glory! . . . Alleluia! . . .'

As, on the verge of awakening, I watch this teeming disorder of the human brain, which is always the same and increasingly various, I listen for one simple laugh. I look for one single derisive smile. Always I encounter faces of stupid earnestness. They are positively not putting it on, unless earnest self-deception had become second nature. They are not pretending to be such fools. They are such fools . . .

He soon had his readers in a mood to discuss how Jesus of Nazareth analysed his own failure, how having disciples was truly 'my greatest mistake', how the tales spread about his miracles almost smothered the whole affair. 'Everyone. Buddha and St. Benedict, every saint in the calendar is half buried under a cairn of marvel-mongers' lies. Mankind would have smothered itself in its own lies long ago, if history were not so plainly incredible. Truth has a way of heaving up through the cracks of history. Or we should be damned without hope.'

Sometimes he was persuaded that a true antagonism existed between Age and Youth, and mostly for sure he had championed the young more persistently than anyone of equal capacities. But sometimes he wilted:

What does appear now is this fact of the slowing down of terrestrial vitality. The years, the days, grow longer; the human mind is active still, but it pursues and contrives endings and death. The present writer – but remember his age – sees the world as a jaded world devoid of recuperative power. In the preceding sections of this book a wishful disposition is manifest to think that Man will be put out of his entanglements and start a new creative phase of human living. In the past two years, in the face of our universal inadequacy, that optimism has given place to a stoical cynicism. The old men behave

301

for the most part meanly and disgustingly, and the young are spasmodic, foolish and all too easily misled.

Some of these paragraphs were intended to appear in the revised edition of *A Short History of the World*, published after 1945, but none of them could be specified as the final word. And, indeed, if the term was to be strictly applied it should be retained for 'The Betterave Papers No. 1': The Story of Harold Swansdown up to date. Told under protest by Woodfrid B. Betterave at the uncalled-for insistence of H. G. Wells, which appeared in the *Cornhill Magazine* in 1945, having been prepared at the end of the previous year. One part of the discussion concerned the disposal of *The Happy Turning*, although not quite so authoritatively as his other final words.

'See that the mud flies, my boy. You will have quite a market for it and some of it will stick. Some of it ought to stick; I'm not all that proud of myself.' And a few moments later he specified who the licensed mudslinger might be expected to be. 'You might be a member of the Right Club. You might be a Roman Catholic Tory. You couldn't do it better. You have done everything you were made to do.'

Thus the great Prophet offered a few prophylactic guards against the mudslinging that he knew must come. 'Either that, or "Oh, Wells," they would say, and leave it at that.' If this was the choice, he would prefer the mud, but even he might have underrated the deluge of Christian fury, licensed and un-licensed, which would descend upon him for generations thereafter. This was an accolade all on its own, the kind of venom reserved for the greatest of the humanists – Voltaire, Swift and Montaigne himself.

He died on 13 August 1946, just a few weeks before his eightieth birthday, at his Hanover Terrace home which he had learned to love. His illnesses had accumulated, but he had never seemed to be the near-physical-cum-mental wreck which Beatrice Webb had described more than five years before. He had played his own part in helping to win the war which should never have been allowed to happen. One of his last utterances concerned the explosion of the A-bomb and how he hoped to treat it for a film sequel to *The Shape of Things to Come*, upon which, with Moura's assistance, as in so many other matters, he was engaged. He had in one sense more right to speak on that subject than any other citizen on the planet, having warned of the perils half a century before. Among other points he said: 'Man should face his culminating destiny with dignity and mutual aid and charity, without hysteria, meanness and idiotic misrepresentations of each other's motives.' He set that example in his last days, as on so many previous crises in the history of our century.

Writers, great and small, sometimes decide to rest on their laurels, and soon their reputations may rise. Others, driven by their artistic or political urge or a combination of the two, can never stop; they constantly search for new worlds to conquer, new events to assimilate, new ideas to develop. H. G. Wells was pre-eminently one of these, and in his last years he displayed all these old qualities with a new intrepid recklessness. His enemies pounced, and they have been pouncing ever since.

His friends knew him better. One of these, one of the most perceptive and devoted, was J. B. Priestley. Reviewing the literary figures who dominated the age just before his own, he wrote, not in an obituary notice where a laudatory tone might be expected, but in a deliberate judgement on the whole period: 'Of all the English writers I have known, he was the most honest, the frankest, the one least afraid of telling the truth. If he has often offended public opinion, that is chiefly because English public opinion feeds itself with cant and humbug.'* No small tribute from a writer who also sought to strip aside the folds of English hypocrisy. Among the haters of hypocrisy in our literature, with Byron and Hazlitt at their head, HG takes his place.

Another observer of the same generation, hardly less percep-tive, continued to stress HG's youthfulness, his fascination with the young, his faith in the young. 'He trusted the generous

* J. B. Priestley, *Margin Released* (1962), p. 167.

303

impulses of adolescence – however ignorant, preposterous, and easily extinguished, and he appealed to the young. No-one understood better, too, their ridiculous amorous predicaments. (Had he not shared them?)' Thus wrote Desmond MacCarthy on his last novel.

> In youth, taking the clue from our own natures which at that time seem easily alterable for the better, we are ready to believe that the same is true of the world. For at every period of life we judge not only other people but the world by ourselves. When our passions die down we see the foolish, the vain side of passion, and when our life cools, we cease to believe that enthusiasm and energy are sufficient to change fundamentally our environment. But which is right – youth or age? Wells, until the end of his life, thought youth was right.

And he was always ready to take incalculable risks with his own reputation to say so. Desmond MacCarthy was an older man speaking for the young with real wisdom, but the young could also speak for themselves. A young Bruce Bain, returning from the war, soon found himself writing for *Tribune* under the name of Richard Findlater.

> In the Red Sea, bored and angry the airmen heard that H. G. Wells was dead; a vision that left us flat, bewildered, with a conviction of personal loss. We leaned uneasily over the rail, and watched the empty sea as we moved on towards a new England. In the wake we left behind the memory of magnificent anger, faith and a friend-ship, for Wells had been a friend to us all. *

He had had a special appeal for Bruce since he came from the same class in the same kind of London: 'I was in the conspiracy with Wells, and with Wells I chaffed and fretted against the limitations of a dead society. Wells gave the satisfaction of purpose, he made life mean something.' That was also the Wells

* *Tribune*, 23 August 1946.

who had recruited into his army of liberation the young George Orwell. Orwell would not retract one word he had uttered in their recent quarrel. That was not *his* method of controversy, but in his notice written for the *Manchester Evening News* he offered his own far-seeing conclusion.

> No writer of our time, at any rate no English writer, has so deeply influenced his contemporaries as Wells. He was so big a figure, he has played so great a part in forming our picture of the world that in agreeing or disagreeing with his ideas we are apt to forget his purely literary achievements. In his own eyes it was a secondary, almost an unimportant thing. He had faults of intellect and of character, but very few writers have had less literary vanity.

The compliment was all the more valuable since George Orwell himself shared that sense of proportion: the cause mattered much more than any dispute about his capacities.

But what of the women, young and old, whom he was alleged to have seduced and abandoned? The best verdict was given on behalf of them all by the one most splendidly endowed with the gift of tongues. 'Rebecca, bless her, is fully able to take care of herself,' wrote HG in one of his last postscripts.* Not only did she do so, but she took excellent precautions to look after all or almost all the others, too. So outraged was she by one biography which purported to explore all these intimate topics that she cited not only her own case but that of most of the others, not a monstrous regiment but an array of individual characters who could never have appeared in any size or shape at all before the age of liberation.† He was no Don Juan who discarded women so readily; he was more often discarded himself. And, if this report suggests too pitiful a picture, it was Rebecca who also under-lined: 'This tale of multiple disaster is the more extraordinary because the women who left him all felt enduring affection for him and were his domestic friends in his old age.' His hold over

* *H. G. Wells in Love*, p. 234.
† *Sunday Telegraph*, 17 June 1973.

305

them, like the original seductions, derived from his charm which was in turn derived from a combination of qualities. 'It is never easy to say', wrote Rebecca in that same review, 'why Wells with no personal advantage but a bright eye made everyone else in the room seem a dull dog.' But that is what he did do, without any posing or posturing, just being his natural self. 'His company', wrote Rebecca, 'was like seeing Nureyev dance or Tito Gobbi sing.' And when he met Rebecca or anyone like her – not that there was another human specimen quite like that – how his life could take a new lease, how the pages in his books would be lit by a new light, how our whole world could acquire a new purpose and splendour. Rebecca could remember those wondrous confrontations: 'One had, in actual fact, the luck to be young just as the most bubbling creative mind that the sun and moon have shone upon since the days of Leonardo da Vinci was showing its form.' That was Rebecca in love, and she never forgot. It was why, on the day of his death, she wrote to Marjorie Wells, the member of the family to whom she felt closest: 'I loved him all my life and always will, and I bitterly reproach myself, for not having stayed with him . . .'* Whatever else that was, it was not a cry of hatred and revenge.

So he remained until his dying day a servant of truth, a champion of youth, and a man who could not live without the companionship of women – some of them, in his case, among the most powerful and attractive women of the century. But, alas, that did not make him a feminist or even an unqualified champion of women's rights. At the height of the suffragist or suffragette campaigns, he had looked for other ways of human advancement, and had never quite been prepared to acknowledge his error. No-one knew of his failing in this field better than Rebecca, and if she could not win his final conversion who could? But she more than the others knew what compensations could be offered by her Nureyev, her Gobbi, her Leonardo.

A few of his latter-day critics or biographers who claimed to have made scandalous discoveries about his treatment of women

---

* Gordon Ray, *H. G. Wells and Rebecca West* (1974), p. 193.

called him a misogynist. It was a pity Rebecca was not still alive
to unloose one of her own special invectives on this particular
absurdity: she could have done it even better than HG himself.
It seems that this strange notion may have been unloosed by
Malcolm Muggeridge in one of his last spasms of Christian
charity. He could shake any stage upon which he appeared with
terrible anathemas, preferably with a sexual connotation,
against his opponents, all the more virulent if they were dead
and could never answer back. He had once alleged, without a
scrap of evidence, that Jonathan Swift was a lifelong victim of
GPI, and he apparently reflected, with an equal lack of
evidence, on the woman-hating, woman-baiting proclivities
of H. G. Wells. Thus the finest upholders of the humanist
tradition may suffer at the hands of the persecutors even beyond
the grave.

Indeed, the more the case is examined, the more the
conclusion is established that H. G. Wells should take his place
in the company beneath Jonathan Swift's epitaph in St Patrick's
Cathedral in Dublin. Since HG himself might have objected to
the Latin we give it in Yeats's translation:

> Swift has sailed to his rest
> Where savage indignation
> Can no longer lacerate his breast.
> Imitate him, if you dare,
> World-besotted traveller; he
> Served human liberty.

He did, and still does; but never more so than in the terrible war
which his wisdom and courage could have averted.

Chronology

Year	Age	Life
1866		Born 21 September, Bromley, Kent, to a lower layer of a middle-class family: father a gardener, shopkeeper and cricketer; mother a maid and housekeeper.
1873	7	Entered Thomas Morley's Bromley Academy.
1880	14	Apprenticed to Rodgers & Denyer, drapers in Windsor.
1881	15	Pupil-teacher at Alfred Williams' school in Wookey, Somerset; pupil at Midhurst Grammar School; apprenticed to Southsea Drapery Emporium.
1883–4		Under-master at Midhurst Grammar School; wins scholarship and bursary at Normal School of Science, South Kensington.
1884–7		Studies under T. H. Huxley at the Normal School of Science; begins to write; first published work, 'A Tale of the Twentieth Century', appears in May 1887 in the *Science Schools Journal*.
1886		Sets eyes on his cousin Isabel, falls in love.
1887		Teacher at Holt Academy, Wrexham.

Year	Age	Life
1888	22	Returns to London after illness, working as a teacher; 'The Chronic Argonauts' published in *Science Schools Journal.*
1890	24	B.Sc. degree.
1891	25	Tutor for University Correspondence College; marries his cousin, Isabel Wells; 'The Rediscovery of the Unique' published in the *Fortnightly Review.*
1892	26	Meets Amy Catherine Robbins ('Jane').
1893	27	Elopes with Jane; in poor health; publishes *A Text-book of Biology*; becomes full-time writer.
1895	29	Divorce from Isabel; marries Jane; they settle in Sevenoaks, then in Woking; *The Time Machine; Select Conversations with an Uncle; The Wonderful Visit; The Stolen Bacillus.*
1896	30	*The Island of Dr Moreau; The Wheels of Chance*; meets George Gissing.
1897	31	*The Invisible Man; The Plattner Story and Others; Thirty Strange Stories; The Star.*
1898	32	Hit by poor health again; travels to Italy; *The War of the Worlds.*
1899	33	*When the Sleeper Awakes; Tales of Space and Time.*
1900	34	Moves to Sandgate, Kent; *Love and Mr Lewisham.*
1901	35	*Anticipations; The First Men in the Moon*; birth of first son 'Gip', G. P. Wells.
1902	36	*The Sea Lady; The Discovery of the Future.*
1903	37	Joins Fabian Society, the Co-Efficients; birth of second son, Frank; *Twelve Stories and a Dream; Mankind in the Making.*
1904	38	*The Food of the Gods.*
1905	39	*Kipps; A Modern Utopia.*

Year	Age	Life
1906	40	Affairs with Dorothy Richardson and Amber Reeves; meets Gorky in New York; *In the Days of the Comet*; *Socialism and the Family*; *The Future in America*; *This Misery of Boots*; *The So-Called Science of Sociology*.
1908	42	Resigns from the Fabians; *First and Last Things*; *The War in the Air*; *New Worlds for Old*.
1909	43	Birth of Wells's daughter, Anna, to Amber Reeves; Wells and Jane move to Hampstead; *Tono-Bungay*; *Ann Veronica*.
1910	44	*The History of Mr Polly*.
1911	45	*The New Machiavelli*; *The Country of the Blind and Other Stories*; *Floor Games* (for children); moves to Easton Glebe, Essex.
1912	46	*Marriage*; meets Rebecca West.
1913	47	*The Passionate Friends*.
1914	48	Birth of Wells's son, Anthony, to Rebecca West; visits Russia; *The Wife of Sir Isaac Harman*; *The World Set Free*; *An Englishman Looks at the World*; *The War That Will End War*.
1915	49	*Boon* (originally published under the pseudonym Reginald Bliss); break with Henry James; *The Research Magnificent*; *Bealby*.
1916	50	*Mr Britling Sees It Through*; *The Elements of Reconstruction*; *What Is Coming?*; visits Western Front in France and Italy.
1917	51	*The Soul of a Bishop*; *War and the Future*; *God, the Invisible King*.
1918	52	*Joan and Peter*; joins Ministry of Information under Lord Northcliffe; meets Lord Beaverbrook.
1919	53	*The Undying Fire*; *History Is One*; contributor to *The Idea of a League of Nations*.

Year	Age	Life
1920	54	*The Outline of History*; *Russia in the Shadows*; visits Russia; meets Lenin, Trotsky and Moura Budberg.
1921	55	Visits USA; the Washington Conference; *The Salvaging of Civilization*.
1922	56	*Washington and the Hope of Peace*; *A Short History of the World*; *The Secret Places of the Heart*; unsuccessful as a Labour parliamentary candidate for London University.
1923	57	*Men Like Gods*; *The Story of a Great Schoolmaster*; *The Dream*; stands for Parliament again but defeated.
1924	58	Meets Odette Keun; *A Year of Prophecies*.
1925	59	*Christina Alberta's Father*.
1926	60	*The World of William Clissold*.
1927	61	*Mr Belloc Objects to 'The Outline of History'*; Death of Jane Wells; *Meanwhile*; *Collected Short Stories*; *Democracy under Revision*; *Collected H. G. Wells* (Atlantic Edition) completed in USA.
1928	62	Lectures at the Sorbonne; *The Open Conspiracy*; *Blue Prints for a World Revolution*; *Mr Blettsworthy on Rampole Island*; introduction to *The Book of Catherine Wells*.
1929	63	First broadcast on BBC; *The Autocracy of Mr Parham*; *The Adventures of Tommy* (for children); film script of *The King Who Was a King*; meets Moura again in Berlin; meets Antonina Vallentin.
1930	64	Moves back to London.
1931	65	*The Science of Life: A Summary of Contemporary Knowledge about Life and Its Possibilities* (with Julian Huxley and G. P. Wells); diagnosed as diabetic; *What Are We to Do with Our Lives?*
1932	66	*The Bulpington of Blup*; *The Work, Wealth and Happiness of Mankind*.

Year	Age	Life
1933	67	*The Shape of Things to Come.*
1934	68	Talks with Stalin and with F. D. Roosevelt; *Experiment in Autobiography.*
1935	69	Works with Alexander Korda on film version of *The Shape of Things to Come; The New America.*
1936	70	Awarded Hon. D. Litt by London University; *The Anatomy of Frustration; The Croquet Player; The Man Who Could Work Miracles; The Idea of a World Encyclopaedia.*
1937	71	*Brynhild; The Star Begotten; The Camford Visitation.*
1938	72	*Apropos of Delores; World Brain; The Brothers.*
1939	73	Visits Sweden; *The Fate of Homo Sapiens; Travels of a Republican in Search of Hot Water; The Holy Terror.*
1940	74	In London during Blitz; speaking tour of USA; *The Commonsense of War and Peace; Babes in the Darkling Wood; All Aboard for Ararat.*
1941	75	*Guide to the New World; You Can't Be Too Careful.*
1942	76	*Phoenix; Science and the World Mind; The Conquest of Time* (final revision of *First and Last Things*).
1943	77	*Crux Ansata.*
1944	78	*'42 to '44: A Contemporary Memoir*; thesis for Doctorate of Science ('On the Quality of Illusion in the Continuity of the Individual Life in the Higher Metazoa with Particular Reference to the Species Homo Sapiens').
1945	79	*Mind at the End of Its Tether; The Happy Turning; The Betterave Papers.*
1946		Dies in London, 13 August.

Index